A. R. Myers, M.A., Ph.D., F.S.A., F.R.Hist.S., is now Professor of Medieval History in the University of Liverpool. A Yorkshireman, he was educated at Huddersfield College and Manchester University, where he gained his First Class Honours in History in 1934. His education in knowledge of human nature was advanced most rapidly during his wartime career in the Royal Navy, whether on active service in the North Sea, the Atlantic, or the Mediterranean, or in shore establishments at Winchester and Hove. His final naval rank was that of Lieutenant-Commander.

He has contributed numerous articles and reviews to various historical journals at home and abroad; his books include *The Household of Edward IV* (1959), *English Historical Documents 1327–1485* (1969), *London in the Age of Chaucer* (1972) and *Parliaments and Estates in Europe to 1789* (1975). He is President of the Record Society of Lancashire and Cheshire and, from 1973 to 1976, was President of the Historical Association of Great Britain.

A. R. MYERS

# ENGLAND IN THE LATE MIDDLE AGES

*Eighth Edition*

PENGUIN BOOKS

Penguin Books Ltd, Harmondsworth, Middlesex, England
Penguin Books Inc., 625 Madison Avenue, New York, New York 10022, U.S.A.
Penguin Books Australia Ltd, Ringwood, Victoria, Australia
Penguin Books Canada Ltd, 2801 John Street, Markham, Ontario, Canada L3R 1B4
Penguin Books (N.Z.) Ltd, 182–190 Wairau Road, Auckland 10, New Zealand

—

First published 1952
Reprinted 1953
Second edition 1956
Third edition 1959
Fourth edition 1961
Fifth edition 1963
Sixth edition 1966
Seventh edition (incorporating illustrations) 1969
Eighth edition 1971
Reprinted 1972, 1974
Reprinted with revisions 1976, 1978

—

Copyright © A. R. Myers, 1952, 1963, 1971

—

Made and printed in Great Britain
by C. Nicholls & Company Ltd
Set in Monotype Baskerville

PARENTIBUS MEIS
MAGISTROQUE E. F. JACOB
SACRUM

# CONTENTS

# PART III

## 1471–*c*. 1536

# FOREWORD

'Good wine needs no bush'; but every vintage may, perhaps, be allowed a few words of explanation. First, as the late R. G. Colling-wood remarked, 'there are in history no beginnings and no ends'; and continuity has been particularly evident in English history. Nevertheless, to split up history into periods and to analyse their distinctive characteristics may help our understanding of man's development. Secondly, the present reaction against political history, like the emphasis on continuity, may have gone too far. To limit history to 'dates and kings and battles' was a mistake; but equally mistaken is the recent tendency to exclude politics and war as much as possible from the now fashionable social history. Isolated in this way, social history can all too easily slip into inconsequential antiquarianism or doctrinaire determinism. For many people the social, intellectual, and artistic aspects of history are the most attractive; but they cannot be rightly appreciated without reference to the political framework. If we must remember the continuity of history, we also need to remember the unity of human affairs and the intimate connexion between all aspects of man's activities. Thirdly, I must apologize for the limitations which brevity imposes. I regret that there has been scope for only an outline picture, lacking the detailed brushwork which would have made it truer to life. The remark once made by that brilliant historian Eileen Power with regard to English medieval towns might well be applied to other fields of history – the only generalization one can accurately make is that there are no generalizations; yet how hard it is to comply with this dictum in a volume like this, small in size and wide in subject! The failings of this book, from this and other causes, would have been more numerous but for the assistance of friends, all of whom were far more generous in their help than I had any right to expect. Professor G. Barraclough and Mr J. Griffiths read the whole of the text; Professor E. F. Jacob examined Part II of the work; Dr R. W. Hunt inspected the chapters on religious and educational movements; Mr R. T. Davies weighed the sections on the literature of later medieval England. My warm thanks are due to all these scholars for pointing out errors, omissions, and ambiguities.

*July 1951*                                                      A. R. M.

# INTRODUCTION

THERE is now less contempt for the middle ages than there was when Milton dismissed it as a dreary tale of battles between kites and crows; but late medieval England is still often looked upon as dull and barbarous, a sort of dark age before the morning splendour of Elizabethan England. For many historians the great Bishop Stubbs with his view of late medieval England as an anti-climax after the great days of the thirteenth century is, perhaps, in part responsible for this impression. Yet an age which gave us Chaucer and Malory, ballads and carols, and the triumphs of Perpendicular Gothic might accuse subsequent generations of barbarism in destroying so many of the products of its culture; and late medieval England should have this especial attraction for us, that in exploring its activities and achievements we can experience some of the pleasure of the traveller in a foreign land strange enough in outlook to stimulate, yet near enough to his own in culture to offer points of contact and sympathy, and sophisticated enough to display a rich complexity. Not only does the period offer this triple attraction, but the materials for our study are usually much more copious than are those for any earlier time in England's history. We are thus in a better position to understand the lives and thoughts of ordinary people; and an increasing awareness of the individual man and delight in earthly realism has left us in the art of this age a sharper characterization of its men and women than did the self-effacing idealism of an earlier time.

It is not for these reasons only that the period claims our attention. Its history is also of special interest for its relevance to the problems of our day. Our grandfathers, lulled into confidence by three generations of peace, security, and technical advance, could view late medieval England with condescension; for had they not finally solved its problems of war and disorder, poverty and ignorance? Yet, unfortunately for us, their confidence was ill-founded and not even unique. Vastly different as it was in so many ways from Victorian England, the thirteenth century was also an age of comparative peace and economic expansion, able to point to its own amazing creativeness, and to feel assured that, whatever troubles might lie ahead, it had found the key to the universe. It, too, was followed by a period of exhausting wars, economic difficulties, and the gradual, bewildering break-up of its code of values. Late medieval England experienced disillusionment, and a desire for new aims and new verities. There were radicals convinced of the need to abolish what they considered the corruptions of the existing order, bitterly opposed by alarmed conservatives who felt that if concessions were made the whole structure of faith and society would collapse. There were complaints that the lower classes were becoming outrageous in their demands, and that unscrupulous capitalists were squeezing out the craftsmen and causing unemployment. Preachers vigorously denounced the selfishness and ambition of their own time, and what seemed to them its exclusive love of pleasure and display. There was a widespread feeling among thinkers and writers that the time was out of joint; and in late medieval literature and art there runs a strain of melancholy, a preoccupation with death, a sense of coming disaster. Yet the difficulties were finally overcome, and the forebodings proved to be exaggerated. We who cannot be sure of a happy issue out of our troubles would do well to approach late medieval England in a humbler spirit than did our grandfathers, and learn from its problems, its cares, and its achievements.

The lesson of the time is not all sombre; in its history, as in its tales, can be found adventure and a creative spirit. It was an age of contradictions as vivid as the bright colours which it loved; an age less sophisticated than ours which could, like a child, turn quickly from sorrow to mirth and find pleasure in simple joys and customs, and a less complex society which could recover more quickly than ours from the ravages of war. There is also the fascination of watching new life, new techniques, new forms of society, new modes of thought and expression unfolding in the old order, until in the sixteenth century the new culture became self-assertive and mature – destroying much that was of value in the old order, but also fashioning an England which was to advance to fresh triumphs of hand and mind.

It has long been recognized that the signs of transition became more marked from the time of Edward IV onwards, and recent work has brought out clearly the importance of the Yorkist period in this respect. Nevertheless, in Part III of this book reasons are advanced for the view that the new forces did not dominate the old ways of thought and activity until the fifteen-thirties, and that that decade is therefore the most suitable point at which to end the story of medieval England. But the origins of the new order go back much further than the beginning of the Tudor dynasty: some of the forces which disrupted medieval society, such as nationalism, capitalism, and individualism, stretch at least as far back as the fourteenth century in England. Indeed, the high middle age, dynamic as it was, had present in its very methods and outlook the seeds of decay. Edward I's determination to restore the prestige of the monarchy gravely weakened its resources, and the militant aristocracy's lust for war was to lead eventually to the subjugation of that aristocracy; the thirteenth-century synthesis of faith and reason was built up by dialectical methods which, in the hands of fourteenth-century thinkers, served to undermine it, and the High Gothic harmony of idealistic symbolism and naturalistic detail led by its own momentum to the mannerism of the fourteenth century and the earthly realism of the fifteenth.

The late middle ages, then, far from remaining static, were characterized by constant change – developments not as rapid as those of our own time, but swift enough to produce in three centuries a new culture, based, indeed, on the old, but differing markedly from it in fundamentals. Change was slow, and hard to see, since men still venerated the past, and still looked back, not forward, to an ideal. It was still presumed that innovation and experiment were bad, and were to be tested, not by empirical methods, but by their degree of correspondence with traditional beliefs and authorities. In a changing world this meant an increasing discrepancy between theories and facts. Take, for instance, the ideas of chivalry; its feats of heroism in single combat, its crusades and adventures, its code of feudal loyalty and courtly love were appropriate to the feudal order, but by the end of the thirteenth century this had lost its vitality. Yet the militant aristocracy of the late middle ages professed to find in chivalry its guiding principles, and the chroniclers who, like Froissart, wrote to please noble patrons echoed their beliefs. The outward forms of chivalry remained and flourished; tournaments and the trappings of chivalry became more splendid, chivalrous courtesy and etiquette became stricter and more complex, orders of knighthood increased in number and in pomp. But in human relationships, especially those of rulers, the spirit of chivalry was dying; by the late fifteenth century the crusading impulse, for example, was dead, though kings like Edward IV and Henry VII could still pay lip-service to it.

In other spheres the widening gulf between professed aims and reality is evident; the formal homage to the unity of Christendom, to asceticism, to thirteenth-century theories of usury or the just price grew less and less sincere. Growing nationalism took pride in England, and in its increasingly distinctive speech and institutions, rather than in Christian unity, and came more and more to regard the Pope as a foreign prince rather than as the Vicar of Christ. Individualism, creative and dynamic, undermined the control of the group, and capitalist merchants and clothiers shook off the regulations of the gilds. Increasing scope for personal initiative in rural society, and the rise of the yeomen and gentry, broke up the old village community and made the hierarchial conception of society more and more unreal. The ideas and way of life of the increasingly important middle classes were in some respects out of harmony with the outlook of the medieval Church (as in the new emphasis on the value of personal initiative, thrift, industry, comfort, and family life), and in other respects opposed to the medieval order (as in the growth of anti-clericalism and anti-sacerdotalism). The increasing interest in the material world, reflected in the improvement of techniques, in specialization, and in new artistic aims, still worked as yet within the framework of medieval Christian society. Veneration was still paid to the traditional intellectual authorities and methods; but in reality the growing subtlety of logical analysis was destroying belief in the validity of human reasoning. On the one hand this intellectual agnosticism drove educated men in despair to seek refuge in mysticism, and, less worthily, to give credence to popular superstitions, such as witchcraft – for if nothing was disprovable anything was possible; and on the other, the increasing concern with the nature of proof and of man's apprehension of the external world prepared the way for scientific experimentalism and a mechanical view of the universe.

By the end of the fifteenth century the Italian Renaissance was at last beginning to produce in England a conscious revolt against some important medieval ideals. Speculations on the spiritual world, and endless disputations on the theory of knowledge were for the humanists replaced by delight in the visible world and a boundless interest in man, in his desires and his capacities. Ideals, methods, and customs which had existed for centuries were now criticized and ridiculed; religious and economic forces helped on the downfall of the old order, and in the fifteen-thirties Henry VIII added the might of the Crown to the assault. The old order, as a coherent whole, was ended; medieval ideas and institutions had to adapt themselves to a new world or disappear either in sudden overthrow or lingering decay.

It is not surprising that in England the monarchy should have been a very effective means of delivering the *coup de grâce* to the medieval order; for in this country the Crown had been strong earlier than in any other state of Western Europe. Moreover, the close of the middle ages saw, in other countries such as France and Spain, the victory of strong monarchy, and all classes turned to the Crown for honour, wealth, protection, and leadership. Yet in England, home of the first strong monarchy in Western Europe, the Crown was, in this age of the apotheosis of kingship, unusually limited in the exercise of its powers. Even Henry VIII had no subservient paid army, police-force, or bureaucracy, but had to rely on the support of the politically powerful classes. This anomalous position, so fundamental for the distinctive constitutional development of the country, had been established by the history of late medieval England. The fourteenth century and much of the fifteenth century were a time of political weakness for the monarchy, when its increasingly inadequate resources and growing subservience to the magnates forced it to make concession after concession to the aristocracy and to the rising middle classes. But the early strength of the Crown had given it enough impetus for its administration and law, already predominant, to go on expanding during this time; and the lords and gentry exercised their influence largely by capturing control of the royal machinery of government. When the Yorkists and early Tudors revived the strength of the Crown, its power was limited by such instruments of its own as Parliament, with its control over legislation and taxation, and the justices of the peace, with their supervision of almost the whole field of local government. To subdue or destroy these royal institutions was harder for the monarchy than to suppress outdated feudal franchises, or to lead a growing nationalism into an attack on the independence of the Church, which was already so much subject to the influence of the Crown. In England, therefore, medieval notions, such as rule under law and by consent, persisted when they were fading elsewhere.

In Part III of this book it is argued that this triumph of the Crown over the Church in the fifteen-thirties marks the close of the middle ages in more spheres of life than the ecclesiastical. It is harder to find a beginning for the late medieval period in England as clearly defined as its end; but in many ways the opening of the fourteenth century seems to mark a transition from the high middle ages. The defeat of Pope Boniface VIII by Edward I and Philip IV gave spectacular proof of the growth of the lay spirit and of nationalism, and of the decline in the strength of the Papacy. The creative impulse of the twelfth-century Renaissance had now spent its force, and the first damaging attacks were being made on the Thomist synthesis of faith and reason; the agrarian prosperity and economic expansion of the high middle ages were followed by depression and contraction; the beginning of the Scottish and French wars in the twelve-nineties closed a period of comparative peace with Scotland and France, and opened a long era of hostility; the successful use of long-bow archers at Falkirk in 1298, together with the rapid decay of the feudal levy, inaugurated a new age in warfare and hence in the structure of society; and the idealism of High Gothic art, united and co-ordinated in the service of Christian scholasticism, was just beginning to fade. All these and other signs of transition were spread out over a generation; but for convenience we may select as our starting-point the accession of Edward II. This date is justified by more than convenience, for in an age and country in which the king was the mainspring of government a change of monarch was of great importance. Moreover, when the character of the new king was such as to strengthen rather than diminish the constitutional and economic tendencies of the time, his accession was likely to be of particular significance. Let us begin our survey of late medieval England, then, with the accession of Edward II.

# PART I · 1307 — 1399

## CHAPTER I

## *The Tragic Dilemma*

PERHAPS the most important fact about the political development of medieval England was the strength of the monarchy at a comparatively early date. But for this, the evolution of distinctively English institutions such as the Common Law and Parliament would have been impossible. Under John (1199–1216) and Henry III (1216–72), however, the Crown had lost some of its prestige and power. Edward I (1272–1307) came to the throne determined to recover both. He saw to it that the government was effectively under his control and that royal claims were asserted to the full, not only in England but in Wales, Scotland, and France; and such a policy involved wars too great for the resources of the Crown. Edward tried in vain to put fresh life into the feudal levy, and the newer method of raising an army by payment was expensive. His castle-building in Wales was very costly, and the effort necessary to wage war simultaneously in Scotland and France prompted him to arbitrary acts which aroused widespread resentment. Such acts, together with his subsequent repudiation of his promises not to repeat the offences, and his high-handed acquisitiveness, made the barons restive. If he had lived to continue the exhausting struggle in Scotland, he might have been faced with an outburst comparable to that of 1297.

The twenty-year-old Edward II thus succeeded in 1307 to a difficult situation. His father had left him with a load of debt, and policies which could neither be abandoned nor continued with safety. The monarchy was confronted by the tragic dilemma from which it was not to escape throughout the century – whether to choose a policy of war, which would in the long run weaken the resources of the Crown as it strengthened those of the magnates, or to prefer a policy of peace which would harm the king's prestige and encourage factious opposition. The magnates showed their resentment against Edward I's autocratic régime by imposing on his successor a coronation oath more stringent than that previously in use. The situation demanded a monarch with the highest talents of statesmanship; unfortunately Edward II was weak and wilful. The king was expected to be the mainspring of government, and Edward had no head for business; the militant aristocracy wanted a warrior king, and Edward, though athletic and courageous, was not warlike enough for them. He took pleasure in music and in unaristocratic occupations such as rowing, play-acting, driving, racing, thatching, and digging. But it was not so much the unkingly character of these diversions which quickly alienated the magnates, as his inordinate affection for the young Gascon adventurer, Piers Gaveston. To call Gaveston an upstart and a foreigner merely throws light on baronial prejudices, for he was the son of a loyal and prominent Gascon knight and a natural-born liegeman of the Crown. There may have been more truth in the charge of unlawful intimacy with the king, and Marlowe's view of their relationship is probably nearer the truth than some modern historians have supposed. But it was not this aspect of the connexion which alienated the barons; it was the fact that Edward's affection caused him to neglect the counsels and companionship of those who regarded themselves as his natural counsellors and exclusive associates – the barons. And Gaveston, brave and able, but vain and tactless, not only ousted the magnates from what they considered their rightful influence over the government, but insulted them by his caustic wit. Within a year of the king's accession the lords in parliament declared that loyalty was due to the Crown rather than to the king's person, and in 1310 they forced Edward to agree to the appointment of a committee of twenty-one lords to draw up ordinances for the reform of the government. If the Ordinances were made in a spirit of faction, they did at least rest on the far-reaching principle that the law was superior to the king. Edward had to assent to them; but he wrecked his chances of splitting the opposition by his infatuated support of Gaveston, which lasted until, in June, 1312, the favourite was captured and beheaded by one of the opposition leaders, the Earl of Warwick. Gaveston's death did not bring peace, for Edward was now irreconcilably opposed to the murderers, and neither side was strong enough to crush the other. The leader of the opposition, Edward's first cousin, Thomas of Lancaster, held five earldoms and had great territorial influence, but lacked energy and constructive ability. The indecisive struggle of Edward and Lancaster paralysed the government of the country.

It was therefore not surprising that by 1314 Robert Bruce was master of nearly all Scotland, and raiding the northern shires of England. When the king marched north to relieve Stirling, the key to the passage of the Forth, Thomas of Lancaster and the opposition lords refused to obey his call, partly from rancour and partly from fear that a royal victory in Scotland would facilitate a royal victory in England too. Certainly the Battle of Bannockburn discredited Edward as a defeated and fugitive king. Not only was Scottish independence assured, but the Scots raided the north of England with impunity, and the damage they did in the next few years inflicted severe blows on the prosperity of the border counties. King Robert's brother invaded and ravaged Ireland with such effect that English power shrank to a narrow territory round Dublin. Edward's prestige sank so low that he had to accept from the Ordainers in parliaments fresh humiliations; these included severe limitations on his expenditure and the appointment of Thomas of Lancaster as commander-in-chief against the Scots in 1315 and chief councillor of the king in the following year. But Lancaster showed himself so supine and inept that he did nothing against the Scots and brought all administration to a standstill. By 1318 the moderate section of the opposition had became so exasperated with his incompetence that they brought his authority to an end.

This moderate 'middle party' tried to infuse more efficiency into the administration; but it was discredited by a Scottish victory at Myton-in-Swaledale in 1319. Edward disliked it, for it aimed to uphold the Ordinances, and, as it was more business-like than Lancaster, it was more effective in curbing his freedom. With the help of two baronial favourites, the Despensers, father and son, Edward tried to build up a royalist party. Though able, the Despensers were greedy, especially in a dangerous area – South Wales. The marcher lords had in the past been allowed great powers to enable them to combat the Welsh; Edward I had struggled in vain to curb their power. During the troubles of his son's reign their independence had grown, and they were now a very important and turbulent element in English politics. When Lancaster revived the outcry against favourites the marcher lords supported him with enthusiasm and, joined by the 'middle party', succeeded in 1321 in banishing the Despensers. The king roused himself to unwonted vigour, recalled the Despensers, and marched against his enemies. In March, 1322, at the battle of Boroughbridge, Lancaster and his forces were defeated by the newly-acquired technique of combining archers with dismounted men-at-arms and pike-men. Lancaster and some other leading opponents of the king were executed; others were imprisoned.

At a Parliament held at York in 1322 all the Ordinances were annulled and the royal authority was reasserted; but Edward's triumph did not last many years. The Despensers were abler and less greedy than is sometimes supposed, and various royal officials made valuable reforms between 1322 and 1326 in the Household, Chancery, and Exchequer. But Edward's government was, on the whole, inept, and the Despensers were widely hated as covetous and oppressive. Like his great-grandson, Richard II, Edward did not realize how narrow was the basis of his power. During the previous decade of civil strife the power of the lords had increased as that of the Crown had diminished; most of the lords were hostile to the government, and the middle classes were not yet strong enough to be an effective support for the monarchy, even if Edward had wooed them.

In 1325 Edward's queen, Isabella, who resented the Despensers' influence over the king, was sent to Paris to negotiate with her brother, Charles IV, about the restoration of Gascony. Soon she persuaded the trustful Edward to send her their son, Edward of Windsor, to do homage for Gascony. In Paris she met various exiles, including Roger Mortimer, the greatest of the marcher lords, who had been imprisoned after Boroughbridge and had escaped in 1324. Isabella became his mistress; the pair betrothed the young Edward to Philippa, daughter of the Count of Hainault, and with her dowry obtained men and arms. When in September, 1326, they invaded England, Edward was soon deserted by almost all the chief men of the realm, including his own brothers; and the Despensers were quickly hunted down and killed. A Parliament was summoned in the king's name and in January, 1327, he was constrained to abdicate; the assembly recognized his son as king in his stead. Edward II was imprisoned, but Isabella and Mortimer felt too bitter and unsafe to allow their captive to remain alive. In September, 1327, he was murdered in Berkeley Castle.

Edward III might be ruler in name, but Isabella and Mortimer were rulers in fact. Mortimer used his power to acquire lands and influence in Wales and Ireland, and, in 1328, the title of Earl of March. The dislike aroused by his ruthlessness and greed was increased by his foreign policy. Lacking the resources and authority to resist the Scots and French, he adopted the realistic but intensely unpopular course of making peace with both. By a treaty of 1327 Charles IV restored only Bordeaux, Bayonne, and a strip of coast between them; and in 1328 Robert Bruce was recognized as King of Scots in complete independence of England. In October, 1330, Mortimer's rule was ended by an alliance of Henry, Earl of Lancaster, Thomas's brother, who detested the government of Isabella and Mortimer, and the young king, disgusted by his mother's behaviour and his own subservience. Mortimer was executed and Isabella was placed in comfortable captivity. Edward III, now eighteen years old, proclaimed that he had taken over the government.

In the young king the lords found a monarch after their own heart. Though capable of outbursts of temper, he won and retained popularity for most of his reign by his regal bearing, his charm, his generosity, and, above all, his conformity to baronial ideas and tastes. He loved display and pageantry and sumptuous buildings; he was adept in all knightly accomplishments and delighted in tournaments and warfare. Successful war was very popular, but war could not always be successful and was in any case a great strain on the Crown's resources. But Edward was not interested in administration and finance, and was scarcely in a position to plan carefully for the future. To have tried to rebuild the royal authority after the disasters of his father's reign without recourse to foreign war would have been very hard; and Edward's early victories solved for the time being the problem of the monarchy's relations with the barons. But when victory was followed by defeat the problem returned, intensified.

Edward's first military enterprises were in Scotland, which was weakened and confused by the death of Robert Bruce in 1329 and the accession of his son, David II, as a child of five. Edward supported a band of disinherited Scottish magnates, led by Edward Balliol, and with English help they won victories at Dupplin Moor (1332) and Halidon Hill (1333). Edward Balliol was crowned king of Scots, but only at the price of ceding to the English king a large part of the Lowlands. This discredited him in the eyes of the Scots, and the war ended in 1341 with the complete expulsion of the English. Edward's government was not, however, weakened by this ultimate failure, for by this time English attention was occupied by the greater struggle in France.

The most fundamental cause of dispute between England and France was the English possessions in France. As the power of the French kings grew, it became increasingly hard for them to acquiesce in English authority in any part of the French kingdom; but apart from the importance of the Gascon trade to English interests, it would have been politically impossible for the English monarchy to withdraw willingly from France. Even a policy of peace with France and of reduction in English claims would be a severe blow to the king responsible for such a course, as the fates of Richard II and Henry VI were to show. Edward III was quite averse to such a policy, and this, together with French penetration and attrition, would in itself have been enough to produce a conflict.

The atmosphere of hostility which developed from this fostered other causes of dispute. Dispossessed French feudatories sought refuge in England, and, more important, the great towns of Flanders, the best customers for English wool, appealed for aid to Edward against the King of France, with whom they were in conflict. Edward tried to build up a system of alliances against France in the Netherlands and the Rhineland; Philip VI, King of France, replied with counter-alliances and supported the Scots in their war with England. English and Norman sailors indulged in sea-fights and in raids on one another's coasts. In 1337 the two countries drifted into the Hundred Years War. It has been said that the cause of this long struggle was Edward's claim to the French throne through his mother, Isabella, against the first king of the Valois line, Philip VI; but Philip had succeeded to the throne in 1328 and Edward had done homage to him for Gascony in 1329. It was only in 1340, when the war had already been waged for over two years, that Edward assumed the title of King of France, and then chiefly to please his Flemish allies, by removing from them the reproach that they were fighting against their lawful king.

From 1337 to 1340 such fighting as occurred took place mainly in Flanders and Picardy; but it was indecisive. In 1340 the English won a great naval battle off Sluys; but they made no good use of their victory, and affairs in Scotland and Gascony were going badly for them. Edward ascribed the lack of success in the war, especially in

Flanders, where he had led the English forces himself, to the obstruction of the treasurer, Roger Northburgh, Bishop of Coventry, and of the chancellor, Robert Stratford, Bishop of Chichester. Edward dismissed them from office and turned on the latter's brother, John Stratford, Archbishop of Canterbury, whom he regarded as the ringleader of the opposition. At a Parliament in 1341, however, the lords supported Stratford and demanded that none of their number should be tried except in Parliament and by their peers, and, moreover, that there should be parliamentary control over the audit of accounts and the appointment of ministers before a grant was made. Edward, though very loath to do so, was forced to yield, for his wars had put him very much in debt; but five months later he revoked the offending statutes. Nevertheless, he was in future careful to choose ministers who had the confidence of the barons and to work harmoniously with them. From 1341 to 1369 there was almost complete harmony between the king and his magnates; for not only was Edward careful not to act counter to their prejudices and interests, but he won their cooperation by conducting a successful war in a wealthy foreign land.

In 1340 a truce had been made with France, but in 1341 a disputed succession occurred in Brittany, and soon England and France supported the rival claimants to the dukedom. In 1345 Edward denounced the truce and in that year and the following one, Henry, Earl of Lancaster, son of the king's ally of 1330, made three successful raids from Gascony far into enemy territory. In 1346 Edward himself led a small army from the Cotentin through Normandy and nearly to the walls of Paris, almost unopposed; then he turned north to join his allies the Flemings. Overtaken at Crécy, in August, 1346, by a much larger French army, he won a brilliant victory by the tactics of Dupplin Moor and Halidon Hill. Long-bow archers broke up the opposing army and stopped its cavalry charges; and the enemy, reduced to confusion, was finished off by the dismounted English men-at-arms. This was one of the first battles in Western Europe in which cannon were used, though they were too small and inefficient to be of much help, except by their noise.

This victory brought Edward great prestige as a general, but no strategic gains. From Crécy he advanced to Calais, which he had to beseige for almost a year before it surrendered. The inhabitants were expelled and replaced by Englishmen; the town was to remain in English hands for over 200 years. The campaign had been exhausting enough for Edward to accept a truce in September, 1347; and a month later he returned to England, his army laden with booty. His prestige was at its height, for these last years had seen other English victories. David, King of Scots, had made a diversion in the north of England to help his French ally, but in October, 1346, he was severely defeated and captured at Neville's Cross by the Nevilles, Percies, and the Archbishop of York. He was lodged in the Tower of London, where he was joined next year by Charles of Blois, the French-supported claimant to the duchy of Brittany.

Edward's popularity was assured by these successes, and increased the prosperity brought by the war to various classes in England. Apart from the prospects of rich booty and valuable prisoners to hold to ransom, the wages paid by the king for service in his army benefited different orders of society, from nobles to simple archers. The lords and knights enjoyed fighting, and successful warfare offered many chances of advancement to the ambitious. The supply of food and clothing for the army enriched not only the contractors but large numbers of their suppliers in town and country.

This war boom received a severe check from the Black Death (the dreaded bubonic plague, or the even more lethal pneumonic and septicaemic plagues), which had originated in Central Asia and reached Italy in 1347. It came to England in 1348, spread during 1349 all over England and Wales, and reached Scotland in 1350. In view of its connexion with dirt and insanitary conditions it is not surprising that its worst effects were felt in the towns, and that it was the poor who found it hardest to escape. The mortality is not easy to compute, but it was undoubtedly very high; it is generally thought that the plague carried off a third of England's population. And though the epidemic abated towards the end of 1349, it revived in 1361, 1362, and 1369 almost as disastrously. Indeed, there were outbreaks of the plague in England until the late seventeenth century, when medical knowledge improved, and the brown rat, which did not carry the plague fleas, began to drive out the black, which did.

The economic and social effects of this huge and sudden death-roll were bound to be great, even if they were not as revolutionary as was once thought. The ravages of the plague did not, however, weaken the martial ardour of the king and his lords. It was while the Black Death was raging that Edward developed his Order of the Garter, pattern of all later orders of chivalry, and celebrated St George's Day, 1349, with much splendour in his new chapel at Windsor. His military victories helped his Order to exert a profound influence. Foreign rulers became proud to be elected to an Order whose colours (and perhaps its motto) emphasized the English claim to the French throne; St George had been invoked as the patron of all knights, but the Order's success resulted in his appropriation by the end of the century as the patron saint of England; and the Order greatly encouraged the development of lay and national orders of chivalry in Western Europe. The quixotic King John of France was so impressed by the new Order that he instituted with much pomp the Order of the Star. Unfortunately for France, his taste for chivalric splendour was stronger than his statesmanship, and he was soon involved in a deadly quarrel with his son-in-law, King Charles the Bad of Navarre, who secretly proposed to Edward III a partition of the French kingdom. An alliance with Charles encouraged Edward to renew the war in 1355; and devastating raids were made from Bordeaux and Normandy far into France. On such a raid from Bordeaux Edward's eldest son, the Black Prince, was overtaken in September, 1356, by a far more powerful army under King John, near Poitiers. There he won a victory as complete as that at Crécy, again largely by a skilful combination of long-bow archers and men-at-arms. King John was taken captive and joined the King of Scots in the Tower of London.

Edward naturally sought to exact terms from his prisoners. In October, 1357, David II accepted the treaty of Berwick, whereby he was freed in return for a promised ransom of 100,000 marks. The efforts necessary for a poor country to pay such a huge sum, together with the feuds between the Scottish lords and the enmity between David and his nephew and heir, Robert, the Steward of Scotland, all combined to prevent Scotland from giving any trouble during the remaining years of David's reign. King John proved equally amenable in negotiation; but France, though terribly weakened by English devastations, aristocratic faction, a peasant rising, and a revolutionary government in Paris, would not accept the extreme terms to which he agreed. Edward was, however, as incapable, for lack of resources, of capturing any more strongholds as the French were of opposing him in the field; so in May, 1360, the two sides came to terms at Brétigny. By these terms, as modified in October at Calais, Edward renounced his claim to the French throne, but received in full sovereignty Calais, Ponthieu, and the whole of Aquitaine, besides a promise of the vast sum of 3,000,000 gold crowns as a ransom for King John. The English organized great festivities to celebrate so brilliant a settlement.

As so often happens after a victorious peace, the rejoicings were short-lived. The English had not the resources to hold what they had won, especially as they had aroused French national feeling against them. It proved very hard to collect from an impoverished land the ransom which had been promised; and the inhabitants of the ceded territories were unwilling to submit to English rule. The English were slow to give up their captured strongholds, which were held largely by mercenaries who refused to surrender. Even when they did so, they were determined not to be deprived of their predatory livelihood and joined together to form 'Free Companies' which brought fresh misery to France. Officially disowned but secretly encouraged by Edward III, they not only pillaged but engaged in open warfare, and in 1364 they won at Auray a decisive victory for John de Montfort, the claimant to the duchy of Brittany who was allied to the English.

English intervention in Spain proved more costly. In 1367 the Black Prince invaded Castile in support of King Pedro the Cruel and heavily defeated his half-brother Henry of Trastamara and his French allies at the battle of Nájera. This proved a Pyrrhic victory, for the campaign ruined the Black Prince's health, his army was ravaged by dysentery, and Pedro was eventually defeated and killed. The whole affair depleted English resources and produced a fervent ally of France on the southern flank of Gascony. The heavy expense of the Castilian expedition made necessary the levy of a hearth tax on Aquitaine, and the discontent aroused by this was used by many lords of the duchy as a pretext for revolt. They were helped by the French government, which welcomed the opportunity of destroying the effects of the treaty of Brétigny. In 1369 an ultimatum was sent to Edward III, who at once resumed the title of King of France; and the war began again.

The fortunes of the antagonists were now very different from those of a generation earlier. The English, with their memories of Crécy and Poitiers, thought in terms of raids and pitched battles; but the French now avoided action except in very favourable circumstances. Since the outbreak of the war English strategy had always been weak; now their tactics proved inadequate as well. And whereas the French now had in Charles V an able king, very different from John II or Philip VI, and skilful generals, such as Bertrand du Guesclin, Edward III was sinking into his dotage and the Black Prince was stricken with dropsy. While in England it became increasingly difficult to raise money for campaigns that brought no successes, in France there was a great wave of determination to expel the English. What had been gained in 1360 was soon lost; and measures of repression, such as the Black Prince's destruction of the town of Limoges in 1370, merely angered the French into fresh resistance.

The English continued to make raids which were not only costly but futile, for the French stuck to their guerrilla tactics. By the end of 1373 Duke John had been driven out of Brittany; and when Edward III died in 1377 all that was left of the English conquests was the four fortified towns of Calais, Brest, Bordeaux, and Bayonne, and the coastal lands about them.

This striking change of fortune in France had, of course, important repercussions on the balances of forces in England, where for a generation after 1341 Edward III had enjoyed an unchallenged supremacy based primarily on a successful foreign war. To ensure the maximum support for that war he had made many important concessions, ranging from parliamentary control of taxation to the domination of the magnates in his councils. Edward's whole way of life had pleased the barons, and he had married his numerous children to members of great baronial houses. But though he had done much to conciliate the magnates, he had done nothing to weaken their power, built up by the civil strife of his father's reign and greatly strengthened by the prolonged warfare in France. He had, in fact, voluntarily ceded to the lords an influence in the government for which they had striven against royal opposition of a century and a half. Once the French war ceased to be victorious, Edward's ascendancy at home was gone, but the baronial influence in the government remained. Failure abroad encouraged disunity at home; and Edward's marriage policy, though not the novelty it has often been called, nevertheless had disastrous consequences, for through it the baronial factions the more easily found leaders in the royal house itself.

One of the protagonists in these quarrels was John of Gaunt, Edward III's fourth son. Married in 1359 to Blanche, heiress of the great Lancastrian inheritance, in 1362 he was created Duke of Lancaster. He sought to gain popularity by joining in the attacks on the king's ministers provoked by the failure of the war after 1369. When in 1371 the chancellor, William of Wykeham, Bishop of Winchester, asked Parliament for supplies for the war, a storm broke out. Since the great officers of the Crown were, as usual, ecclesiastics, the widespread discontent with the reverses in France, took an anti-clerical form, as Edward's wrath had done in 1341. Parliament petitioned the king that, since clerics could not be brought to account for their actions, none but laymen should be appointed great officers of the realm. John of Gaunt supported this anti-clerical agitation and gave his protection to John Wyclif.

The government was now largely under Gaunt's influence, but the new administration was no more successful than the old one had been. The royal mistress, Alice Perrers, the courtier nobles, and the rich London financiers who supported Gaunt were accused of feathering their nests at the Crown's expense. A strong opposition arose, headed by the Black Prince and his niece's husband, Edmund Mortimer, Earl of March. Edward III had married his third son, Lionel, to the greatest heiress of the day, Elizabeth de Burgh, only daughter of the Earl of Ulster. Lionel's only child by Elizabeth was Philippa, who was married to Edmund Mortimer, himself a great magnate with wide lands and influence in the Welsh marches. He was the great-grandson of Queen Isabella's lover, and the ancient rivalry of Mortimer and Lancaster was now renewed.

The discontent against the government burst out in the Parliament of 1376, which became the longest and best-reported Parliament yet held and famous as the 'Good Parliament'. Inspired by the Black Prince, the Earl of March, and the bishops, the Commons vigorously attacked the administration. Their leader and mouth-piece was Sir Peter de la Mare, steward of the Earl of March, the first speaker of the Commons of whom we have any clear picture. Through him the Commons accused various courtiers of corruption, especially Lord Latimer, the chamberlain, and Richard Lyons, a London financier; and the two, in spite of royal opposition, were condemned by the Lords to forfeiture and imprisonment. This was the first example of the process of impeachment. Alice Perrers was banished from Court, and Parliament insisted on 'afforcing' or strengthening the royal Council with nine lords and prelates without whom no business was to be transacted. The power of the 'Good Parliament' was weakened, however, by the death of the Black Prince in June, 1376, and as soon as it was dissolved, a month later, Lancaster seized power again. Latimer and Lyons were released, Alice Perrers returned to Court, Peter de la Mare was imprisoned, the councillors nominated in Parliament were disregarded, and all the work of the Good Parliament was undone. In January, 1377, a new Parliament was summoned; the Commons elected Gaunt's steward, Sir Thomas Hungerford, as their speaker, and complied with Gaunt's wishes. In spite of episcopal opposition he remained in power until the old king died in June, 1377, deserted by his courtiers and robbed by his mistress before she fled of the very rings on his fingers.

The new king, Richard II, only son of the Black Prince, was at this time ten years old. The government was in the hands of a council of nine in which by a compromise the various aristocratic interests were represented, but this attempt at a coalition ministry was not a success, since the various factions were so opposed to one another. The war with France went from bad to worse. England, exhausted by the struggle, was faced by both the Castilian and the French navies, and lost command of the sea. Even the voyage from Dover to Calais was dangerous, and Gravesend, Hastings, Rye, and the Isle of Wight were ravaged. Expeditions were sent to Brittany and Gascony, but in vain. Indeed, it was probably only the deaths in 1380 of the able Charles V and his great Constable, Bertrand du Guesclin, which saved the English from being driven out of France altogether. The new king, Charles VI, was still a boy, and France was soon made impotent by the quarrels of the king's powerful uncles.

Fruitless expeditions were more costly than successful ones; and with Scottish invasions to repel, and the need to re-cover command of the sea, it is no wonder that the government had to ask Parliament for heavy taxes. But the usual forms of taxation affected especially the propertied classes which dominated Parliament, and these were increasingly reluctant to provide money for a war which offered no prospect of success. The Commons therefore resorted to poll or head taxes, which would hit every one; in fact, the levy of 1380 pressed most hardly on the poorest, and in the early summer of 1381 touched off the Peasants' Revolt. This rebellion was due to a complex combination of political, social, and religious factors, such as resentment of the government's weakness and mismanagement, hatred of the landed classes' policy of repression in the labour shortage following the Black Death, visions of better conditions inspired by the French wars and the social changes of the time, and dissatisfaction at the wealth and worldliness of the higher clergy; the poll tax was the last of a generation of grievances. The revolt affected areas as far apart as Hampshire and the Scottish borders, Wirral and Norfolk; and, owing to the supineness of the government, the rebels of the home counties occupied London. Disaster was averted only by the courage of the young king, and the issue of pardons for rebellion and of charters conceding demands such as the abolition of serfdom, servile tenures, and trade restrictions. Once the peasants had dispersed, pathetically trusting in these pardons and charters, the ruling classes recovered their courage and reasserted their rights. It was thought in the past that the revolt resulted in the virtual extinction of serfdom; but on the contrary, the reaction which followed the rising delayed emancipation. When a deputation of peasants came to Richard to ask him to confirm their charters, he exclaimed 'Villeins (serfs) ye are still and villeins ye shall remain', adding that promises given under duress counted for nothing. The king was not altogether hostile to the villeins; he was later to veto a proposal of the Commons in Parliament (who represented upper-middle-class interests) that villeins should not be allowed to send their sons to school. But after 1381 he could look for no support from a crushed and disillusioned peasantry.

He was soon to need all the support he could get. As he grew up he saw how the royal authority had been weakened by his grandfather's policy, and hence he opposed the continuation of a war which weakened the monarchy and brought poverty and disorder to the realm. In the middle eighties he began to build up a party of confidants devoted to himself and his policy. The idea of peace without victory was, however, unpopular, and this widespread reluctance to admit defeat was exploited by some lords. Not only did they profit in wealth and prestige by the war, but they were indignant that the authority which they had enjoyed in the royal councils for half a century should be threatened; and in 1386 they made Richard dismiss his chief ministers, including his able chancellor, Michael de la Pole, Earl of Suffolk, who was impeached and imprisoned. Richard was too high-spirited to submit quietly, but he was short of money and his opponents were powerful and ruthless. They denounced his policy of peace as cowardice and a betrayal of English interests. In 1387 the king's youngest uncle, Thomas, Duke of Gloucester, together with the Earls of Arundel and Warwick, raised an army and defeated the king's forces. The victors caused the summoning in February, 1388, of a Parliament which earned the epithet of 'Merciless'. The king's chief supporters were executed, exiled, imprisoned, or otherwise removed. Their accusers or 'appellants' rewarded themselves and their friends profusely with money, honours, and appointments, and seemed firmly in control of the government.

Within little more than a year, however, Richard was able to reassert himself. The appellant lords had alienated many of their supporters by their conduct. Though they had criticized Richard's ministers for their lack of jingoism, the appellants negotiated with France. Their incompetence allowed the Scots to inflict the severe defeat of Otterburn on the English in 1388; and their régime cost a great deal with nothing to show for it. And, after all, it was traditional that the king had normally the right and duty to govern.

Gloucester may have hoped that Richard would discredit himself by tactless and high-handed actions as speedily as he had done in 1386; but the king made no attempt to recall his exiled friends or to undo the work of the Merciless Parliament. He did not even exclude the appellants from his Council. The result was that in domestic affairs the years from 1389 to 1397 were fairly calm. Nevertheless, Richard was moving quietly towards a more personal rule. He cultivated the moderate section of the aristocracy and began to look outside the baronial ranks for more devoted support; and, as a check to the hated Gloucester, he drew closer to his uncle Lancaster.

To restore the royal authority Richard felt that he needed allies abroad as well as at home. He therefore made a truce with France and sealed the rapprochement by a marriage. His beloved first queen, Anne of Bohemia, had died in 1394, and in 1396 he married Isabella, the seven-year-old daughter of Charles VI. The diehards, led by Gloucester, strongly opposed this alliance, but it suited Richard's purpose well. Not only did it end a big drain on his resources, but the French king promised to aid him as strongly as possible, if necessary against any of his subjects.

Another useful ally would be the Papacy. It was not easy to conciliate the Pope, in view of anti-papal legislation in England in 1390 and 1393 and the rising anti-papal sentiment in English nationalism. Moreover, since the Great Schism in the Church began in 1378, France, now Richard's ally, had adhered to a rival Pope. However, the Pope whom England acknowledged, Boniface IX, was so afraid of losing England's obedience to his rival at Avignon that in 1398 Richard managed to arrange a Concordat.

Richard's alliance with European powers and abandonment of continental ambitions harmonized with an attempt to reassert royal authority in Ireland. That country had been nominally under English rule for over 200 years, but the English kings had always neglected it to further their imperialist aims in Scotland and France, so that now royal authority was hardly even nominal beyond a small area round Dublin. Successful royal intervention might revive the Crown's authority not only in Ireland but in England too. Accordingly, in 1394 Richard went to Ireland for just over seven months – a visit too short to enable him to subdue the Irish by force, but long enough to arrest the decay of English power. The expedition was useful, too, in helping Richard to build up his military forces, especially from his own estates. If the king was not to be at the mercy of the private armies which his magnates had developed in the French wars, he must raise an army himself. Just as the retainers of other lords wore their masters' badge, so the king's men-at-arms and archers wore his cognizance of a white hart.

By 1397 the king felt strong enough to strike. Gloucester, Arundel, and Warwick were suddenly arrested, and lords of the king's party 'appealed' them of treason, as his friends had been appealed in 1388. Owing to the reconstruction of Westminster Hall, Parliament met at Westminster in an open-sided temporary building, and through the open sides could be seen Richard's retainers wearing his white hart, and called up in strength. This Parliament executed, imprisoned, or deprived his opponents, and was then adjourned to Shrewsbury, near to Cheshire, one of the strongest centres of Richard's military power. At Shrewsbury it declared illegal all the acts of the Merciless Parliament and rehabilitated defenders of royal authority as far back as the Despensers. By an unprecedented act the Commons granted to the king the duties on wool and leather for the rest of his life.

Shortly afterwards Richard seized an opportunity to exile Gaunt's eldest son, Henry. Now that Gloucester and Arundel were dead, Richard was afraid to be left face to face with the might of the house of Lancaster. When Gaunt died in February, 1399, the king forbade Henry to enter into his inheritance and extended his term of banishment to lifelong exile. This blunder turned the greatest magnate of the realm into his bitter foe and gave the opposition an able leader. It also unsettled all the propertied classes; for if even a duke of Lancaster could be debarred from his inheritance by mere royal decree, would any man's possessions be safe? Such an act was all the more dangerous because since the Parliament of Shrewsbury Richard had been making himself unpopular with the politically powerful classes. He tried to exercise a strict control over local government, he used prerogative courts of law, with their authoritarian tendencies, he demanded large loans, and he exorted from suspected persons sealed blank charters which he could later fill up as he pleased if they offended him.

Confident of the divine right of his royal prerogative, and elated by his success, Richard did not realize how slender were the foundations of his authority. He had a fatal incapacity to judge situations and read men's minds; and he chose this critical time to leave his kingdom for Ireland, where his lieutenant, Roger Mortimer, Earl of March, had just been killed. But as Richard was childless, his heir-presumptive had been Roger, whose death left only his six-year-old son between Henry of Lancaster and the succession to the throne. Yet Richard not only went to Ireland, but appointed as regent his incompetent uncle, Edmund, Duke of York. A few weeks later Henry of Lancaster landed at Ravenspur on the Humber, and was warmly welcomed by the northern lords, especially the powerful Henry Percy, Earl of Northumberland. Lancaster acted with such speed and skill that York and Richard's other incompetent lieutenants in England were out-manoeuvred. When Richard reached Conway he found only a tiny band of supporters awaiting him.

From Conway he could have escaped by sea, to Ireland, to Gascony, or to the French Court; instead he delivered himself into Henry's hands. Recent research has revealed that he was tricked by Henry, who swore solemnly that Richard should remain king if the Lancastrian inheritance were restored and Henry were made hereditary steward of England. Once in Henry's hands, however, Richard was hurried to London and imprisoned in the Tower. A Parliament was summoned in his name, but the day before it was to meet some sort of renunciation was wrung from him. Lancastrian propaganda said that he had abdicated, voluntarily and with a cheerful countenance. When the Lords and Commons assembled, they were faced with an empty throne. Richard's supposed deed of abdication was read out, and thirty-three charges against him were recited. The few who were brave enough to protest that he should have a hearing were overruled, and Henry of Lancaster at once rose to claim the Crown by descent, conquest, and the need for better rule. The fact was that a great magnate had taken advantage of discontent to seize the throne by force. His title by descent was weak, and the claim to make a revolution because of 'default of governance and undoyng of the gode lawes' was a weapon which could later be used against him. His troubles soon began. In January, 1400, some of Richard's adherents, who at first had been too stunned to act, rose in his favour. Their revolt was crushed, and Henry's government decided that the royal prisoner in Pontefract Castle was too dangerous to be allowed to live. A fortnight later he was dead.

The favourite explanation of Richard's failure is that he was always mentally unbalanced, and finally mad. It is true that he was temperamental, tactless, and emotional, too fond of flaunting his authority instead of exercising it unobtrusively, and a bad judge of character and situations. After his victory in 1397 he grew increasingly reckless, capricious, and tyrannical, and it may be that in these last years he became mentally unbalanced. Nevertheless, it should be recognized that not only his failings but his talents worked to his destruction. He preferred beauty and refinement to war; and, just as Henry III had been despised by the magnates, Richard found his tastes and qualities, from his patronage of art to his introduction of the use of handkerchiefs, regarded as extravagant and effeminate. To concentrate on the defects of Richard's character is to underestimate the difficulties of the situation. Some of his policies were the same as much-praised Tudor aims – to strengthen the authority of the Crown as the surest safeguard against aristocratic faction and civil strife, to end the waste of resources in the French war, and to assert instead the power of the English Crown in the British Isles. To have achieved these aims an abler king than Richard would have needed a more favourable situation. Richard reaped the harvest of his grandfather's policy, and lacked the strong support of the middle classes which was such a pillar of Tudor government. Not until Henry V's renewal of the French war had brought defeat and civil war in its train would the aristocracy be decisively weakened, the Crown's resources strengthened, and the rising middle classes convinced that a strong monarchy was essential to their safety and prosperity. Only then would the Crown be able to achieve the aims for which Richard II had striven in vain. Only then would the monarchy escape from its tragic dilemma.

## CHAPTER II

# The Government of the Realm

THE barons might demand that the administration of the realm should be in accordance with their outlook and wishes; for were they not the proper leaders of society and the natural councillors of the king? But except in revolutionary years, such as 1310 or 1388, none but a few extremists denied that it was the king's right and duty to govern; indeed, failure to govern efficiently was one of the grounds for the deposition of Edward II.

In governing, the kings of England had certain advantages. England was small enough for the important parts of it to be within reach of the central government. The Scottish marches and most of Wales were, it is true, only very weakly controlled by this government; but the economic strength of the kingdom lay, roughly speaking, south-east of a line joining Exeter, Chester, and York. Moreover, England was fairly well united. The turbulence and power of northern or Welsh marcher lords were at times a great menace to the monarchy; but the English kings did not have to contend with great baronial houses, almost independent of royal authority, controlling compact blocks of territory, in the way that the French kings had to struggle against the might of Flanders and Brittany, Burgundy and Aquitaine. They were undisputed military leaders of the nation, with valuable powers of organizing military and police arrangements throughout the realm. By the fourteenth century they had been able to secure that the law of the royal courts – the common law – should normally extend its influence throughout the land, except in the marches; and they had enjoyed since Anglo-Saxon times the right to financial aid from their subjects for the defence of the realm. Moreover, although in this century two kings were deposed, there was no open challenge to the position of the monarchy. Edward II and Richard II made, in form at least, voluntary abdication of the throne. Both Edward III and Henry IV stressed their hereditary right; both claimed to exercise undiminished all the rights and prerogatives of their predecessors, and in both cases this claim was, in form, universally acknowledged.

In actual fact, both Edward II and his great-grandson had been deposed by their barons, and this could not fail to weaken the power of the monarchy. We have seen how Edward III tried to conciliate his magnates, a policy which seriously depleted the resources of the Crown. When the century began the crown lands had been insufficient for the king's needs, and he was driven increasingly to ask for financial aid from his subjects. Whatever might have been the legal theory, in practice it was necessary to obtain consent for such financial grants, which were almost always grudging and hardly ever adequate; hence the kings had constantly to be disposing of their lands, thus diminishing their revenue still further. During the thirteenth century the inadequacy of the Crown's resources had driven the kings to make repeated confirmations of Magna Carta, confirmations so frequent that the Crown's obligations to observe Magna Carta and subsequent concessions had by the early fourteenth century become part of the national tradition.

Thus, although in 1307 the king was the mainspring of the government, there were already some important limitations to his power. Another check on the personal will of the king was connected, paradoxical as it may seem, with the growth of the royal administration, which by the end of the thirteenth century was already highly developed and complex. In the older departments of government, esprit de corps and traditional methods already often acted as a brake on the king's wishes. The Exchequer, for example, which had evolved in the twelfth century, already had an elaborate routine to which it was strongly attached; and if the king tried to resort to novel financial expedients or to short-circuit the lengthy Exchequer routine, he might find himself hampered by silent obstruction. Moreover, in a department as old as the Exchequer some of the posts had become hereditary. By the early fourteenth century one of the two important offices of chamberlain of the Exchequer belonged to the Earl of Warwick, and under Edward II we have the curious spectacle of one of the heads of the baronial opposition having the right to nominate to an important post in the king's administrative machine. These drawbacks were not so evident in the case of the Chancery, then the great secretarial department of the royal government, but a similar departmental tradition was growing up there too, and, as with the Exchequer, the Chancery's organization and methods dated from a time when royal activity had been small, and its routine meticulous and slow.

Where speed and adaptability were essential, as in the recruitment of armies and the organization of military expeditions, the Exchequer and Chancery were not suitable instruments. It is not surprising that during the thirteenth century the kings had developed in their household another financial and secretarial department, more completely under their control, and more adapted to new situations and needs than the older offices of state. Even in a royal household in the thirteenth century the only place private enough for transacting important or confidential business, and for storing valuables, was usually the king's bedroom or chamber, and the closet opening off the chamber, the wardrobe where the king's clothes were kept. By the time of Edward I the Wardrobe had become, in effect, a new treasury and a new chancery, entrusted, among other matters, with military administration. The new department would have been of little use to the king if all its orders had had to go through the Exchequer or Chancery routine, and be authenticated by the Exchequer seal or the great seal kept by the chancellor. Hence the Wardrobe built up financial resources and secretarial methods not subject to Exchequer or Chancery control, and it had its own seal for authenticating documents – the privy seal.

It was a long time before the barons realized the importance of the Wardrobe as a weapon of royal power. But by

1310 they had done so, and in the Ordinances of 1311 they resolved to make of it an office of state, the head of which should be appointed only with the consent of the magnates. At the same time they determined to subject its activities to the control of the Exchequer and Chancery. The king struggled hard against this, but the opposition succeeded in depriving the Wardrobe of much of the resources which it had hitherto diverted from the Exchequer. Lack of money partly explains the defeat of Bannockburn, which was regarded by the barons as a defeat for the royal household. Eventually Edward II, no longer able to rely on the Wardrobe and the privy seal as effective weapons in his political and military struggles, began to develop the Chamber and the secret seal instead, as instruments of royal authority; but though he managed to obtain independent control of some resources for the Chamber, he never succeeded in raising it to the importance which the Wardrobe had enjoyed.

When Edward II had been deposed, the Chamber sank into obscurity; but a few years later Edward III revived his father's policy. By this time the keeper of the privy seal was, owing to the baronial opposition of Edward II's reign, becoming a great officer of state; Edward III therefore created a new seal, the griffin, for the use of the Chamber. Besides this, the Wardrobe was revived when he wished to prepare for war against France, and played the same military and financial role as it had done under Edward I. It was jealousy of the important role of the Chamber and Wardrobe which goaded the treasurer and chancellor to be obstructive in 1340, so leading to the crisis of 1341. After 1341, however, the king abandoned his attempts at personal rule for the sake of wholehearted support for the French war by the magnates and the great officers of state. The system of Household control, which under Edward I had barely sufficed to finance wars on a small scale waged largely in Britain, proved altogether inadequate for the administration of the great continental compaigns of the Hundred Years War; hence the Chamber and Wardrobe lost their former importance, and their activities were brought into line with those of the Exchequer and Chancery.

In the reign of Richard II, even when he was in the ascendant, the Chamber and Wardrobe played a less prominent part than they had done in the reigns of Edward II and III. This has led some historians to minimize the importance of the Household in Richard's schemes. It is true that his personal seal, the secret seal or signet, did not have the same controversial importance as the privy seal had had under Edward II, or the griffin seal in the early years of Edward III. Nor was the clerk of the signet, the secretary, as yet the important official he later became; though it was in Richard II's reign that the secretary first became of administrative consequence and head of a staff of signet clerks. But the remarkable ebb and flow in the prominence of the signet and the secretary with the vicissitudes of Richard's fortunes shows that these instruments were of value to him until in 1397 he gained complete control of the Exchequer, Chancery, and privy seal. Richard at times made considerable use of the Household for military organization; recent research has shown what a high degree of confidence he placed in his chamberlains and in the knights and esquires of his chamber, and what an important part they played in building up the personal rule of the last two years of his reign.

During the thirteenth and fourteenth centuries the royal Wardrobe had at times so much to do with organizing the king's military affairs that in the fourteenth century a sub-department, the Privy Wardrobe, was gradually evolved to store arms and armour. As the king was constantly travelling, and arms and armour were too bulky and heavy to be constantly on the move, the Privy Wardrobe was gradually separated from the royal household and settled in the Tower of London. There this store of military equipment (including guns and ammunition) was convenient for continental expeditions.

By the early fourteenth century the feudal method of raising an army – as an obligation of land tenure – was nearly dead. Edward I was the last king to try to make it the basis of his military organization, and in 1385, after a long interval, the feudal army was summoned for the last time. Already Edward I had begun to raise troops by indenture or contract, whereby a commander settled with the king the conditions of specified military service – the number and type of troops, the length and place of service, the rate of wages, and the obligations and rewards to be rendered. The advantages of this indenture system over the dying method of service by the feudal tenure showed themselves in the Scottish campaigns; and when Edward III was confronted with the raising of troops for a great continental war, the indenture system received a tremendous impetus. The feudal levy was hard to assemble, and incoherent and un-disciplined when it met; whereas the new system made even the greatest commander anxious to bring a full contingent of troops, and encouraged discipline and the subordination of commands. The feudal army was reluctant to serve abroad, and its duty was limited to forty days; but inden-tured troops would readily fight in France, for as long as the Crown could pay them. The indenture system was eventu-ally to breed a great menace to the Crown, but for the time being it saved the king trouble. Once the contract had been made, it was the commander's responsibility to produce, equip, and organize his men. The lords, prominent in mak-ing such indentures, had their own household officials, and their own budgets for military organization. For the king the most immediate problem was how to find the vast sums which such a system demanded for a prolonged and large-scale war. He and his ministers tried every possible expedient, but were driven increasingly to rely on taxation. Those who paid the piper wished to call the tune, especially when the war ceased to be successful; and in the latter years of Edward III's reign and during that of Richard II, a special political organization under a treasurer of war, responsible to Parlia-ment where the taxes were voted, superseded the expanded Wardrobe as the directive authority under the king for the campaigns abroad. Richard II's few campaigns within the

British Isles were, however, still administered in the old way by Household officials.

Besides the heavily-armed and armoured knights, the hobelars (light horsemen), and the archers produced by the indenture system, the king had a less important source of supply of soldiers. This was the ancient principle that all able-bodied men were bound to arm themselves and serve to keep the peace and defend the realm, and by the statute of Winchester (1285), as later modified, every free man between 16 and 60 had to provide himself with suitable weapons, according to the value of his lands and chattels. The men thus armed were organized in the various hundreds and linked up for the whole shire under the control of the sheriff. The force so formed, the shire levy, was available for use not only as a civil instrument for public purposes, but also as a military weapon for local defence. In practice only a part of the whole militia was usually mobilized when it was needed, and supported by the contributions of those left at home; the contingent to be mobilized was chosen by special officers known as commissioners of array, usually of the country-gentry class. They were supposed to choose the strongest and best-armed men; but the methods of Shallow and Falstaff were not unknown in the fourteenth century.

The king's household officials do not seem to have had the share in naval affairs which they had in the affairs of the army. By the fourteenth century there was already an office for naval administration, supplies in the Tower of London, and a 'clerk of the king's ships'. He did not have many to look after; towards the end of Edward III's reign, for example, there were probably about twenty ships, most of them small. In time of war the chief naval requirement was the transport of men, provisions, and other supplies for the army. If it came to a fight at sea, it was merely a land-battle on the water, with no thought that naval tactics were a separate branch of military science. Merchant vessels could easily be fitted when necessary with forecastles, aftercastles, and fighting-tops, and thus according to the ideas of the time be made completely ready for war. Hence most of the navy could in time of war be raised by impressment or contract from the chief ports. The Cinque Ports, for example, were bound to supply for the service of the crown fifty-seven ships for a period of forty days each year; and in 1347, at the siege of Calais, from which one of the first lists of the English fleet has survived, the king evidently had more than half the ships in England in use as warships. These methods were a heavy burden on English traders in times of prolonged warfare, such as the reign of Edward III. The war-time navy was usually organized under two admirals, normally of the knightly class; the authority of one extended from the mouth of the Thames northwards, and that of the other from the Thames south-westwards. In view of the dangerous hostility between the sailors of Yarmouth and those of the Cinque Ports, this was a sensible arrangement. The admirals were appointed for the duration of hostilities only; in time of truce or peace their clerks went back to the government departments – Exchequer, Chancery, or Wardrobe – from which they had been drawn. The king also saved money in peacetime by hiring out his own few ships to merchants for trading voyages. It is therefore not surprising that, in spite of Edward III's fitful claims to the dominion of the sea, it was at times impossible to prevent French raids on the English coasts, or piracy in home waters, or even battles between the sailors of English ports hostile to one another.

Just as the growing specialization and routine of the Exchequer and Chancery had to some extent removed them from the king's personal control, so his personal influence over the Crown's judicial activities was not what it once had been. The Court of Common Pleas, with its own records, its own chief justice, and a well-developed procedure, had already become quite separate from the royal household before the beginning of the fourteenth century. By this time the Court usually met at Westminster, and the judges were becoming specialists. In the thirteenth century they had been royal clerks, but by the reign of Edward III these had been replaced by lawyers who had made their career at the bar.

The most important part of the Court's jurisdiction was that exercised over common pleas – that is, over actions between subject and subject, especially suits connected with land. An appeal in error lay from its decisions to the Court of King's Bench. The official title of the King's Bench was 'curia regis coram rege' –the king's court held in his presence – and its two distinctive spheres of competence – jurisdiction in error and in criminal cases – sprang from a close connexion with the king's person. At the beginning of the fourteenth century the King's Bench still travelled about with the royal household and when the king wished it cases were heard before him and his counsellors, but during the century the King's Bench lost its former close connexion with the king and his Council.

Thus by the end of the fourteenth century the Courts of Common Pleas and King's Bench, like the other great common-law court evolved in the Exchequer, the Court of Exchequer, worked to a growing extent independently of the king; but the extent of their independence, like that of the Exchequer and Chancery, must not be exaggerated. In spite of an attachment to precedents, settled routine, and esprit de corps, the justices were very conscious that they were royal servants, bound to safeguard the king's interests. In 1387, for example, Chief Justice Tresilian and his fellow-judges pronounced that the parliament of 1386 had encroached unwarrantably on the royal prerogative. It is anachronistic to accuse them of cowardly subservience; they were probably quite sincere in their decision, and regarded themselves as maintaining the most lawful tradition of government. It is true that the independence and intractability of the common-law courts inclined Richard II to favour exceptional tribunals, such as the Courts of the Admirals, of the Constable and Marshal, of the Steward and Marshal, as more expeditious and more inclined to favour royal authority and interests. But all the departments of government were still in fairly close contact, and the justices of the Courts of Common Pleas and King's Bench, and the judges of the Exchequer Court, known as barons of the Exchequer, were often called in to advise the king and his counsellors, even at the end of the fourteenth century.

Counsel was indispensable to the conduct of the king's business, however autocratic the king tried to be, and counsel by this time took various forms. For the conduct of everyday affairs a small Council advised the king, and this was the mainstay of the king in government and a most effective force in administration, either in conjunction with him, or, as often, on its own. It was natural that such an important body should change in character with the changing political and social conditions of the fourteenth century. In the reign of Edward I the permanent or continual Council was normally a body of expert administrators rather than of magnates. It consisted essentially of the chief ministers, the principal officials of the royal household, some justices and Exchequer barons, some Chancery and Wardrobe clerks; to these were added a variable number of prelates, barons, knights, and royal confidants. From the time of Edward I some of the councillors swore an oath to give good advice, serve the king faithfully, and keep his secrets; but the mere taking of such an oath did not entitle a man to attend, and the advice of unsworn members could be just as important as that of the sworn. The kings insisted that they had the right to consult whom they pleased, and that it would therefore be an unwarrantable limitation of their prerogative for the Council to be fixed in numbers and composition. The magnates took quite another view. They regarded themselves as the natural counsellors of the king, and in times of crisis tried to enforce their claim. At such times they were supported by the country gentry and the merchants, who did not want the arduous task of government themselves, but liked to blame those in authority when things went wrong; they then demanded a Council of great men and of fixed composition, on which they could pin responsibility.

Edward II had fierce struggles with his barons over the personnel of his Council, but Edward III, especially after 1341, pursued a policy of conciliation towards the lords, and did not summon to his Council any who had not the confidence of the magnates. His policy greatly strengthened baronial influence on the government, and as he sank into his dotage the dominant aristocratic factions struggled for pre-eminence in the Council. When the boy Richard became king the lords secured the appointment of a Council of fixed composition, dominated by themselves, and throughout his reign there were conflicts over its personnel. Partly because the opposition lords, whenever they were in the ascendancy, pressed for a Council of fixed and publicly known composition, the Council tended by the end of this reign to be better defined in personnel and more exclusively aristocratic than it had been before.

By this time the Council exercised direction over the various aspects of the king's government and was usually consulted on all questions of policy, both domestic and foreign. As the king was supposed to be the source of justice, the Council had a good deal of judicial work, often because of the alleged corruption of the lesser law courts or their inability to provide a remedy for wrongs. For more than a century important judicial cases and questions of policy had been reserved for the consideration of special solemn assemblies, in which originally the justices and principal officials of the government were prominent to give expert advice. The word parliament, which had originally meant simply any important talk or discussion, was gradually limited to these assemblies. Edward I had summoned many of the magnates to his Parliaments, for the barons claimed to be the king's natural counsellors, and might make trouble, as they had done in Henry III's day, if they felt that they had no influence in important matters of law and policy. In any case their cooperation was usually necessary to implement important decisions, such as war. But Edward I had summoned which lords he pleased, whereas in his son's reign the chief magnates insisted that they had a right to be summoned. Edward III, in accordance with his policy of conciliating the barons, tacitly acceded to this demand, and in his reign the lords, spiritual and temporal, were not only always in a large majority in the Council in Parliament, but the same men were summoned time after time. The justices and royal officials in the Council in Parliament tended to sink from principal councillors to mere advisers; and whereas Edward I would have as many as thirty such officials at a Parliament, Edward III rarely invited more than ten, and sometimes only five or less. By the reign of Richard II the lords could claim that they alone were the king's councillors in Parliament, whose advice was essential on all important matters of law and policy, and they resented upstarts being summoned to sit among them. They asserted that the king and lords assembled in Parliament constituted the highest court in the land, and, beginning in 1376, even ventured at times to try the king's ministers and confidants for misconduct. They said that the lay lords, and perhaps the prelates, habitually summoned to Parliament were peers of the realm; and as long ago as 1341 the king had been forced to agree to a statute enacting that when the king was prosecutor, no peer should be judged except by his peers in full Parliament. But we must beware of antedating the stages in the development of Parliament. By 1399 the lords had not yet established a hereditary claim to a summons; the king still exercised some choice in the summons of lords to Parliament. Parliaments were still held very much at the king's discretion, and normally his government largely determined the order and nature of business transacted. Parliaments were, in fact as well as in form, still to a great extent the king's.

By 1399 representatives of the Commons were always summoned to Parliaments; whereas when the century began their presence had not been essential. Representatives were originally summoned primarily because the king wished to give the utmost publicity to his financial needs, and to obtain the fullest possible cooperation for the collection of taxes through the communities of the shires and boroughs. At the beginning of the century these communities were not anxious to be represented, for they had to pay their representatives' expenses at a high rate; and if the king did summon knights and burgesses they were not considered part of the Parliament. They appeared before the king's councillors in Parliament merely to listen and to answer questions put to them. Although the role of the Commons was thus so humble, the classes to which they belonged, the country gentry and the merchants, were by now of some political importance. During the reign of Edward II both king and magnates found it worth their while to cultivate the support of these classes, and so representatives were summoned to Parliaments more frequently. Even more important for the Commons was the next reign, for Edward III's war policy entailed such vast expenditure that his normal revenues were quite inadequate, and he constantly needed help from taxes. The first instinct of the representatives was to regard taxation as a very extraordinary evil; but when, by the middle of the century, they realized that it was becoming a regular feature of national life, they insisted on control of taxation – not only, as hitherto, of taxes on movable property, but of customs duties which the king had previously negotiated direct with the merchants. Edward resisted this claim, but finally yielded to it. Faced with common demands, the knights and burgesses began during this reign to meet together in one body, the knights, in view of their superior social status, taking the lead. Until the sixteenth century it was always a knight who acted as speaker of the Commons, and spoke on their behalf in full Parliament before the king and lords.

During the reign of Edward III the Commons began to frame or sponsor more and more petitions, and by the end of the century this had become a well-established right. In the time of Richard II it became increasingly frequent for bills put forward by the lords to be sent to the Commons later, and in 1382 a statute was repealed on the grounds that the Commons had not given their assent to it. But, as with the history of the lords in Parliament, one must not antedate developments. Both public and private petitions could still be presented to Parliament without the participation of the Commons. At the end of the fourteenth century the king still often rejected petitions wholly or in part, or granted something different from what the petition asked. Then, although the Commons liked to criticize those in authority when things were going wrong (especially if financial burdens were involved), they did not want the dangerous responsibility of sharing in the government. When, for example, in 1348 they were asked for advice on the conduct of the war, they pleaded that they were too ignorant and simple to advise on such high matters; and in 1399 they obtained a declaration on the king's behalf that the judicial work of Parliament appertained to the king and lords alone, and that the Commons had no share in it. Above all, it must be remembered that functions now usually regarded as exclusive to Parliament were then by no means confined to it, and that the ordinary work of government normally went forward without it. In the fourteenth century even legislation could be, and often was, extra-parliamentary. The Council still made ordinances on important matters; indeed, it needed the deposition of Richard II to establish clearly the principle that royal ordinances were inferior to parliamentary statutes. Moreover, the Crown often exercised a wide discretion in the application of statutes, such as the well-known Statute of Treasons, 1352; and the king often dispensed from the operation of statutes. Thus individual merchants might be allowed to trade with a particular country in spite of statutory regulations, or clerks might be permitted to accept a papal provision to a benefice, notwithstanding the Statute of Provisors of 1351; and thousands of licences authorized the gift of land to the Church, notwithstanding the Statute of Mortmain of 1279. There were many subjects, such as the doctrines, constitution, and recognized jurisdiction of the Church, on which Parliament had no power to legislate. In 1387, and again in 1397, Richard II secured judgements that Parliaments could not limit the royal prerogative; but for his deposition these judgements might have become a clearly established doctrine.

The knights and burgesses who attended Parliaments might describe themselves as ignorant and simple to escape responsibility and please their social superiors; but in reality many of them, especially the knights, had had much experience in public affairs. Since the thirteenth century the Crown had constrained the knightly class to be increasingly active as unpaid agents in local government. It is true that since Anglo-Saxon times the monarchy had had sheriffs to safeguard its local interests, and that in the fourteenth century the sheriffs still had important functions. Until the appointment of lord-lieutenants under the Tudors the sheriff remained the leader of the shire-levies; he was normally responsible for seeing that the men of the lower classes in his shire were organized in groups called tithings for police and surety purposes and for the holding of the old local courts, the shire and hundred moots; it was his duty to arrest suspects and carry out penalties adjudged by the courts; royal writs were addressed to him, and prisoners awaiting trial were entrusted to him; and through his bailiffs he usually collected the Crown's older sources of revenue from the shire. The sheriffs had long been generally hated, for they had great opportunities for oppression and extortion. The kings suspected them of feathering their nests at the Crown's expense, and were not loath to win popularity by clipping their wings. As new needs arose in local government, the functions to which they gave rise were entrusted to new officials, and even some of the sheriffs' previous powers were taken away from them. By the fourteenth century the kings had well developed the system of itinerant justices who toured the country in circuits, and these were a useful check on the sheriffs, as well as valuable links between central and local government. Their visits were, however, too rare for the Crown, which needed resident local agents.

These the king found in the country gentry, whose unpaid services he called upon in an increasing variety of ways – as jurors, as assistants to the itinerant justices, as commissioners of array, as tax-collectors, and as coroners. At the beginning of the thirteenth century it looked as though the office of coroner had a great future; but the Crown had had misgivings about it, possibly because the office was elective and therefore too insecurely under royal control. The kings developed instead the office of keeper of the peace, filled by men of the knightly class appointed by the Crown. In the fourteenth century the powers of the keepers of the peace were greatly and frequently extended, and towards the end of Edward III's reign they became known as Justices of the Peace. By the end of the century they were exercising very extensive police, judicial, and administrative functions, ranging from the arrest of offenders to the trying of felonies and misdemeanours committed in the country, and from the fixing of maximum wages and prices to the supervising of the administration of the shire. The Quarter Sessions, which originated in an act of 1362, were already becoming a veritable governing body for the county. This development saved the Crown money, but was a source of weakness and danger; for the J.P.s were often closely connected to the magnates who were overawing the king, and were in any case independent in spirit.

Local government was not yet by any means entirely in the hands of the Crown's officials, paid or unpaid. Apart from the towns, including all the large ones, which by the end of the fourteenth century had bought the right of self-government, many administrative and judicial functions which we should regard as belonging to the Crown were then in private hands. Since at least the days of Edward I the Crown had kept a close watch on those who claimed to exercise such functions in liberties and franchises, as they were called; but this did not mean that all such franchises were rapidly whittled away. For defect of good order and justice the king could, and did, take a franchise into his own hands; but he was not necessarily hostile to all franchises on principle. Indeed, in the south-east of England franchisal jurisdiction usually dovetailed smoothly with royal jurisdiction. Cooperation and profit-sharing were often the most prominent features of the relationship between the Crown and great franchise-holders like the Bishop of Ely or the Abbot of Peterborough. Indeed, the same official was not infrequently employed simultaneously by the king and the privilege-holder. Sometimes men who began their careers as bailiffs or stewards for some great lord ended their days in the service of the Crown, and such transitions were all the easier because the magnates modelled their administration on that of the king. As Bishop Stubbs observed, 'every baron on his own property practised the method and enforced the discipline which he knew and shared in the king's court'.

The greatest franchises were to be found in the north and west. The wide powers of northern lords like the Nevilles and Percies and the almost regal authority of the bishops of Durham could, perhaps, be justified by the perpetual state of unrest on the Scottish border in the late middle ages. These lords needed great authority to enable them to resist sudden Scottish raids and attempt to keep some order in the lawless border region. But on the Welsh marches things were otherwise; Welsh independence had disappeared in Edward I's reign, yet the Welsh marcher lords – over a hundred of them – still exercised very great powers, claiming them, moreover, by right of conquest and not by grant of the Crown. During the fourteenth century the great franchise-holders were consolidating their legal position and increasing their practical powers, and the lords of the Welsh and Scottish marches played a very prominent role in the politics of late medieval England.

A greater threat to order and justice than the power of the marcher lords was, however, the perversion by magnates all over England of the expanding system of royal administration. This, in one sense a sign of the growing unity of England, was nevertheless a creeping disease which affected not only the outlying members of the body politic but also its vital centres: victims of the bribery or intimidation of sheriffs and justices, commissioners and jurors appealed in vain to a Parliament or a Council dominated by the very magnates responsible for these offences.

This growing political and administrative power of the lords was closely linked with economic and social development; and to these we must now turn.

CHAPTER III

# Economic and Social Developments

In the late middle ages England was still predominantly an agricultural country, in normal times self-supporting in essential foodstuffs. Though trade and industry had become more important than in Norman times agriculture was still the occupation of the majority of the people – as it was to remain until the nineteenth century.

In most of the richest and important parts of the country the open-field system was the usual method of cultivation. It prevailed in the middle south, the midlands, Lincolnshire, and East Yorkshire. The normal type of settlement in these areas was a village community of a cluster of houses standing in the middle of its territory, the most important part of which was the arable land, divided into two, three, or four great fields. In these, the villagers held their land in scattered strips; so, too, did the lord or lords of the village, if they had any land in the village. The strips were usually separated by unsown furrows, so that the cultivated area would have seemed very open to modern eyes. The intermingling of the strips necessitated cooperation in cultivation. It was very difficult for one man to plough or sow or reap his strips at a different time from another, and the weeds in a lazy man's strips were of great concern to his neighbours. Cooperation was necessary for other means of livelihood, too. The quantity of hay which a villager might draw from the common meadows, the number of pigs and poultry which he might support in the woods and wastes round the village, were regulated by custom, in accordance with the size of his arable holding, and his social standing in the village.

Nearly all these villages were under a lord; often under the control of one, but frequently divided between several. Conversely, four or five villages might be grouped in one great manorial unit. At the beginning of the fourteenth

54

century most of these villagers were unfree, the more substantial often being known as villeins, the poorer ones as
cottars. They tilled their lord's land, could not leave their
holdings, and were in some respects their lord's property,
part of the livestock of the estate. The affairs of these unfree
peasants were therefore regulated by the manorial court of
the lord or lords of the village; but the custom of the manor,
by which disputes were normally settled and the agricultural year was regulated, was declared by the suitors of the
court. The villagers were organized into tithing-groups for
police and surety purposes, and it was often the head men of
these tithings who were trusted to declare the custom of the
village. Great lords had councils, just as the king had his,
and these sometimes overrode manorial custom; but usually
appeal to custom decided most of the village's affairs.

School text-books used to describe 'the medieval manor'
as if there were one uniform system of agriculture and rural
organization all over England. But geographical variations
alone would have made that impossible. The open-field system of the midlands could not be worked in the woodland
pastures of the Kentish weald, the fishing, bird-hunting, and
cattle-rearing country of Romney Marsh or the Fens, the
mountains of Wales or the Lake District, the rugged country
north of the Tees, or the moors and heaths of Lancashire
and Devon. Regions like Kent, so near to the market of
London and to industrial Flanders, and East Anglia, pro-
ductive and populous, were likely to develop faster than the
poorer, more remote and sparsely populated north and west.
And geographical differences were reinforced by historical
ones. Down the western side of England, for example, from
the Lake District to Cornwall, the variety produced by local
conditions was increased by Celtic influences, and the
diverse and important contrasts to the midland type of rural
organization may be seen in this western region. Here were
found such non-midland features as small open arable fields,
with little rotation of crops; an intensive cultivation and
manuring of the 'in-field', and a primitive cultivation of the
'out-field' until its fertility was exhausted for the time being;

the lord's demesne small, if any, and the dependence of several settlements on a sometimes distant manor; division of land among co-heirs, and the importance of rents and dues rather than of labour services; the prominence in this hillier and wetter region of sheep-walks and cattle-ranches rather than of arable land. Even the settlements were not of the midland type. Instead of the large village, straggling down its village street, we find hamlets of a few houses, or even isolated farms, often because of the needs of pastoral farming, the lower fertility of the soil, or the readier accessibility of water supplies.

There was variety not only between the various regions of England but within the open-field system itself. On fertile soils a three- or even a four-field system might be ventured, to reduce the amount of arable land which had to be left fallow at any one time; whereas on poorer soils only a two-field system might be possible, in view of the inadequate supply of manure from the small, lean cattle of the time and the insufficient knowledge of crop rotation. In the stimulating agricultural boom of the thirteenth century, with an expanding market and a rising population, efforts were made to increase the productivity of the land, and great lords especially, ecclesiastical and lay alike, devoted themselves with zest to the business of farming. For them Walter of Henley and other writers on estate management composed their treatises. Intakes or assarts from the waste round the existing fields provided fresh arable land, so that by the end of the thirteenth century there was more land under the plough than ever before or possibly since, and devices for increasing the fertility of the soil, such as the spreading of marl or the cultivation of peas, were increasingly used. The boom brought still more variety, for the pace of advance varied not only with the fertility and climate but with the intelligence of the cultivators and the landlords. Some of the great Benedictine abbeys, for instance, set an example of high farming which included the specialization of certain manors to pursuits such as sheep-rearing or dairy-farming; just as the Cistercian wool-growers of Rievaulx or Fountains responded to an age of rising prices and an expanding market by organizing their manors by groups, ewes being kept on one, wethers on another, and hoggets on a third.

And divergencies were stimulated not only by the differing business capacity of the various landholders, but by varying opportunities – especially in the marketing of the produce. Remote settlements, such as hamlets in the Pennines, were often isolated enough to conform to the old text-book standard of self-sufficiency; the hamlet would itself satisfy all its ordinary needs except the salt indispensable for the winter curing of meat, the iron necessary for tools, the tar used for sheep scab, and a few other wants. But in the villages of the south and east and midlands there was usually much more intercourse with the world outside than is often realized. Ecclesiastics, royal and manorial officials, and pedlars would visit the village, and substantial peasants journey away from it to attend a law court or make a pilgrimage. Many villages were on important highways, and in such cases a constant stream of travellers would pass through them and stay at the inn or the abbey. Fairs and markets were numerous, and great fairs like those of Winchester or Stourbridge brought merchants not only from other parts of England but from abroad. The home counties were already producing for the London market. Many villages formed part of great estates, a relationship which usually involved much movement. By the early fourteenth century all great estates were farming for the market; and most crops were taken to some fixed centre (the abbey on monastic estates or the chief residences of the lord on secular ones), or were marketed for cash. In either case carting was necessary, and this was usually performed, not by professional carriers, but by peasants of the manor in which the crop was produced, which meant that simple folk might go a long way on such carrying expeditions. The peasants of the Fenland abbey of Ramsey, in the villages near the monastery, carted as far as Huntingdon, St Ives, Cambridge, Ipswich, Colchester, London, and Canterbury. In fact, the amount of carting to be done for the great estates was so large that the great landholders found it worth their while to maintain in good order the roads which connected their estates; largely because of this the roads of the country were on the whole in better condition at the beginning of the fourteenth century than they were to be for the next four centuries. And besides the carting of the great estates, there was transport for war purposes. Sheriffs and lords in the south of England, for example, would be told to provide carriage for arms and victuals to the north for the Scottish campaigns, and such carriage would take many peasants on long journeys from their villages. So, too, did building operations which required carts for sand and timber, stone being so heavy that it was borne as far as possible by water.

There was thus more variety and movement at the beginning of our period than was formerly thought; and there was also more change taking place in the fortunes of the peasantry. Recent research has shown that even in the thirteenth century there was much buying and selling of land by free peasants, leasing and exchanging by unfree, even in the open-field villages of the midlands. A generation ago it was thought that as the use of money spread there was a correspondingly steady, if gradual, emancipation of the bondmen. It is now known that this conception of what happened is too simple, and indeed, in places the spread of money economy might mean, not emancipation, but a renewal of serfdom. In the far north and north-west of England, remote from markets and supplies of money, labour-services of the peasants were commuted early; whereas in the midlands and south-east in the thirteenth century there had been an increase in the labour-services exacted on great estates – even a revival of services already commuted. The reasons for these apparent paradoxes are to be found in the influence of trade and the type of farming. In the far north, where the market mattered little and the amount of arable land was small, lords valued dues in money or in kind more than labour-services; but in the south-east the importance of arable land was great, and the thirteenth century was an age of rising prices and an expanding market. Great lords, seeing the profits to be made out of business-like farming in such conditions, realized that costs of production would be lower if they exploited to the full the labour-services of their peasants instead of hiring labour; and as the expanding market encouraged them to increase the arable acreage of their estates, they were prompted to increase or revive the labour-services of their unfree tenantry, for the tilling of the extra acres. We now know of many struggles of thirteenth-century villeins against these increased burdens, struggles which were usually in vain, for the lords had a strong claim to increase the obligations of their bondmen at will, and the villeins could look for no protection from the king's courts, which were only for freemen.

The increase in labour services was not universal. Villeins usually performed their services unwillingly and the supervision necessary to secure a profitable efficiency was proportionately greater for a few bondmen than for many. The lord of a small estate might well find that such labour, inelastic in form as well as reluctantly given, was not worth the cost. If there was a plentiful supply of cheap wage labour available, as was the case in many parts of populous East Anglia, for example, it would pay him to commute the labour services due to him and use the money to hire husbandmen for his lands.

Even on big estates the desire to exact such dues gradually dwindled in the fourteenth century. This was not because of any important advance in the technique of arable farming, replacing labour by machines, nor because the magnates had lost their appetite for wealth – on the contrary, they wanted more revenue, not less. Standards of living in noble households had risen with the growth of trade, as they had risen in many great monasteries with relaxations of the Rule; and there was increasing social emulation in the form of magnificent hospitality, chivalric pageantry, or costly buildings and clothes. It was quite another reason which had led the magnates to commute labour services – an agricultural depression.

If economists fail to agree why twentieth-century booms are followed by slumps, it is not surprising that the reasons for this fourteenth-century depression, about which the information is so meagre, are still not clear. The growth of population in the thirteenth century had outstripped, for the labouring classes, the means of subsistence; this led to widespread malnutrition and increasing susceptibility to famine and plague. This growth seems to have stopped towards the end of Edward II's reign, and this meant a falling-off in the demand for food. The troubles of the reign were bad for production, especially in the north, where the Scots brought great devastation after Bannockburn. These factors synchronize with the beginning of the agricultural depression in many places in England; but such purely English phenomena cannot explain why the slump hit other countries of Western Europe at about the same time. One of the wider causes may have been that in the latter half of the thirteenth century the export of cereals from the newly-developed lands of Eastern Germany began to affect the markets of Western Europe, as the wheat of North America was to do six centuries later. Such new competition may have been the more serious because the thirteenth-century expansion in production in England and Western Europe may already have become too great for the available market, in view of the poverty of most of the people. The lack of sufficient demand for foodstuffs was made worse by the increasing costliness of handicraft products and imported goods compared with agricultural commodities. And, beginning with the anarchical interregnum in Germany (1250–72), Western Europe dissipated much of its newly-found agrarian prosperity in two centuries of great wars and civil strife. As far as England was concerned, the Hundred Years War was a continuation of chronic warfare from about 1295 – if not earlier.

Whatever the relative importance of these, and other, causes, the social consequences of the slump were important. The first onset of depression often prompted great lords to increase labour services, or to exact labour dues already commuted – as happened on the estates of Christ Church, Canterbury – in an effort to increase production and lower costs. But as the depression was deepened by the financial burdens of the Hundred Years War and the mortality of the Black Death, the lords gradually sought financial security by leasing their demesnes for rents. The speed of the process varied greatly according to the state of the local market; but the first demesnes to be leased were usually marginal lands and isolated, outlying estates. This development began before the first onslaught of the Black Death, which therefore did not start the commutation of labour services, as was once thought. Indeed, after the pestilence labour was so scarce, and the wages demanded by the peasants were so high, that landholders, alarmed and shocked, often renewed their demands for labour services. Nor, contrary to the old view, did the lords always find it impossible to let villein tenements; for the peasant population had apparently been so numerous before the Black Death in relation to the available land that in many areas even the heavy death-roll left enough land-hunger to provide new tenants for the vacant holdings. By about 1390, however, the amount of land which the lords were trying to lease was so great in relation to a population depleted by further attacks of the pestilence that, as recent research has shown, lords often began to experience a dearth of applicants. The Black Death hastened already existing tendencies. The Ordinance and Statute of Labourers (1349 and 1351) set up, it is true, justices of labourers with powers to fix maximum wage rates and enforce them under heavy penalties; and in the following two decades the Sessions of the Peace show that determined efforts were made to enforce the Ordinance. But labour was so scarce that employers often paid wages higher than the regulations allowed and received strange peasants without asking whether they were fugitive villeins. As costs increased, however, without a corresponding rise in market prices, lords were moved either to lease their land and stock or to turn arable into pasture. Cattle and sheep-rearing demanded less labour than arable farming, and wool production was fairly profitable. By the end of the century some landholders were beginning to find even cattle and sheep-rearing unprofitable, and to lease their flocks and herds as well as their plough-lands; though, as in the case of

Ramsey Abbey, the leasing of all the lord's demesnes was in some instances not completed until the fifteenth century.

The men who took up these leases were often the richer peasants of the estate. In a time of slump and high wages, when great lords found farming no longer profitable, lesser men, working with few hired labourers, more familiar with local opportunities, more adaptable in their farming, and with much smaller overhead expenses, could usually cope much better with the situation. Even during the thirteenth century there had been more buying and selling of land than is often realized, and some peasants had prospered while others had lost. Then, however, the divergencies of wealth and standing among the peasantry did not increase nearly as much as they did in the following century, when the customary framework of rural society had begun to crumble. Once a lord had leased his demesne he no longer had a personal interest in maintaining the integrity of peasant holdings, for he was no longer concerned to ensure the supply of labour services for his own tilling. Moreover, the leasing of the lord's lands in itself often increased the disparity among the peasants of the village. Thus the developments of the fourteenth century fostered the growth of a prosperous farmer class on the one hand, and a rural proletariat on the other.

By the close of the century there were therefore already considerable differences in standards of living among the peasantry in the more advanced parts of England. In the poorer and more primitive north the labourers often lived with the farmer who employed them. In such a case the house often consisted of a gabled barn, in which the labourers slept on the hay in the loft. The great two-leaved door at one side of the hall opened into a nave flanked by stalls. In these were sheltered the horses, cattle, pigs, and poultry of the household. At the upper end of the hall the bunks of the farmer and his family were ranged round the walls, and in the middle of the floor was an open fire. Some of the smoke from this found its way through a louver in the roof; the rest hung about the rafters, counteracting the smell of the livestock and driving away the fleas which the animals bred.

In the nucleated villages of the south and midlands it was less common for the labourers to live in the houses of the richer peasants. The very poor lived in round, tent-shaped hovels made of wooden posts filled in with wattle, clay, or turf. A little higher in the social scale was the cruck house, whose rectangular tent-like appearance was derived from the pairs of great timbers fastened together at the roof ridge. Cruck houses still exist, though with walls added later to give more head room, as at Didbrook, Gloucestershire. The use of wood or 'cob' and shingles or thatch was natural, in days of difficult transport, in well-wooded arable and well-watered regions, just as the use of stone walls and roofs was fitting in stony regions like the Pennines or the Cotswolds. As yet, only the very rich had wall chimneys and glass in the windows; and even for the wealthy glass was still so valuable that it was often set in transportable frames. Poor men's houses had only a fire of wood or peat in the centre of the floor and shutters to the unglazed windows. 'Full sooty was hir bour, and eek [also] hir halle', says Chaucer of his 'poor widow'; and the two rooms as well as the soot seem to have been typical of many peasants' huts. If the poorer peasant had three rooms, the third apartment often sheltered, not members of the family, but the few pigs, sheep, and poultry which he possessed. In the midlands and middle south, where an effort was still made to bequeath the peasant's holding undivided, the old parents were often accommodated in a room, sometimes with a separate entrance, at one end of the family dwelling. Unmarried brothers and sisters might be allotted small huts on the plot of land which usually surrounded the cottage; but if they married they had to leave to keep the holding intact. Even the heir had few household goods; a chest, a trestle table and stools, a cauldron, brooms, wooden platters, bowls, knives, spoons (but no forks), wooden or leather jugs, a salt box, straw palliasses, and rushlight-holders were often all the furniture; a wooden four-poster bedstead was a treasured possession, to be handed down as an heirloom, and only the wealthiest peasants possessed one.

In the 'close' or garden surrounding the cottage vegetables were often grown, and poultry was maintained. Bees were usually kept, too, for sugar was very expensive and honey was useful for making mead which, together with ale, cider, and home-brewed wines, formed the peasant's staple drinks. There was also a fruit tree or two, and perhaps a few herbs for simple remedies, as usually no apothecary was to be found in the village. The peasant usually had the right to pasture pigs, sheep, and a cow or two on the waste round the village; and the woods provided not only (strictly illegal) rabbits and game, but wild fruit, and also wild flowers, such as violets, primroses, lilies, or roses, which were then used for seasoning. Herrings, codfish, and ling were in great demand, but because of transport difficulties fish was not easily obtainable in villages far inland. The peasant's food varied greatly with the region, the weather, and the season. As there was not enough fodder to keep all the livestock through the winter, most beasts were killed and salted at Martinmas, and spring was a lean time, both for men, who were then often short of food, and for their surviving beasts, which became weak and gaunt until the grass started to grow again. Fasting in Lent was often a necessity; and after a winter passed in dark, draughty, smoky huts, living on salted beef and smoked bacon, dried peas and beans, the remains of last year's wheat or rye (or oats in the north or barley in the west), and a few winter greens, men welcomed the spring with fervent joy. Poets did not sing of autumnal splendour then; their delight was in the 'merry month of May', and the light, warmth, vitality, and freshness of spring. Fresh food was a great treat; and the lack of enough milk, butter, and cheese, especially in winter, meant that resistance to epidemics was low. The diet was also deficient in fruit and greenstuffs; fruit was thought dangerous to health, and vegetables were used mainly as seasonings for soups and meat, with the result that scurvy was prevalent, especially at the end of winter. If peasants fell ill, they relied chiefly on local women wise in the lore of herbs and other traditional remedies. Physicians were very rare in villages; but this was probably an advantage in most illnesses, in view of the constant blood-letting and queer remedies advocated by the medical lore of the time.

By the late fourteenth century the wealthier peasants in the more advanced parts of the country enjoyed a standard of living much higher than that just sketched, and might aspire to rise higher still. There were not at that time the sharp distinctions between social classes which existed in many countries of Europe. The various degrees of the peasantry merged into one another; and at the top of their class the substantial tenant farmers differed little in social standing from the wealthier freeholders, the franklins. Both were coming to be regarded as yeomen, and economic and military developments enabled many prosperous yeomen to enter the ranks of the gentry. Typical of these was the Paston family; Clement Paston was a yeoman farmer in Richard II's day, but his son, William Paston, rose to be a justice of the Common Pleas – William Paston, Esquire, of Paston Hall.

Yeomen, squires, and knights might rise not only by successful farming, education, well-planned marriages, and assiduous service to the king, as these early Pastons did, but by commending themselves to some great lord. A knight, for instance, might honourably serve as steward of the lord's household, or of his estates, or lead a contingent of troops for him to the wars: in return he expected the lord's help and favour. This patronage by the landed aristocracy was of course not new, and under one form or another remained a great force in the countryside until the late nineteenth century; but at a time when the landed aristocracy was increasing its power the favour of a great lord was of especial importance for lesser men who wished to rise, or even to maintain their existing footholds in society. In most parts of the north, for example, the outlook in the late fourteenth century was very dark for the man who did not enjoy the favour of Henry Percy, Earl of Northumberland, Ralph Neville, Earl of Westmorland, or John of Gaunt, Duke of Lancaster.

It was very pleasing to great magnates to find able men seeking to serve them. Such service had to be rewarded, however, with food and shelter, or pensions, or land, or other gifts. And for other reasons great lords found their expenses mounting. Luxuries found during the long wars in the more cultured land of France were introduced into English society, either because of real appreciation of them or because of social emulation. This and the sophisticated chivalry of the age meant increasing pomp and display, which manifested itself in magnificent tournaments, elaborate banquets, colourful heraldry, and more splendid houses. Such rivalry and display was fostered by the chivalrous court of Edward III, with its cult of the Round Table, and the luxurious court of Richard II, which encouraged greater extravagance of dress and speedier changes in fashion. Armour became more costly, as it covered the body more completely and was more intricately made. Great lords were finding it more expensive to live, at a time when the profits from their estates were often dwindling. This must have spurred them on in their claims to political power, and in their desire for a continuation of the French war, with its chances of gain at the expense of the French and the Crown.

The Hundred Years War benefited other Englishmen besides the magnates. The first three Edwards had relied a good deal for loans on the great Italian bankers of the time, especially the Florentine houses of Frescobaldi, Bardi, and Peruzzi. When in the early years of the Hundred Years War the magnitude of Edward III's borrowings, and his failure to repay them, helped to cause the bankruptcy of the Bardi and Peruzzi, Edward turned to rising English capitalists to finance the war. In return for large loans, a small group of English financiers were given various concessions – the most important of which was a temporary monopoly of England's chief export, wool. By the middle of the century most of these English financiers had lost their fortunes as quickly as they made them; but a few of the most astute retained enough wealth to found noble houses. One of them was Sir John Pulteney, member of the Drapers' Company and four times mayor of London, who founded the fortunes of the Pulteneys, later Earls of Bath. Still more successful was William de la Pole, a Hull merchant active in trade and in the royal service, especially as a baron of the Exchequer; he and his descendants built up landed estates, which were eventually concentrated in East Anglia. His son was created Earl, and his great-grandson Duke, of Suffolk; both found favour with their kings, to whom both became chief ministers.

Such cases show that the best way to rise rapidly into the aristocracy was to make oneself useful to the king, and also that those who amassed wealth in trade were usually not content to remain urban patricians, but wished to migrate to the country and become landed gentry. The fluidity of English society and the weakness of class barriers, helped by the early unity of the country under a strong Crown, enabled them to do this with comparative ease; so that in fourteenth-century England there was not the cleavage between urban and rural societies which existed in contemporary Germany.

The close bond between town and country was remarkable. The industrial regions of Western Europe were then Flanders and Northern Italy; and all English towns, except London, were small even by contemporary European standards. A medium-sized English town would have only 3,000 or 4,000 inhabitants, and its houses stood amid gardens, orchards, and even farmyards. Even London still had gardens and paddocks within the walls. The towns would seem to us ill-paved, smelly, insanitary, and their people quick to succumb to frequent plagues; but they were still in close touch with nature. It was easy to walk into the surrounding country; and, especially in the smaller towns, burgesses often owned cattle, and even held arable tenements, outside the walls.

Even small towns had their walls, for the country was weakly policed. The ordinary police took the form of neighbours turning out in the hue and cry when called upon to do so by the constable or the sheriff and their men. But the walls served as more than a protection against disorder; they were useful to the ruling classes of the towns in maintaining their privileges against the outside world. For in view of the deepening rural depression the burgesses who dominated the towns were becoming exclusive in spirit. Their constant aim was to maintain and extend such rights of self-government, and monopoly of local trade and industry, as they had bought from their lord, whether king, noble, or prelate. They were careful to uphold these privileges, not only against aliens, but against all other Englishmen, including the burgesses of other English boroughs and the inhabitants of their own town who had not been admitted into the ruling circle. Constant supervision was necessary to shut out interlopers, especially in trade and industry; and walls greatly facilitated such supervision, as the gates were always closed during the hours of darkness.

As to the form which this supervision took, it must be remembered that the towns developed at very varied rates. In the fourteenth century some market towns still had no craft gilds, or only embryonic ones, many had them well established and functioning smoothly, whereas in the bigger towns the gild system had already begun to break up. In their prime the craft gilds were composed of master craftsmen, who were both manufacturers and merchants; they not only made the goods but sold them in their own workshops. The affairs of each craft, including prices, workmanship, the welfare of its workers, and the suppression of interlopers and sharp practices, were controlled by the whole body of masters. An apprentice who had completed his training under a master was qualified to become a full member of the gild. There was thus no permanent wage-earning class in the craft. This system needed a fair equality of wealth between the master craftsmen for it to function satisfactorily. It assumed a limited and stable market, in which the master could be his own salesman.

These conditions had already passed away in the largest towns of fourteenth-century England, especially London. The market had expanded, and some masters had become richer than others. It was not easy for the small master to distribute his wares over a wide area, and the wealthier masters began to specialize in distribution, rather than in manufacture, thus growing wealthier still. They began to monopolize the government of the craft; and, in order to maintain profits by lessening competition, to keep out would-be entrants by high fees and other devices, including an expensive livery. Hence the gild, which had thus been turned into a narrow oligarchy, often achieved a new status as a livery company; many of the London companies received their first charters under Edward III. When the crafts were reconstituted as chartered companies the members were secure in their control; and in any case a poor man would have had too little capital to compete with the wealthy traders. Already, therefore, in large towns there was a clash of interests between the capitalists and the artificers; the latter were organized as a separate body out-side the livery, the yeomanry or bachelor gild, consisting mainly of small masters confined to the manual parts of their trade. Many of the yeomen were in fact trained workmen employed by the livery men; these yeomen tried to use their gild to keep up wages and organize strikes, aided by the unapprenticed serving men of their craft.

In the larger towns of the fourteenth century there was also a clash of interests between various sections of the capitalists themselves. In Richard II's time the victualling gilds of London wanted a monopoly of the import of food-stuffs into London, and even elsewhere in England; but the non-victualling gilds opposed this strenuously, fearing that such a policy would mean higher prices for food. The slogan of cheap food won the non-victualling gilds much popular support; but the victuallers had the backing of the cloth-workers because of their hostility to the drapers. So bitter did the struggle become that some of the Fishmongers, disgruntled at the recent victory of the non-victualling gilds, were even suspected of admitting the rebels into the city in 1381. London was already so important that its internal feuds naturally linked up with the struggles between the king and his opponents. The victualling gilds were supporters of the king, the non-victuallers of the opposition barons, who also wanted cheap imported victuals, such as wine. Great was the satisfaction among the non-victualling gilds when the Merciless Parliament of 1388 executed the high-handed mayor, Brembre, leader of the victualling gilds and staunch supporter of the king. Eventually both sides had to make concessions, but the advantage rested with the non-victuallers; and during the following century the mercers, the grocers, and the drapers were the most influential of the great companies.

This result was aided by the growth of the cloth industry, whose expansion benefited the great merchants – mercers, drapers, grocers, and others – who dealt in cloth, but harmed the urban clothing crafts, since the cloth industry was mostly developing, not in the chartered towns, but in the countryside. The rapidly expanding use of fulling-mills from the late twelfth century onwards achieved by water-power what had so far been done by hand or foot. Running water to work the mills was found in the Cotswolds, the Pennines, and the Lake District, and by the beginning of the fourteenth century the cloth industry was already moving to these districts. Worsted cloth, made particularly in East Anglia, did not need fulling, and was therefore not so dependent on water-power, but even worsted manufacture tended to move into the villages, because of the restrictive policy of the town crafts. Their attempts to keep up the price of their wares hastened their decay, for the unorganized village cloth-workers were willing to take lower wages. Already by Chaucer's day this rural cloth industry was being organized by the capitalist clothier, who brought the wool and distributed it for carding and spinning to country cottages, where spinning was an occupation so characteristic of girls that virgins came to be described as spinsters. He collected the spun wool, and took it to the weavers, thence to the shearers, the fullers, the dyers – from craftsman to craftsman until the finished cloth was ready for him to carry on his pack-horses to market. All this needed capital; but if that was forthcoming, this method could easily beat the craft-gild organization of the older towns in catering for an expanding market. The development of the rural cloth industry in late medieval England was thus due rather to this advance in technique and organization, than (as is sometimes alleged) to Edward III's invitation to Flemish weavers to settle in England.

Indeed, Edward III's reputation for a far-sighted policy of prosperity and free trade has suffered since the researches of George Unwin and his pupils. The king's economic policy was determined largely by financial necessity, and in so far as his actions had a long-term effect, they were to the detriment of trade, for his exhausting wars tended to depress commerce as well as agriculture. English overseas trade had, it is true, other difficulties to face in the late fourteenth century. The pestilences of that age must have reduced demand, as did the growing strength of powerful foreign trade rivals. The Hanseatic League of North Germany, for example, already tried to exclude Englishmen from the Baltic trade, important for the supply of timber, pitch, tar, ashes (used in cloth making), and fish. Until the sixteenth century English exports, except for cloth, consisted chiefly of raw materials – metals, wheat and other foodstuffs, wool, and leather – and by the fourteenth century English exporters of some of these commodities, especially wheat, were facing the increasingly powerful competition of the newly-colonized lands of East Germany. Moreover, the production of gold and silver in Western Europe was barely adequate to meet growing demands for currency; and the shortage was probably accentuated by the constant drain of bullion to Asia. Countries like India did not need many European products; whereas Western Europe greatly desired the spices, silks, and other luxuries of the East. There were constant complaints in late medieval England of the shortage of good money and of the drain of gold and silver abroad. Serious deflation was averted only by devaluations of the currency – profitable to the Crown but, in the circumstances, also stimulating to trade. In any case, the poverty of the mass of the population in Western Europe and the monopolistic spirit of the merchant class tended powerfully to end the trade expansion of the thirteenth century.

The exclusiveness of the English merchants, together with

the Crown's financial necessities, had a depressing effect on what, at the beginning of the fourteenth century, was England's most important export – wool. In late medieval England there was a remarkable development of the cloth industry; but that cannot account entirely for the decline in wool exports. An analysis of the customs figures has shown that the average annual exports of English wool in the early fourteen century were almost 40,000 sacks. The centres of fine cloth-making were then not in England but in Flanders and Florence; and the best grades of English wool were the most prized in Europe. No wonder that the chancellor sat in Parliament on a woolsack, symbol of the nation's wealth! By the middle of the fifteenth century, however, the average annual exports had sunk to less than 8,000 sacks. In the early fourteenth century alien merchants were still able to engage in the English wool trade with some degree of freedom, and they it was who exported more than 60 per cent of the sacks. The most important of them were the Italian merchant-bankers, most of whom were eventually ruined by their financial transactions with the first three Edwards. Edward III then granted a monopoly of the wool trade to a small group of English capitalists in return for financial assistance; but by 1350 his excessive demands had bankrupted each in turn. Moreover, such a close monopoly had annoyed all the various interests concerned in the production and export of wool, each of which wanted something different from the rest; but after many hesitations the compromise which would guarantee money to the king and displease the least number of people was found to be that of the Staple.

The institution of the Staple involved two things – the Staple, a fixed place through which the export of wool was compulsorily directed, and the staplers, a corporate company of merchants handling the wool which passed through the Staple. The wool trade was therefore to be in the hands of a monopoly, wider than that of the forties, but still a monopoly; the staplers usually numbered three to four hundred. Owing to the conflicts of the divergent interests involved, the Staple was moved about from town to town, both in England and on the Continent. By the last quarter of the century it had settled down at Calais, which had the advantage of being located in English territory as well as being easily accessible to the merchants of Flanders. The monopoly did not apply to the trade with Italy, which the Italians were still allowed to dominate; but the bulk of the trade was with the Low Countries, and from this aliens were shut out. The king was pleased with the system, for the Company of the Staple was a firm basis and instrument for the taxation of wool; but the staplers did not intend to bear the weight of his heavy taxes and loans on wool. Their monopoly enabled them to pay low prices in England, which hit the growers, particularly the great ones who had specialized for the wool market, and to charge high prices abroad, which injured the English wool trade. The only advantage of this policy to England was the unintentional encouragement it gave to the English cloth industry, sheltered as it was by this difference between the domestic and the foreign prices of wool.

The establishment of the Staple is only one instance, though an important one, of the growth in the late fourteenth century of a restrictive and anti-alien policy, which had important effects on the merchant class. The great capitalists of the early years of Edward III, who had united all other sections of society against them and had lost their fortunes so quickly, were gone, and the fourteenth century closed with a more modest but more widely diffused prosperity. English merchants, expecially those of London, were becoming more numerous and more important in the country's life; and their struggles against powerful foreign competitors, such as the Hansards or the Italians, stimulated them to share in the growing nationalism of late medieval England.

## CHAPTER IV

# Religious and Educational Movements

SOMETHING of the contrast between the expansion and confidence of the thirteenth century and the arrested development of the following age, which can be seen in economic affairs, can be found also in the life of the Church. In both cases it is easy to make the contrast appear too violent and too simple. Many peasants suffered by thirteenth-century economic forces; many wool merchants benefited by those of the fourteenth; and the regions of England were too varied for one generalization to fit them all. So in spiritual matters, there was much that was amiss in the thirteenth century, and there were saints in the fourteenth; and in such a complex institution as the Church had become there were countless gradations. Yet nevertheless, a certain contrast between the two centuries does make itself felt. The twelfth and thirteenth centuries had seen great efforts to achieve reform, order, and cohesion in the Church, in organization, in dogma, and in philosophy; and, above all, the monks in the twelfth century and the friars in the thirteenth had given to Western Europe a new sense of devotion and spiritual joy. But in the fourteenth century we find a widespread sense of decline, a feeling that abuses were gaining ground instead of being overcome. Signs of vitality there were; but some of these, such as the popularity of the mystics, were due partly to a growing sense of frustration at the increasing legalism of established religion.

This sense of unfulfilled promise is greatest in the case of the regular orders. Holiness was still to be found among the monks, and the friars were by no means inactive in the performance of good works. It is, moreover, easy to stress too much the prevalence of unseemly behaviour among the monks. It was the business of episcopal visitors to reveal and correct what was wrong, not to record success or sanctity;

hence episcopal registers have much to say about corruption, and very little – perhaps only 'all is well' – about satisfactory houses. It must be remembered, too, that in the middle ages, unlike the present day, it was almost impossible for a monk who had mistaken his vocation or had developed psychological illness to leave his monastery and return to the world, and, consequently, maladjusted monks remained in their houses as a constant source of moral infection to their colleagues.

Nevertheless, when all allowances are made, the sense of disappointment remains as it did for the fourteenth-century contemporaries of the monks and friars. Perhaps from the eighth century, at any rate from the tenth, until the twelfth, the monks had played the most vital role in England's mental and spiritual life; then in the thirteenth century the friars had swiftly advanced to the centre of the stage. But by the fourteenth century neither monks nor friars occupied such a position; and though many of them might still be leading worthy lives, they were not transforming the Church and the world in the way that their predecessors had done.

Even in the most favourable circumstances it would have been hard to preserve undimmed through many generations the flame of devotion which had consumed St Ailred of Rievaulx, St Gilbert of Sempringham, or Agnellus the Franciscan. Every religious society has experienced the difficulty of maintaining the brightness of the early vision clear through the mists of time and the narrowing horizons brought by increasing organization. Their very success had contributed to the difficulties of the monks and friars. The holiness of their first generations aroused great enthusiasm. Men had tried to show their veneration by lavishing wealth on the orders; and wealth had slowly driven out the early single-mindedness and devotion, and in many ways had brought with it 'the world's slow stain'. Even Orders like the Cistercian, which had made particular efforts to shun the world and its temptations, found themselves increasingly immersed in the activities of the landowner and the magistrate. The more intimately connected they became with the world around them, the more infected they generally were by the morals and outlook of the secular society of their day. The abbot and chief officials of a wealthy monastery found much of their time and energy spent in defending its rights and administering its estates. It seemed to them a solemn, even a sacred, obligation to maintain the privileges of their house unimpaired; but such a view meant that the things of Martha tended to drive out those of Mary, and that to its tenants and subjects the monastery appeared not as a holy community but as a property-owning corporation, tenacious of its legal rights. Whenever civil commotions offered an opportunity, as in 1327 and 1381, the inhabitants of monastic towns rose in bitter mood against their masters.

The lure of wealth had ensnared the friars, too. The English sections of the mendicant Orders seem to have departed from the original ideals less than the friars of some other countries; and this may, perhaps, be one reason why no house of the reformed Franciscans, the Friars of the Strict Observance, was founded in England until the close of the fifteenth century. The friars were active, and, in many respects, still popular. They were skilfully trained as preachers – to go to hear a friar preach was a recognized holiday attraction; their racy stories, direct moral appeal, and emotional style gave them great power to move their hearers. As confessors they were equally popular with kings and queens and with humble folk. They did useful work by serving as suffragan bishops, performing the spiritual functions of bishops who either found their sees too large for them, or were absent for long periods on political business. They still maintained their reputation for learning, and had produced a galaxy of famous scholars at Oxford in the thirteenth century. Nevertheless, it was widely felt that they had lost the vision which had given them such spiritual power in the early days of their Orders. Poverty had been both an outward sign, and much of the inward reality, of the friars' original and distinctive message. St Francis had aspired to 'follow naked the naked Christ'; and this spectacle of joyful renunciation of human selfishness for love of God and man had been so moving that St Dominic too, had vowed his Order to absolute poverty. Now, however, far from being characterized by their love of Lady Poverty, the friars were accused of greed. By subterfuges they enjoyed the use of much property, and the parish clergy complained that they exploited the sermon and the confessional to attract bequests and gifts for their churches and houses. Chaucer's picture of the friar so skilled in professional begging that he would wheedle a farthing from a poor widow may have been unkind, but it represented a view widespread among the laity.

The extent to which the monks and friars had yielded to the world naturally varied, and one monastic Order succeeded in avoiding any compromise. Before 1343 only two Carthusian houses had been established in England, as long ago as *c.* 1179 to 1181 and *c.* 1227. Between 1343 and the end of the century six were founded. Only one more, the wealthiest of all – that of Shene in Surrey (1414) – was added before the Reformation. The Carthusian Rule represented a partial return to the anchoritic, or hermit, ideal; and that silent and solitary life of contemplation in separate cells was proof against the temptations which overcame less secluded Orders. Only the austere Carthusians could proudly claim 'nunquam reformata quia nunquam deformata'; and the purity and zeal which they maintained undiminished through the generations aroused great admiration and respect.

The puritanism of the Carthusians helped to save them from the financial worries which increasingly beset houses of other monastic Orders in this period. As fervour waned, expenses grew. The number of meals had increased and the food had become richer and more varied than was envisaged by the Rule, with 'pittances' or extra dishes above the standard diet. Although St Benedict intended his monks to be vegetarians, by the fourteenth century the prohibition of meat was a dead letter in most houses. In the thirteenth century there had been repeated struggles against such relaxation of the Rule, but by the fourteenth the authorities were acknowledging defeat, and regulating what could not be stopped; for example, in 1316 a papal bull made large concessions in the matter of meat-eating. And food was not the only thing which was putting up expenses. This century saw an increase in the custom of giving monks pocket-money and cash allowances and the rise of a system of holidays (with pay). Besides, long before this time the manual labour envisaged by the Rule had been replaced by reading, meditation, administration, or diversions, and so the number of domestic servants kept was sometimes greater than the number of monks in the house. Monks now totalled less than one-third of the monastic population. Monasteries wished to have the increased comforts which were now becoming available – glazing of windows, panelling of walls, provision of cubicles and bedsteads, construction of chimneys and carrells (i.e. studies), provision of clocks, and so on; but all these amenities cost money. With so many people travelling, the duty of hospitality bore heavily on houses on or near frequented roads. Guests were expected to contribute alms, but these were often quite inadequate to pay for their keep. The most remiss were often the very distinguished visitors; Edward II's queen, Isabella, once left her pack of hounds for two years at Canterbury, after a visit, to the impoverishment of the monks. The burden became so heavy that in this century some of the most frequented monasteries began to establish inns nearby. A financial load which could not be evaded, however, was the taxation which the kings were now demanding from monasteries, as from the rest of the clergy, especially in time of war, and the increasing burden of episcopal or papal fees.

All this increased expenditure came at a time when agricultural profits were growing less and benefactions from the laity to the monasteries were dwindling. The centralized accounting which business-like abbots had often established in the thirteenth century as an aid to planning and economy was now frequently in decline; the various officials of the abbey were often left with great freedom of action over the revenues they collected, sometimes not accounting for them at all. It is therefore not surprising that in the early fourteenth century the number of monasteries in financial distress increased.

The problem may have been eased a little by the decline in the number of monks. Opportunities for literate men outside the monasteries were increasing; and enthusiasm for the monastic life waned as life outside became less grim. The decline in the number of monks and regular canons, relatively small in the first half of the century, became catastrophic owing to the Black Death; about 1350 the numbers were almost exactly halved. But after 1360 there was a quick recovery; though at the end of the century the numbers were still only about two-thirds of what they had been in the early thirteenth century. The nunneries also suffered severely from the Black Death; Wothorpe nunnery, near Stamford, was left with only one nun, and had to be dissolved. But in the nunneries the problem was usually the opposite one of overcrowding. Middle- and working-class women could earn their living in many ways; but women of the upper classes who failed to find husbands were prevented by the conventions of the time from seeking 'gainful employment', and there was often nothing for them to do but to enter a nunnery, regardless of whether they had any vocation for the life. This use of the nunnery as an aristocratic spinsters' club was not conducive to austerity and zeal; and though an endowment on admission was usually expected, often more women were admitted to nunneries than their resources could adequately support. Although nunneries had hitherto been recruited exclusively from the nobility and country gentry, some needy houses began in this century, with the rise in social importance of the merchant class, to admit tradesmen's daughters, if their dowry was large enough.

Both monks and nuns often used unbusinesslike ways of raising money which in the long run only increased their difficulties. There were, however, methods financially sounder, such as the elementary teaching of boys and girls, which nunneries often undertook. A valuable help was the possession of relics, such as the body of a venerated person, e.g. Edward II at Gloucester. The most popular shrine in fourteenth-century England was that of St Thomas Becket at Canterbury, and the cathedral priory was greatly enriched as a result. Privileges of indulgence for visits to the monastery were also useful; for pilgrims made offerings. But perhaps the most important way of increasing the revenue was the appropriation of churches. The cure of souls in the parish would usually be provided for by the institution of a vicar or a perpetual curate at a low wage, while the monastery took the rest of the income. This custom was not new, but became more frequent in the fourteenth century.

As usually practised, these appropriations were opposed to the interests, both spiritual and material, of the parish churches and their parishioners. Popes such as Urban V tried to check the practice; but it was too useful to the monasteries to be stopped, and besides, it was not only they which drained away the revenues of parishes. Episcopal registers contain an enormous number of memoranda of dispensations granted to rectors for non-residence. Such a rector might be busy in the service of the king or some great lord; or, like Wyclif, wish to reside at a university; or, less worthily, be an idle absentee pluralist. There were in the fourteenth century rectors who dwelt in their parishes and lived useful, and indeed saintly, lives; but the number of appropriated churches and absentee rectors was very great, and though from the early thirteenth century onwards bishops, councils, and popes had tried to insist on a living wage for vicars, vicarages were often too small in value to attract well-educated incumbents. Absentee rectors and monasteries were apt to regard parishes merely as a source of income. The chancel of the parish church was the responsibility of the rector; and while individual rectors sometimes rebuilt chancels, it was very rarely that the proprietors of appropriated churches seem to have done so. There is often a striking contrast between the insignificance of the chancels of such churches, which received only cheap repairs, and the splendour of the naves rebuilt by the parishioners in the fourteenth or fifteenth century.

Such naves are a visible reminder of the part which the Church still played in the life of the people. Family worship did not occupy the important place which it enjoyed among the seventeenth-century Puritans or in Victorian England; worship centred on churches, altars, and shrines. For the majority, who could not read, knowledge of the Christian faith depended on visual aids such as stained-glass or wall-paintings, or on oral instruction; children might be taught something by their parents or passing friars, but their chief source of instruction was the parish priest. In view of the poverty of most of the resident parochial clergy, and the lack of facilities for their proper theological training, it is not surprising that lay folk's knowledge of their faith was often confused and scanty. But ignorance or superstition did not necessarily imply indifference; on the contrary, there was in this century a widespread spirit of inquiry. This partly explains why people flocked to hear the preaching of friars, whose education and training in exposition were far superior to those provided for vicars and curates.

It was easy to see that the lack of adequate wages and education for the parish priests was an evil, and the contrast between poor, conscientious parish priests and rich, worldly monks and bishops is a frequent one in fourteenth-century literature. But it was one thing to recognize the abuse, and quite another to do anything about it. Attempts at reform would obviously arouse the hostility of the powerful groups who benefited by the existing system. They would have the backing of the monarchy, for the impecunious king made extensive use of church livings to provide incomes for his civil servants without cost to himself. It is true that pluralism and absenteeism were tackled seriously by the Church of Rome in the Counter-Reformation and the Church of England in the nineteenth century; but in each case it was at a time when the Church was plainly in grave danger unless drastic action was taken. In fourteenth-century England, before Wyclif at any rate, there seemed to be no peril, and in any case the Church's coercive authority was unimpaired. The critic of the existing order not only aroused hostility as a trouble-maker but risked suppression as a heretic. The thirteenth century had been an age of definition in organization as well as in dogma. The relationships between the various sections of the clergy, the rights and duties of clergy and laity, of seculars and regulars, and of the various orders of the hierarchy, had been ever more minutely regulated by ecclesiastical legislation. This was a natural development, especially as a means of settling serious disputes, such as, for instance, those between parish priests and friars, abbots and monks, monks and bishops. It meant, however, that it became increasingly difficult to criticize any aspect of the existing order without challenging legal decisions of the Church; and to persist in such criticism was heresy.

It could be, and was, argued that the proper function of the laity was not to criticize but to obey; but the increasing literacy and professionalism among the laity provided a growing challenge to this view. Earlier in the middle ages the clergy had gained authority not only because of their sacred calling, but because of their monopoly of literacy and learning, which naturally gave them immense influence in political and social life. But by the fourteenth century many laymen were literate and many, such as lawyers, judges, stewards, or bailiffs, had acquired professional skill and knowledge. There was a new tendency abroad, perhaps fostered by the development of the Convocations of Canterbury and York, to regard the clergy as only one profession among others, and to regard their claim to special and extensive legal and economic rights with a jealous eye. Until Wyclif's time there was no question of attacking established dogma, but anti-clericalism was already widespread. In one sphere especially was there much resistance to clerical pretensions – the jurisdiction over land and property. There had long been opposition to the claims by the courts of canon law to jurisdiction in such matters. Now there was a growing awareness that the lands and revenues which the Church enjoyed had been bestowed by pious laymen, and an increasing conviction that what had once been given might be taken away if it were misused. When in 1312 the lands and revenues of the suppressed Order of Templars were transferred to the Knights of Hospitallers, it was carefully noted in the Act that but for the statute the lands in question would have reverted to the several lords of the fees. This century saw the first appointments (even though only for short periods) of laymen to the great offices of state, for consciously anti-clerical reasons.

When such anti-clericalism was reinforced by the growing nationalism of the times, the result was a potentially formidable anti-papalism. It was not yet pressed to the logical extreme; people were not yet prepared for this, and Crown and Papacy benefited too much from each other's help to want a decisive struggle. The pope's spiritual supremacy was not yet challenged (except by Wyclif and the Lollards), but there was a growing feeling that English resources belonged to Englishmen and that in the end nothing could stand against that. Yet the increasing expenses of the papal curia and the increasing centralization in the Church provided the Papacy with both the necessity and the means of exacting increasing financial support from the various provinces. Strong protests were made against such exactions in the Parliament of Carlisle in 1307; and when the Hundred Years War and the residence of French popes at Avignon made the Papacy seem to Englishmen an ally of the national enemy, resentment no longer stopped at protests. In 1351 was passed the first Statute of Provisors, against the papal claim to provide to English benefices, and in 1353 the first Statute of Praemunire, declaring that jurisdiction over presentations to benefices belonged to the king's court, and providing for the punishment of those who sought from the papal curia any legal instruction to the detriment of royal rights. It has sometimes been said that these statutes were due to the king's initiative and had no backing in the country; we now know that they were due not to the king, but to the insistence of lesser patrons. The king could protect his interests unaided, and used such statutes only as bargaining counters in his relations with the Papacy; rarely applied for more than a few months at a time, they were no longer enforced after Edward III's concordat with Pope Gregory XI in 1376. But there was nothing transient about English anti-papalism; in 1366 Parliament declared that King John had had no right to make England tributary to the Papacy, and the Great Schism, which began in 1378, increased anti-papal feeling. To the scandal of two rival popes, each denouncing the other, was added the grievance that each strove to maintain the former papal income from a sadly shrunken obedience, and that the popes therefore attempted to increase exactions, and tolerated or even encouraged abuses if they would bring in revenue. In 1390 and 1393 were passed more stringent Statutes of Provisors and Praemunire, which Richard III used as bargaining counters as his grand-father had done those of 1351 and 1353; but it was already clear that papal authority in England could not endure, if eventually it should suit the king's interests better to strike than to collaborate.

All this will help us to understand why the Lollard move-ment came when it did, and to explain the influence of Wyclif's theory of dominion – that righteousness, not legal forms, is what gives the clergy their title to dominion and property, and that the decision as to whether an ecclesiastic should retain his jurisdiction and property or not ought to be taken by the civil power.

There were other reasons for the development of Lollardy at that particular time. Men's minds were unsettled by war, pestilence, and social changes, and less ready than in the past to accept without question the established order. Great calamities like the Black Death encouraged fatalist views, and found an intellectual expression in the revived Augus-tinian doctrines, with their emphasis on the infinite power and over-ruling will of God. Not only thinkers like Arch-bishop Fitzralph or the 'doctor profundus' Archbishop Brad-wardine, but also mystical recluses like Dame Juliana of Norwich stressed Augustinian views of grace and election. Such writers might be venerated, but their works promoted tendencies dangerous to the existing order; for the emphasis of the Church's authorities was on free-will and the efficacy of good works, ecclesiastically determined, not on the assur-ance of salvation through the grace of an omnipotent and predestinating God.

Dame Juliana was one of a number of fourteenth-century English mystics whose writings were extremely popular in the late middle ages. It is significant that more manuscripts of the works of the Yorkshire mystic Richard Rolle (d. 1349) are said to be extant than those of any other English medieval writer; and great popularity was also enjoyed by other fourteenth-century mystical works, such as Walter Hilton's *Scale of Perfection* and the anonymous *Cloud of Unknowing*. Diverse as these mystics were, they had some traits in common. They made little reference to philosophical speculation or to the precepts of scholastic theology and ecclesiastical authorities. They were much concerned with individual spiritual culture, combining practical advice with transcendental teaching. Orthodox they all intended to be; but their emphasis on 'quietist' personal religion and the possibility of an immediate approach to God, and their reliance on the inner light rather than on authoritative tradition, all tended unwittingly to undermine belief in a sacerdotal and sacramental religion. Their works were especially popular with the middle classes; the country gentry, the merchants, and the craftsmen could usually read by this time, and there is much evidence that they possessed and read mystical and devotional works. It was widely felt that the spirit of official Christianity was now too mechanically legal and authoritarian. Even the grace of God had become so strictly confined to prescribed ecclesiastical channels that it had the appearance of law. Men were groping for a faith which would appeal, not so much to the spirit of obedience to the laws of the Church, but to the heart and the individual conscience.

This was responsible for more than a vogue for mystical works; it helped the spread of Lollardy, especially amongst the middle classes, where it reinforced the growing individualist, anti-clerical, and critical spirit. Aristocratic politicians like John of Gaunt had in the seventies supported Wyclif for his anti-clericalism, but were frightened away when in 1379 he began to attack the doctrine of transubstantiation; and though Lollard teaching contributed little directly, if at all, to the Peasants' Revolt in 1381, the outbreak scared men of great position and wealth still further from it. It is significant that the first stern measures against the heretics were taken in the following year. Lollardy still found support among the lower secular clergy, the gentry, the traders, and the artisans, and in 1395 a group of knights of the shire actually presented in Parliament a bill of Lollard demands. Richard II suppressed their petition, but retained in his household men who were known to favour Lollardy, such as Sir Lewis Clifford and Sir John Montagu*. It was not until the Lancastrian dynasty had come to the throne that the persecution of Lollardy became severe enough to turn the Lollards into despairing revolutionaries and cause men of substance to abandon them.

We shall naturally be curious to know not only why and where Lollardy found support but why such an anti-clerical movement originated in the greatest centre of clerical thought in England, and was at first extremely popular there. An obvious explanation would be that the only trained theologians and philosophers were clerics, and that as Oxford University was the most important intellectual centre in England, it was natural for an Oxford cleric to initiate the movement; but this does not explain why attacks on the existing order should have found any favour in an exclusively clerical community. This was due in part to the fact that Wyclif's views developed gradually; his increasing lack of orthodoxy after 1379 alienated many of his supporters, whereas his earlier attacks on the abuses of clerical property, at a time when he was still orthodox, had delighted the friars, who were prominent at the universities and saw in his views arguments to support their official championing of poverty. But Wyclif's popularity at Oxford was due partly to deeper causes which take us back a long way in the history of thought.

The twelfth-century renaissance of learning had many

*In 1924, in the Scottish Historical Review, XI, 55–92, that distinguished scholar, the late W. T. Waugh, argued that these and other reputed 'Lollard knights' were merely anti-clerical; later work has made it seem likely that they were nearer to heresy than that.

features which seemed to threaten the existing Christian society of Western Europe: the recovery of Roman law, the revival of interest in classical literature, the renewal of pleasure in the external world, and the great number of translations of Greek and Arabic philosophical works. By the middle of the twelfth century it was becoming apparent that there was a serious conflict between the traditional Augustinian theology and the 'new' Aristotle, especially as interpreted by the great Arabic thinkers Avicenna and Averroes. Owing largely to the way in which Greek philosophy was recovered, beginning with the logical commentaries of Boethius in the ninth century or earlier, the West attached great importance to dialectic as a means to the discovery of truth; and the aristocratic complexion of society predisposed it to accept the Greeks' trust in abstract reasoning, rather than the manual labour of experiment, as a path to wisdom. The logic and metaphysics of Aristotle, who was already deeply respected in Western thought, seemed therefore a great threat to Christian theology; and scholars tried hard to assimilate the new learning and resolve the apparent conflict between faith and reason. This issue involved the whole approach to theology, which is summarized in the opening question of the *Summa Theologica* of St Thomas Aquinas (1224–74), whether theology is a science. It was the supreme achievement of Aquinas that he showed the way in which a Christian theologian could use the new material and arrive at a synthesis. Scarcely was his *Summa Theologica* finished, however, than two Oxford Franciscan friars initiated the process of destruction which eventually led to Descartes and the downfall of a medieval philosophy.

Oxford University had in the thirteenth century become renowned through the work of three generations of distinguished scholars, mostly Franciscans; but none had a keener mind than John Duns the Scot (*d.* 1307). His subtle brain greatly reduced the number of theological doctrines which could be established by purely natural reasoning, and he undermined the harmonious structure which Aquinas had erected by denying the necessary validity of his philosophical arguments as to, for example, the immortality of the soul. His maze of self-invented technical terms and metaphysical forms made him the favourite of one school of intellectuals in late medieval Europe, and the archetype of Gothic stupidity, 'the dunce', to the reformers of the sixteenth century. The gap which he had re-opened between reason and revelation, metaphysics and theology, was widened into a chasm by William of Ockham (died *c.* 1350). Duns was a 'realist', believing in the reality of universal concepts, whereas Ockham was a thorough-going 'nominalist', holding that universal concepts are only nominal; thus Duns held that 'mankind', for example, is an objective reality, whereas Ockham and other nominalists taught that 'mankind' is only a mental classification of particular men. The only real knowledge, Ockham said, was the unreflective intuition of the individual object. His mind, sharp as a razor, subjected every proof to the most critical scrutiny; and when he had finished his attack on the traditional philosophical arguments there remained no rational basis for faith. Like Duns, Ockham asserted his complete orthodoxy to the end; but as he held that even the existence of God was not demonstrable by reasoning, he was driven to the position that the only real basis for religion and morality is simply faith and authority.

The influence exerted by Duns and Ockham was profound. It is hardly too much to say that their rival philosophies dominated the universities of Western Europe until the Renaissance, and, in some respects, until the seventeenth century. Ockhamism was, on the whole, the more influential of the two; and, as its arguments were so destructive of Christian theology and morals, the ecclesiastical authorities naturally tended to be increasingly suspicious of all original thinking, unless it was confined to purely academic discussions. By 1340 the Rector of the University of Paris was condemning Ockhamism for creating an attitude of doubt towards the accepted authorities and leading to conclusions such as 'Socrates and Plato, or God and His creatures, are nothing.' Ockham contributed powerfully to the very widespread trait of fourteenth-century thought, that there is an infinite, unbridgeable gap between God and this world. On the one hand, this encouraged an interest in natural science; for if God could not be known by human reason, would not that reason be better employed in investigating the properties and relationships of the natural features of this world? On the other hand, it was accompanied by an increased emphasis on the infinite power and the inscrutable will of God. This caused some influential thinkers of the period, such as Gregory of Rimini, to revive in an extreme form St Augustine's doctrines of predestination and reprobation; for God can foreknow and will what men He chooses to salvation or to damnation. At a popular level, the emphasis of the Ockhamists on faith and authority as the sole basis for religion increased the opportunities for superstition; for if God's power is absolute and His mode of operation unknowable, then not only is anything possible but right and wrong are simply whatever He wills, however outrageous to human reason. If, then, faith and reason were such poles apart, why should not crude, absurd, or even immoral miracles and beliefs be true if faith should assert that they were? The philosophical developments of the early fourteenth century severed natural science and secular learning from theology; but interest in the external world increased, and, insufficiently controlled by reasoning, led to the displacement of the symbolism and introspection of the earlier middle ages by a growing emphasis in the Latin Church on earthy realism, on human drama and human emotion, by a longing to bring God and the saints down from heaven and to see and touch them.

Though Ockham was the last English medieval philosopher of European importance, fourteenth-century Oxford was a centre of speculative ferment. Ockham's influence was strong; but many Oxford scholars were dismayed at its solvent tendencies and its reliance on the uncontrolled decree of authority for every doctrine. Distinguished Oxford thinkers like Archbishops Bradwardine and Fitzralph, advocated a moderate 'realism' as a step towards the reunion of mind and God. They exerted a strong influence on Wyclif, himself a more extreme 'realist' who, however, derived some ideas from Ockham and disciples of his, like Marsilius of Padua – notions such as reliance on scripture and temporal authority as against ecclesiastical law and papal authority. Hence, in his early phase especially, Wyclif's philosophy appealed, on varying grounds, to various shades of contemporary intellectual opinion. Stern measures and repeated efforts by the Archbishops of Canterbury were necessary before Wyclif's doctrines were stamped out at Oxford.

So influential was Wyclifism at the University in the seventies that William of Wykeham, Bishop of Winchester, tried to protect his scholars against the heresy in his great foundation of New College (1379). This was the most important college foundation of the century, not only for its size and magnificence, but for its provisions for college worship and for tuition, and for the youth of its scholars – thus heralding the collegiate system which eventually superseded the university lectures and students' hostels and lodgings prevalent so far. Several other colleges were founded in Oxford and Cambridge in this century, for the training of theologians, canon lawyers, or simply arts graduates; but the number of scholars they supported was as yet only a small fraction of the total student body. There were already a few monastic colleges in Oxford and one or two more were founded in the universities in the fifteenth century; for in the late middle ages some monastic orders, especially the Benedictines, stressed the importance of university studies, and produced one or two noted theologians such as Uhtred of Boldon (1315?–1396) and Adam Easton (d. 1397).

Only a small minority of ecclesiastics, whether monastic or secular, went to the universities, however, although these existed for the education of clerics. Expense was a deterrent, and the curriculum was more suited to the training of theologians, canon lawyers, administrators, and grammar teachers than to that of parish priests or monks. The universities had faculties of medicine, but only physicians were catered for. Surgery was regarded as a manual labour too degrading for a scholar; and it was thought unseemly that clerics should touch naked bodies or possibly cause death. Hence even such a distinguished surgeon as John of Arderne (1306–90?), who made important contributions to the treatment of gout, clysters, and fistula in ano, got his training by an adventurous career as an army surgeon in the Hundred Years War. The humble operations of surgery, such as cupping, leeching, and teeth extraction, were left to barbers. For scholars everything relating to anatomy and physiology as well as disease was referred back to Galen (A.D. 131–201), a final authority from whom there could be no appeal. This reliance on abstract logic and authority meant that physicians had no means of distinguishing between scientific treatment and traditional quackery. Thus John of Gaddesden (1280?–1361), physician to Edward II and a fellow and professor of Merton College, Oxford, in 1314 compiled a book, *Rosa Anglica*, which on the one hand contains a very early reference to the red-light treatment of smallpox, but on the other is mostly a collection of Arab fables and countryside superstitions.

University thought exerted an influence out of all proportion to the numbers of men in direct contact with it. However, it must not be forgotten that most literate men finished formal education at a stage that was untroubled by speculations of University dons. Academic education was still under the aegis of the Church; the teachers were therefore clerics and the curriculum was devoted to ecclesiastical ends. The elementary education provided by the nunneries, or the song schools attached to cathedral, collegiate or parish churches, grammar schools, private chapels or chantries, consisted of singing, reading, and simple instruction in the faith. Such elementary schools furnished all the academic education which humble folk could count themselves lucky to get, and for the more fortunate formed a basis for the work of the grammar school, where the main subjects were Latin grammar and composition. The teaching of these was permeated with dialectic, partly because books were costly and scarce, and learning had to be largely by oral instruction, rote, and disputation; and partly because the work of the grammar school was designed to lead to University studies, where the methods were largely dialectical and theology was the highest aim and crown.

In the late middle ages many educational institutions were still being started under direct ecclesiastical inspiration and for ecclesiastical ends. The founding of chantries became extremely popular, and the chantry priest was appointed primarily to pray for the souls of the founder, his family, and his friends; but such a priest usually had much time to spare, and one of the commonest duties enjoined on him was that of teaching poor boys. By the time that chantries were suppressed in 1547 there were well over 2,000 of them in the country; and though some recent research has questioned both the numbers and the importance of the chantry schools, it seems to be still true that by 1547 they were more numerous than any other type of school in England. It was for religious purposes that Wykeham founded Winchester College in 1382, so that prayers should be said in perpetuity for his soul, and boys should be educated ready to enter his New College at Oxford and eventually become priests to serve the Church in various ways. Even Winchester College, however, marks a step away from the complete subjection to the Church, for at Winchester, for the first time, a school was established not as a mere adjunct to a church or monastery, but as an independent corporation, self-centred and self-governed.

More important still was the growing complexity and sophistication of society, with the rise of a lay culture, and the need for an increasing variety of technical skills outside the orbit of the Church. It is true that in the late fourteenth and early fifteenth centuries private teachers at Oxford provided a business training, instructing their pupils in Latin and French composition, conveyancing, the drawing of wills, the keeping of accounts, the holding of courts, and legal pleading. It is also true that some of the increasingly specialized occupations, for example, the growing civil service, were commonly entered by way of the ecclesiastically controlled song and grammar schools. But many of these clerks in the service of the king or some great lord were engaged in secular activities and could marry if they remained in minor orders. Some increasingly influential occupations were, moreover, in the hands of laymen. Such were the legal profession attached to the royal courts, whose members gained their knowledge of the common law in the 'lawyers' University' evolving in fourteenth-century London – the Inns of Court, and the crafts and trades, whose craftsmen and merchants gained their technical skill in an apprenticeship of several years' duration. Lawyers and gildsmen still maintained very close relations with the Church, and did not dream of challenging her authority in education; but their very existence lessened the Church's influence over instruction, and their needs were one day to influence the grammar schools themselves. In 1385 was established what appears to have been the first English school founded by a layman.

Besides these middle-class professional and business men there existed a very important class whose education owed even less to the Church – the nobility and gentry. Girls seem often to have been admitted to A.B.C. and song schools, but not to grammar schools. Their presence there would, it was thought, have distracted and corrupted the boys, and the education given in grammar schools was considered quite unsuitable for girls, whose natural destiny was marriage – unless they were of the upper classes, when, as an alternative, they might enter a nunnery. Hence her main education took place in the home, where she learned to cook, to spin, to sew, and to embroider, if she were of gentle birth, and to ply a trade or craft, if she were not. Many women of position managed to acquire somehow a knowledge of legal terms and accounts, so that they could help in estate management. If a girl belonged to a family of quality, she must also cultivate skill in dress, polished manners, correct posture and demeanour, and accomplishments such as singing or dancing, for all these were thought valuable for acquiring a husband. Handbooks on such matters were now in vogue – among them the extremely popular Book of the Knight of LaTour-Landry, written in France (*c.* 1371–2). But the most valued way of securing a training in such accomplishments for a girl was to place her out in a noble household. This was also the usual procedure with boys of the upper classes. Taught by the women or chaplain of his father's household until about the age of seven, the boy was then sent as a page to the castle or hall of a neighbouring lord or knight, to learn manners, reading, writing, and the elements of the faith. At fourteen he became a squire and began to acquire skill in the martial arts, and in the pastimes and accomplishments considered proper to his class.

Diverse as the training of the squire and his sister might be, they had some accomplishments in common, including a knowledge of French. Until nearly the end of the century French was still the language of the upper classes, and facility in it was a necessary accomplishment for all who wished to move, or be thought to move, in polished society. In the latter half of the century, however, English was ousting its rival. John of Trevisa, writing in 1385, ascribed this to the effect of the Black Death, which killed off or frightened away many of the old teachers and caused a break in tradition; but the anti-French prejudices engendered by the Hundred Years War probably had their effect as well. In 1362 English was made the language of the law-courts, and next year, for the first time, the chancellor opened Parliament in English. The city of London issued a proclamation in English in 1384 and the earliest known will in English dates from 1387. It is significant that Henry of Lancaster spoke in English instead of French when he formally claimed the throne in 1399, and Gower and Chaucer had already begun to write in English. Henceforth the teaching of French waned in importance, and by the late fifteenth century even ambassadors to France were sometimes ignorant of the language. At the same time ability to read and write English grew steadily in the upper and middle classes. If education had still been limited to ecclesiastics, this development would have been much slower; for the language of the Church and its schools was Latin, and English was of interest to it only for homiletic and didactic purposes.

Once teachers had begun to take account of English, a great difficulty confronted them. During the two hundred and fifty years in which it had been merely the patois of the lower classes (except, perhaps, in the remote parts of the north and west, where the gentry also may have spoken the language) it had had no social or literary conventions to preserve a standard English, and existed only in many dialects. Which of these should be used as the standard tongue? It may seem natural to us that the victorious dialect should have been that of the east midlands, the region in which London and the two universities were situated, and in which the king most frequently held his court. But the very presence of the court and the universities, centres of the use of French and Latin, meant that the east midland dialect had become the most degraded and poverty-stricken of all. Its eventual victory was due partly to the prestige of the man who used it at the end of the fourteenth century – the poet Chaucer.

CHAPTER V

# *The Arts*

THE gradual superseding of the French by the English
language in the latter part of the fourteenth century is the
most important literary development of this period. English
was written, however, in the early fourteenth century; indeed, R. W. Chambers showed that a continuous tradition
of English prose from Anglo-Saxon times onwards survived
the dominance of French among the ruling classes after the
Norman Conquest, and of Latin in the Church, learning,
and administration. This tradition was maintained by religious works. It was essential that the ignorant should be
instructed in the faith, and they might not understand Latin
or even French. Hence we find, even in the twelfth and
thirteenth centuries, English didactic and devotional works,
generally of no great literary merit, with one or two notable
exceptions, such as the *Ancren Riwle*. This was an original
manual, but these works usually drew their ideas, and to
some extent their form, from the dominant French and
Latin literature of the time, of which, indeed, they were
often translations. They usually had only a local appeal, for
they were necessarily written in one or other of the many
dialects into which English was divided, and they had increasingly to borrow French and Latin words to express
their message adequately.

This tradition of religious writings in English was continued in the early fourteenth century, in translations such
as the Lincolnshire Robert Mannyng's *Handlyng Synne* (begun in 1303), a series of some sixty stories in short, rhymed
couplets, warning against the various ways of falling into
sin. It is based on the Anglo-Norman *Manuel des Pechiez* of
William of Wadington, but is much more forceful, and skilful in story-telling, than the original. Another translation,
completed in 1340, made by Dan Michel of Canterbury, is

the *Ayenbite of Inwyt* (i.e. remorse of conscience), a treatise on morals which is a close but awkward translation of the popular French *Le Somme des Vices et des Vertues*. The literary activity of the south of England was less remarkable at this period than that of the north, perhaps because of the greater remoteness of the north from French literary domination. About 1320 was written in the north of England the skilful and popular *Cursor Mundi*, a rhymed poem in nearly 30,000 lines; this ran through the course of the world from Creation to Doomsday, interweaving homilies and legends with Bible stories, and giving special prominence to the Virgin Mary, who became more and more important in the popular devotion of the late middle ages. Another popular northern work was the *Pricke of Conscience*, a popular summary in nearly 10,000 lines of current medieval theology. Whether written by Richard Rolle, the Yorkshire hermit, or not, it shares with his undoubted work a practical and credulous vein. Rolle's authentic poetry has very small literary value; but in his prose his mystical fervour sometimes carried him beyond his usual pedestrian loquacity.

The north was responsible in this period for works of other kinds in English. The miracle plays which had begun as dramatic illustrations to the liturgy had by this time developed in many towns into cycles of vernacular plays, which usually extended in theme from the Creation to the Last Judgement, and were performed annually by the various gilds, often at Whitsuntide, or the new feast of Corpus Christi, instituted in 1311. Of the four most famous cycles which have come down to us – those of Chester, York, 'Coventry' (probably in reality composed at Lincoln), and Wakefield – the first three seem to have taken shape in this period. The twenty-five plays of the Chester cycle may have been initiated about 1377; they preserve more than the other vernacular cycles the devotional impulse which had given birth to medieval drama. The more numerous York plays, though elaborated later, may have originated about 1378. Besides religious works, political songs were composed in the north at this time: there were complaints of the poor against

their oppressors, as in the *Song of the Husbandman,* or tales of
ruin and woe in Edward II's reign, as in the Auchinleck MS.,
now preserved at Edinburgh. The military triumphs of
Edward III were celebrated by Laurence Minot, who sang
of Halidon Hill and Sluys, Crécy and Neville's Cross. His
rugged poems are appropriately vigorous and energetic, and
his stanzas, with their combination of alliteration and rhyme,
portray the horrors of war in a vivid style infused with
savage patriotism.

Although the English language was being employed for
various literary purposes in the first half of the century,
nothing written in English could compare in range and
importance with contemporary Latin writing, or with the
achievements of the French tongue, from the *Chanson de
Roland* to the *Roman de la Rose.* It was the French who in the
last two centuries had cultivated vast new fields, both in
subject-matter, which ranged from adventure or light-
hearted comedy to allegory or courtly love, and in literary
forms, which explored all the resources of metre and verse-
forms, assonance and rhyme. In the fourteenth century the
poetry of Machaut and Deschamps made fresh contributions
to verse technique; and Minot's celebration of the deeds of
Edward III seems naïve and mediocre compared with the
brilliant and sophisticated descriptions of Froissart. It was no
wonder that English writers borrowed and adapted French
themes and forms, as well as an increasing number of French
words, and that even those most remote from French influences could not escape them altogether. That great work
*Piers Plowman* (1362–98) by William Langland (whose
authorship has now been confirmed) is written in west midland dialect entirely in the alliterative form descended from
Anglo-Saxon poetry; and in this, as in its looseness of structure, its want of clarity, its lack of rhyme, its passionate and
fervent mood, it shows the minimum of foreign influence.
Yet the form in which even this work is cast – allegory within
a dream – is derived from the French, who had made great use
of this device. And if we turn to other roughly contemporary
and notable English alliterative poems, such as those two

masterpieces, the lively and well-written *Sir Gawayne and the Grene Knyght* and the fervent and sensitive *Pearl*, the debt to French inspiration is much stronger, even though these two poems were written in remote Lancashire or Cheshire.

By this time the use of English was rising into more courtly circles, but it had yet to prove that as a literary medium it was a worthy rival of French or Italian. In prose some advance was made – not so much in the level of attainment as in the variety of themes for which English was employed. It was so far used chiefly for translations, not for original composition. John of Trevisa catered for students by translating into English two of the standard works on history and science: the *Polychronicon*, compiled by the Chester monk Ranulf Higden about 1350, which he translated in 1387 into racy, if awkward, English, with many interesting additions, and the *De Proprietatibus Rerum* of Bartholomeus Anglicus, finished in 1398, in which he did not dare to deal so freely with his original, for novelty in science was only less dangerous than it was in religion. More popular in appeal was *The Travels of Sir John Mandeville* which, on the pretext of a pilgrimage to Jerusalem by a fictitious knight of St Albans, narrated all manner of geographical knowledge, genuine and fabulous, with the emphasis on the exotic. This wonderful romance, concocted in France, was welcomed eagerly as soon as it was translated into English (*c.* 1377). Apart from its appeal to the popular love of tales of travel and adventure, it opened up new fields for English prose, on whose development its simple effortless style had a good effect. In another sphere an advance was made by the translation of the Bible by Wyclif or one of his followers (*c.* 1382); for, although the English was unduly Latinized in its constructions, it was remarkable as the first complete rendering of the Bible into English, and, in the opinion of some literary critics, the finest large work of English prose yet produced. Although the ecclesiastical authorities tried to suppress a translation used by Lollards to justify their teaching, the tradition of biblical English which this version founded lived on to become one of the bases of the Authorized Version of 1611. Neither this

nor the other prose works mentioned served, however, as a
standard and inspiration in the writing of English at the end
of the fourteenth century. A cultured man like John Gower
(1330?–1408) still felt the magnetism of French or Latin as a
medium of expression, and his first important poem, the
*Speculum Meditantis* or *Mirrour de l'Omme*, is in French. It is an
unrelieved denunciation of the sins of the various classes of
society, for Gower, like Langland, was a moralist and
preacher, though he did not share Langland's sympathy for
the poor, and in his best work composed in Latin, the *Vox
Clamantis,* he expressed his horror at the Peasants' Revolt of
1381. This poem was, however, sincere and vehement,
whereas his venture into English, the *Confessio Amantis,*
finished about 1390, was artificial and uncongenial to him.
Written at the request of Richard II, this book had a plan
which was well devised to connect the hundred or more
tales which it contained, and the stories were fluently told
by a man who had searched widely to find attractive
examples. It is, all the same, heavy-going, for Gower, moral,
industrious, and encyclopedic as he was, lacked (except at
the end of the book) a vital interest in his subject – love. He
had little humour, and in dramatic power and delineation of
character fell far short of his great contemporary, Chaucer
(1340?–1400).

Geoffrey Chaucer produced what English had lacked
since Anglo-Saxon times – literary creations worthy to rank
with the best works of contemporary European literature.
This he did, not by trying to eschew all foreign influence, but
by steeping himself in French and Italian literature and
profiting by what he learned from them; and he was great
enough to learn by experience. In his early work, such as
*The Boke of the Duchesse* (1370), *The Hous of Fame* (c. 1380),
*The Parlement of Foules* (c. 1382), he was restricted by the conventions of French poetry, such as the use of a dream leading
into an allegory. But already his very active career had
brought him into contacts with all kinds of men – first as the
son of a London vintner, then as page and official in noble
and royal households, followed by embassies to Italy and an

important post in the customs; and this had already given him the insight into character which is so important an element of his power. In *Troilus and Criseyde* he transmutes the conventional figures of Boccaccio's voluptuous story into subtle and moving character studies. His later posts as clerk of the king's works, surveyor of roads, and sub-forester gave him further experience of life; and his mature experience was contained in his last and greatest work, the incomplete *Canterbury Tales*. In this the framework of a pilgrimage was a stroke of genius, for it gave him full scope for his gifts. Chaucer had his limitations; he lacked the profundity of a Dante or the spiritual vision of a Bunyan. But his breadth of sympathy and understanding of character, his tolerance and humour, his powers of construction and description, his sense of drama and of vivid imagery, all combine to make him one of the greatest writers in the English language. He was the first Englishman who was a man of the world and created poetry out of what he saw around him. Moreover, his mastery of dramatic characterization was something new in English literature; Criseyde is in many ways the first real character of English fiction. Unlike some great writers, his worth was immediately recognized; and for almost a century every courtly writer of English poetry acknowledged Chaucer and Gower as his masters, and strove to imitate their methods.

In architecture, too, the assertion of English independence can be seen. In both spheres the French had led the way in the thirteenth century. English buildings of that time had some distinctive features, but the Gothic style in which they were built had been evolved by the French, who were erecting the most logical and daring examples of it; and one of the most important English buildings of that period – Henry III's Westminster Abbey – was inspired directly by contemporary French work. In the early fourteenth century English architecture struck out on its own lines. The choir of Bristol Cathedral (*c.* 1311–40) experimented in vault structure and in a hall-church plan, and, as Dr B. G. Morgan has shown, displays the first comprehensive use of a system of geometrical designing by the mason's square in England. Moreover, some of its features foreshadow those of the peculiarly English Perpendicular Gothic – its feeling for horizontality and breadth, its absence of a triforium, its lierne vaulting, and its arcading without capitals, which carries the eye straight up from the ground to the roof. The influence of Bristol can be seen in the cathedrals of Wells and Exeter, the latter of which is the most typical 'Decorated' Gothic cathedral in England. The design of Exeter's west front shows a determination to sacrifice height to breadth not usually found in French churches, and figure sculpture was not confined to the portals, as in France, but spread over the whole façade, as at Lichfield. The square east end contrasts with the French apsidal or chevet plan and the clustered piers are a peculiarly English trait. In some respects, indeed, the English builders now gave the lead in new developments. In England the window tracery now often lost the stiffness of the previous period and the tracery lines became flowing, as in the east window of Carlisle Cathedral or the west window of York Minster (both c. 1330); whereas the French designers rarely adopted the fashion of curvilinear tracery until later, and probably borrowed the idea from England. In France the mouldings, the capitals and bases of piers, and the vaulting of the early fourteenth century changed little from those of the thirteenth; whereas in England mouldings became flatter, and capitals and bases often developed from circular to polygonal. As for the vaulting, the English introduced ridge ribs, tierceron ribs intermediate between the transverse and diagonal ribs, and lierne ribs, which did not start from the springing of the vaulting compartment; thus was evolved the beautiful stellar vaulting, as in the choir of Ely Cathedral, a church unique for its great lantern tower (c. 1324–38).

Fundamentally, however, the divergence between the two countries was not yet great. Building technique advanced in both. Windows could be larger, walls and roofs lighter and more stable than before. Experience had taught a better understanding of the play of thrust and counter-thrust of masonry and the amount of support and buttressing needed at crucial points. And in both countries the religious fervour of the thirteenth century was waning, and the scholastic synthesis of that age was breaking down. The Early Gothic churches had achieved a dynamic union of idealistic conceptions and realistic details, the various arts had been harmonized by their subordination to religious and constructional needs, and the growing interest in the external world was balanced and restrained by the heritage of symbolism and monumentality. But this Early Gothic balance was destroyed by the forces at work within it, and by the early fourteenth century was changing into the luxuriance of Decorated Gothic. The thirteenth-century synthesis was dissolving into extravagance, prettiness, or the meticulous copying of natural forms. The growing interest in movement had in the late thirteenth century made a wind sweep through Gothic foliage, as in the leaves of Southwell Minster, and a new sense of drama had enlivened human forms, as in the Angel Choir at Lincoln; but in the early fourteenth century this movement and drama became conventionalized, and often hardened into mannerisms. Typical of much of the change of character was the fondness of both England and France for the ogee arch – structurally weak but gracefully sophisticated and technically accomplished.

In the second half of the century there spread over England a style which was to hold the field there for the rest of the middle ages and was to be almost confined to that country. The growing antagonism to the French may have stimulated the rapid adoption of the Perpendicular style, just as Scotland's hostility to England and her alliance and close contacts with France made Scotland cling to the French 'Flamboyant' Gothic in the late middle ages. Another recommendation for the Perpendicular style was the fact that it was cheap to build, since the parts were often standardized and could easily be drawn and cut in stone. This relative cheapness probably appealed to a generation of patrons impoverished by war, the Black Death, and declining agricultural profits. Moreover, patrons were beginning to make comprehensive contracts with master-masons, who agreed to carry out specific jobs for a lump sum inclusive of labour;

and it was then in the mason's interest to do the work as cheaply as was consistent with the terms of the contract.

The first famous example of the new style is the choir of Gloucester Cathedral, which the monks began to reconstruct in the fourth decade of the century, financing the work from the offerings made at Edward II's tomb. Mr John Harvey has cogently pointed out that the mason, William of Ramsey, had already introduced an incipient Perpendicular style even earlier in the chapter house and cloister, begun in 1332, of old St Paul's Cathedral, where many elements of the new style were present – tracery with vertical lines, rectilinear wall panelling, the four-centred arch, and the broad 'casement' moulding. Since then Dr Maurice Hastings has stressed the importance of St Stephen's Chapel, Westminster, in the development of Perpendicular Gothic. Nevertheless, the example set by Gloucester Cathedral is remarkable, and all the more so as one of the earliest instances of a striking and graceful feature of Perpendicular architecture is to be found in the cloisters there. Like other features of Perpendicular Gothic, fan-vaulting was comparatively cheap, for its parts were standardized, it was easier to build than rib-and-panel vaulting, and it needed less buttressing. It was not, however, until the next century that it was first used, in the choir of Sherborne Abbey (c. 1430–40), to vault a wide span. The greatest ecclesiastical ventures in Perpendicular of the late fourteenth century were all roofed with lierne vaulting, and each of them illustrates some typical features of the new style. In the choir of York Minster (1361–1400) were achieved immense windows strengthened by horizontal transoms, and primary and secondary mullions, which provided a simpler and more attractive pattern for the glazier. The naves of Winchester and Canterbury Cathedrals (1360–1410, c. 1380–c.1410) are typical in the increased height of the nave arcade and the clerestory, the shrinking of the triforium to a mere line of wall-panelling, and the beauty of the stellar vaulting. The Winchester nave was remodelled by Bishop Edington and Wykeham, whose fine chantry chapels are early specimens of the chantries which were to become so numerous until the Reformation.

The master-mason of Canterbury nave, Henry Yevele, was greatly esteemed by his contemporaries. He did a great deal of work for Richard II, whose love of beauty and splendour made his court a centre of artistic activity and Yevele's finest royal commission was Westminster Hall, with its peerless hammer-beam roof (c. 1399) made by the carpenter Hugh Herland. Owing partly to the abundance of its timber, England had always been noted for its fine timber roofs, which were never used more successfully than in the Perpendicular period. The most splendid form, peculiar to England, was the hammer-beam type, evolved at the end of the fourteenth century, but other kinds of timber roof – the tie-beam, barrel, collar-braced, and trussed-rafter types – continued to be used both for smaller churches (especially parish churches) and for secular buildings.

The abundance of timber meant that wood was used for dwellings of all kinds, except where trees were scarce, as in the Pennines; but if defence was the first consideration, as on the Scottish border, or magnificence was desired, as in the Palace of Westminster, stone was used. Building with brick was unknown in England from Roman times until the early thirteenth century. Commerce with the Low Countries helped to bring to England the use of brick, as did the Hundred Years War, which familiarized English chivalry with brickwork in France. Another architectural effect of the War was the introduction into England of a French type of castle, built on a simple quadrangular plan. An early example of this new type is Bodiam Castle, Sussex, begun in 1386 as a protection against the French, who were then ravaging the south coast. In the fourteenth century the south and east of England were normally not turbulent enough to necessitate the building of castles there, though pele towers and other fortresses were essential in the northern shires against Scottish raids. But even the south-east was disturbed enough, especially in the reign of Edward II and the last four decades of the century, for the fortification of manor-houses to be essential.

Manor-houses varied greatly in detail, but were normally quadrangular, with a courtyard in the middle entered through a gatehouse and drawbridge over a moat which protected the whole group of buildings. Opposite the gatehouse was the entrance to the hall, where most of the household ate, slept, and spent its leisure time. The hall was open to the roof timbers, sometimes with a wall fireplace, but more often with a hearth in the centre of the floor, and a louver in the roof, through which the smoke was supposed to escape. This is the arrangement at Penshurst Place, Kent, the oldest part of which is a typical fourteenth-century manor-house. (It is significant that Sir John Pulteney, who built it, had made his fortune as a war financier to Edward III just as it is significant that the grandest domestic hall of the fourteenth century, at Kenilworth, was built by an 'over-mighty subject', John of Gaunt.)

At the lower end of the hall was the entrance from the courtyard, from whose draughts the hall was somewhat shielded by a screen. On the other side of the screened-off gangway were usually doors into the pantry (< pain, bread), buttery (< bouteille, bottle), and the kitchen, though the kitchen, owing to the risk of fire, might be a separate building. Over the passage formed by the screen was usually a gallery, often used for minstrels on festive occasions. At the other end of the hall were the dais and high table, where the lord dined with his family and sat to administer justice. Beyond the dais end of the hall were the apartments of the lord and his family, often a parlour on the ground floor and a solar or loft above it. Bigger establishments had these arrangements as a nucleus, and other buildings were added haphazard when necessary; for as yet, except in castles such as Beaumaris or Bodiam, no effort was made at symmetry in domestic architecture, whose appeal had to depend on picturesque groupings.

Even in the largest households privacy did not exist. So many people were attached to a great household and the rooms were so few that they had to serve many purposes; thus the king might give audience in his chapel, for in those days there was not the modern sharp distinction between the sacred and the profane, and the proper and improper use of churches. Often royal courts were held in the king's bed-chamber, the king and queen sitting on the bed as the furniture was so scanty. The furniture of the hall consisted essentially of benches, boards on trestles, a dresser for displaying cups, and chests. Normally the only chair would be at the middle of the high-table, for the lord; hence the significance of 'taking the chair' and 'chairman'. The men of the time set much less store than we do on comfort and much more on magnificent display and lavish hospitality. The latter particularly was a potent means for the great to bind to their cause men of lesser rank, who, coming perhaps from two-roomed hovels, if they were poor peasants, found the lord's hall impressive in its splendour.

Some of this splendour was provided by the rich and abundant hangings, woollen covers, and cushions with which the hall was decorated. Great lords were constantly on the move; hence the usefulness of heavy chests stout enough to serve as travelling-boxes, and of magnificent hangings, which could be carried in baggage wagons or on sumpter horses, and used to adorn one castle or manor-house after another. Many of these brightly-coloured tapestries and covers were imported from Paris or Arras; but with the rise of the English cloth industry an increasing number were made in England, especially in London, and Edward III created the office of King's Tapestry-Maker. Too little English tapestry of this period remains for us to estimate its quality. Technical ability was not lacking, at any rate, for English embroidery of the earlier fourteenth century was un-rivalled and was famous throughout Western Europe as 'opus anglicanum'. It was eagerly bought, even by popes, and specimens of it survive in museums from Sweden to Spain. Some of it was still worked by nuns, but much of it was now executed by professionals, especially in London shops. The workmanship was usually delicate and the designs were very fine; the favourite colours for the threads were gold, yellow shading to green, and white to blue. Embroidery was not limited to ecclesiastical vestments; for instance, there is now in the Musée de Cluny in Paris a chasuble made out of a magnificent horse-trapper. This was worked about 1330 in gold thread on red velvet, and is probably the finest heraldic representation of the leopards of England now in existence. In the late fourteenth century English embroidery was still popular, but its quality had declined, and for the rest of the middle ages it never reached, either in skill or artistic feeling, the level of the great age of 'opus anglicanum'.

The development of design in embroidery was closely related to the development in illumination. Smoky halls were unsuited to easel paintings, for which it would have been impossible to provide large enough sheets of protective glass; hence there was a great demand for illuminated books, often still produced in monasteries, but also increasingly the work of professional illuminators. English illumination had enjoyed an international reputation since the early eleventh century; but it was in the early fourteenth that it attained its greatest heights. Ornament, realism, imagination, and tradition were united with a rare discrimination by artists with greater technical skill and naturalism in detail than their early Gothic predecessors had possessed. The feeling for line in which English artists excelled was never more finely displayed than in *Queen Mary's Psalter*, probably made for Edward I or Edward II. In the exquisite beauty of its line-work this volume stands alone, but in variety and brilliance of decoration it is rivalled by its great contemporaries of the East Anglian school, whose finest products were, perhaps, the British Museum MSS. Arundel 83 and Stowe 12, and the Gorleston, Ormesby, and St Omer Psalters. The chief characteristics of this school, whose achievements were fostered by the growing wealth of East Anglia in the early fourteenth century, were (*a*) the profusion of ornament, especially in frame borders and initial decoration, with effective combinations of leaves (e.g. ivy, oak, and vine), animals, and human figures, (*b*) a passion for the droll and grotesque, (*c*) a rich and harmonious colour scheme, and (*d*) the decorative use of coats of arms. Particularly attractive are the characterizations of animal life – cats and dogs, mice and squirrels, butterflies and snails, and, above all, rabbits, a charming link in the tradition which in modern times is represented in the work of Beatrix Potter and A. A. Milne.

After the first third of the century the East Anglian school declined, as can be seen in the Luttrell Psalter (*c.* 1340), for all its sumptuousness and its fascinating scenes of contemporary life. Apart from a few attempts in the late fourteenth century to derive inspiration from French illumination, then flourishing, English illumination did not revive until Richard II's marriage to Anne of Bohemia in 1382 brought in Bohemian and German influence. The resultant style, of which the magnificent Bible of Richard II (B.M. Royal 1 E ix) is a splendid example, was characterized by great softness in the treatment of the faces, a rich, warm, and harmonious colour-scheme, the skilful use of architectural ornament, and the introduction of new forms of foliage, especially light and feathery sprays of acanthus or spoon-shaped leaves, and bell- or trumpet-shaped flowers.

Illuminated manuscripts could be afforded only by the well-to-do and were not available to the mass of the people, whose acquaintance with painting was with the wall-paintings in churches, or in great houses where they sometimes took the place of tapestry. Owing to the practice of lavish hospitality and open house it was much easier for the humble to penetrate into a palace or mansion than it was in the eighteenth or nineteenth century. Like other forms of art, wall-paintings of this period often developed a greater sweetness and had a greater desire to please than those of Early Gothic art, but at the cost of strength and simplicity. Technique became more assured, and the manner more detailed and naturalistic, at the expense of artistic force. Of course, it took a long time for new fashions to seep down to the local craftsman who painted the Last Judgement or St Christopher in the village church, or scenes of chivalry and romance on the walls of the manorial hall; but such local work was not necessarily crude, for its executants were the heirs of a long tradition. Their products were sometimes very beautiful, as in the series of wall-paintings in the village churches of Croughton (Northants) and Chalgrove (Oxon). These two series, like many other local ones, kept to the older limited range of ochre, red, bluish grey, and white, although painting at Court had long ago changed to brighter and more varied colours; and local work tended to be homely and realistic, in contrast to the aristocratic, romantic, and mannered style popular at Court. Of work produced there, some fragments survive of the wall-paintings done for Edward III in St Stephen's Chapel, Westminster, which was sumptuously rebuilt by him but was burnt down in 1834; and the painting of the Holy Trinity beneath the tester of the Black Prince's tomb in Canterbury Cathedral is remarkable, in both form and colour. By far the best extant paintings of fourteenth-century England, however, are the magnificent portrait of Richard II in Westminster Abbey, possibly the finest fourteenth-century portrait in Europe, and the Wilton Diptych (perhaps 1395–6), exquisite in its miniature-like and Italian manner. Several attempts have recently been made to show that these two great works were painted by Englishmen, but their ascription to a French Court artist, André Beauneveu or Jacquemart des Hesdin, has not been altogether disproved.

The picture of Richard II is the finest example of the taste for portraiture which appeared in this century, as the idealized types of thirteenth-century religious fervour and scholastic synthesis gave way to a greater interest in individual appearance. This more worldly mood is reflected in the stained glass of the period as well, and it was in the fourteenth century that the donors of windows were first depicted in the glass. No less than twelve of the early fourteenth-century windows (c. 1303–5) of Merton College chapel, Oxford, show the donor – twice in each window! And in the drawing of saints more attention was paid to realistic and distinguishing detail. This meant a loss of symbolism and dramatic force; the emphasis as in the painting of the period was on grace and sweetness instead, and a more naturalistic rendering of form was combined with a tendency to mannerism. There was, for example, an endless repetition of the so-called 'Gothic curve', an S-like stance of the figures to achieve a willowy grace. The didactic spirit which had previously been such a unifying force in art was often submerged by an interest in decorative motifs for their own sake; such were the careful copying of leaves and other natural forms, the introduction of coats of arms and other heraldic devices, and the increased emphasis on patterned backgrounds, either by the combination of figures and grisaille work, or painted diaper patterns on coloured grounds. Particularly striking was the prominence of ever bigger and more elaborate canopies, which solved so well the problem of framing the figures. All these features may be seen in the windows of York Minster, which form the finest collection of fourteenth-century glass in England. The same windows illustrate the development of technique. The combination of coloured figures with light backgrounds solved better the problem of lighting the church; the drawing became more assured, and the simpler iron-work clarified the pictures. The range of colours was much greater than the reds and blues of the thirteenth century; and the invention of silver-stain in the early fourteenth century, by making possible an almost infinite gradation of tones of yellow, enabled glaziers to paint much more subtle and life-like human heads and hands.

Many developments in painting and stained glass were paralleled by those in the sculpture of the period. Here, too, there was a gain in technique and grace but a loss in nobility and grandeur – resulting partly from increasing specialization, as the supply of sculpture passed from the building-mason to the image-maker. The technical skill of carving such as that of the tomb of Lady Eleanor Percy (*d.* 1328) at Beverley is beyond praise; but a comparison with the magnificent series of tombs in the sanctuary of Westminster Abbey shows how the monumental stateliness and idealized nobility of the thirteenth century had given place to theatrical poses and picturesque exaggeration. This increasing richness of detail is of great value to the historian and antiquarian; much information about changing fashions in dress and armour in the late middle ages can be gleaned from effigies on tombs (and also from the memorial brasses in which England is outstandingly rich).

Effigies in the early fourteenth century were usually made of freestone, which had replaced the Purbeck marble beloved in the thirteenth century, owing to the growing love of painted stonework. It was found that softer and more easily worked stone, which was cheaper than marble, produced as good an effect when coated brightly with paint; any tricky details necessitated by the growing taste for realism could be added in gesso, a kind of gummy plaster. In the latter part of the century, however, freestone and wood were increasingly ousted by alabaster. During the next hundred years English alabaster work became of international repute, and was exported in considerable quantities all over Western Europe, from Iceland to Italy. Alabaster was quarried chiefly in Derbyshire and Nottinghamshire, and the main centre of the trade was at Nottingham, though at first the alabaster was probably sent to London to be carved. It had the advantages that it was almost indestructible, that it could be carved in the minute detail so admired at this period, and that it could be painted without a foundation of gesso. It became extremely popular for reredoses or retables, for the very hardness of its lines brought out the subject-matter when looked at from a distance (as these reredoses were intended to be) in a way that finer sculpture would not have done. Alabaster also became extremely fashionable for effigies, the earliest important alabaster effigy still extant being that of Edward II in Gloucester Cathedral. In this tomb the great prominence of the canopy, with its profusion of buttresses and pinnacles half hiding the effigy underneath, is a typical example of the growth of decoration at the expense of subject-matter which occurred in all the visual arts in the fourteenth century.

In music England did not achieve the same distinction during this period as in embroidery, painting, and sculpture.

Except in singing, for which she had long been distinguished, England did not until the fifteenth century display the musical creativeness shown in the thirteenth. Since at least the beginning of the thirteenth century there had been in England an impulse to sing in parallel thirds or sixths, a form of part-singing which in the fifteenth century became known as gymel (from cantus gemellus=twin song). In the early fourteenth century 'gymel' led to a further development. If there were three voices, the tenor (or bass) would sing the melody, while the alto and treble would improvise above it a harmony consisting mainly of a succession of parallel $^6_3$ chords, i.e. the alto would be singing a third above the notated line and the treble a sixth above it. This important step in the development of harmony seems to have originated in England, whence it spread to the Continent; though in the English form (descant or faburden) the melody is in the lowest voice, and in the Continental form (fauxbourdon) in the highest register. However, the English experimented much with $^6_3$ chords, and in the fourteenth century produced examples with the melody not only in the lowest voice, but in the highest and middle. An example of the latter is a late fourteenth-century setting of 'Angelus ad Virginem', the melody of which was very popular. Readers of Chaucer will recall that in the Miller's Tale Nicholas, the lecherous young clerk, sang this song at night, accompanying himself on a psautery or dulcimer, whereas his rival Absalon, the parish clerk, serenaded the fair Alison on a guitar. Other instruments popular in this period were the harp, the viol (then known as a fiddle), and the shawm, ancestor of the oboe. The flageolet-like pipe and the drum-like tabor (both played by one performer) were favourites for dancing on the village green, while horns, trumpets, and clarions were used in hunting. Organs had long been common in churches, though often they were small choir organs with only flute stops, or portative organs of some twenty pipes, of the type depicted in the next century in Jan Van Eyck's 'Adoration of the Lamb'. Before the end of the fourteenth century the virginals, ancestor of the harpsichord, had appeared, simply a small box suitable to be placed on a table. Its delicate notes could not have been appreciated in the hubbub and size of a medieval hall; and in great households where it was played it must have been another factor to encourage the novel craving for privacy which led the lord and his family to withdraw more and more from the hall to their solar or their bedrooms.

CHAPTER I

## The Nemesis of Lancaster

IN form the revolution of 1399 left the prerogatives of the Crown undiminished; it was only the 'tyrannical usurpations' of Richard II which were swept away. In reality, the authority of the Crown had been greatly weakened. The consequences of the usurpation of 1399 dogged the Lancastrian dynasty like a Nemesis from which in the long run it could not escape. The magnates who had made the revolution had to be lavishly rewarded. This further depleted the already scanty resources of the monarchy, and made it almost impossible for the king to resist the magnates, who expected him to govern according to their wishes or suffer the fate of Richard II. The inadequacy of the royal resources and the weakened authority of the Crown meant that Henry could not maintain order in the realm; it meant, too, that he had constantly to ask parliaments for money, since he dared not resort to the high-handed methods which had cost Richard his throne. The Commons resented these demands, for they thought that the government was failing in its primary duty of maintaining order and good governance. The reasons, they argued, must be inefficiency and extravagance; hence as a condition of their grants they imposed on the king controls which were humiliating and also crippling to his authority, such as appointing auditors for the spending of parliamentary grants, determining the composition of the king's councils, interfering in the expenditure of the royal household, besides presenting criticisms of administration. As the first sharp resentment against Richard II faded, disillusionment with the new government increased.

Disaffection turned into rebellion which, coupled with foreign invasion, made the very existence of Henry's throne precarious. Not until 1408 did the danger recede.

In facing these almost overwhelming difficulties, Henry's temperament was a help, instead of a hindrance as his predecessor's had been. Although hot-tempered, Henry was capable of schooling himself to patience and dissimulation, and in his long struggles he showed tenacity and decision. His troubles soon began, with a conspiracy in January, 1400, of Richard's personal adherents among the magnates, who missed capturing Henry at Windsor by only a few hours. The rising failed, but it sealed the fate of Richard II, who early in February was murdered in Pontefract Castle. The government did not profit so much as it had hoped from his death; the French became more hostile than ever towards the new régime, and by 1402 they and the Scots were circulating a rumour that Richard was still alive, hiding in Scotland. Fortunately for Henry, Scotland was torn by faction, yet an expedition into the Lowlands in 1400 was a complete failure. In 1402 the Scots invaded England and were utterly defeated at Homildon Hill by the Percies, whose prestige was raised as much by this victory as Henry's had been lowered by his failure. Scotland was too crippled by internal feuds to invade England again, and in 1406 all further danger from that source was ended when Prince James, the heir to the Scottish throne, was captured in a ship off Flamborough Head as he was on his way to France.

The menace from Wales was far greater. In 1400 Henry aided the unjust and violent marcher lord, Lord Grey of Ruthin, against a talented Welsh gentleman, Owen Glyndŵr,* and thereby turned Owen into a formidable rebel, who quickly became the able leader of a general rising of the Welsh. Many of the castles of the king and the marcher lords fell into Owen's hands, and three expeditions led by Henry against him failed completely. In 1403 Owen acquired formidable allies. The Percies had been loaded with grants and

*For a more favourable view of Lord Grey, see R. I. Jack, 'Owain Glyn Dŵr and the Lordship of Ruthin', *Welsh History Review*, 2 (1965).

offices for their services to Henry, but their appetite and ambition proved insatiable and in 1403 they made an alliance with the Scots. The allies marched to join the Welsh but Henry managed to intercept the Percies and the Scots at Shrewsbury before they had united their forces with those of Owen Glyndŵr. In the battle of Shrewsbury Harry Hotspur, the Earl of Northumberland's son, was killed, and Hotspur's uncle, the Earl of Worcester, and his ally, the Earl of Douglas, both fell into the King's hands.

The worst crisis of the reign was now over; but the Welsh revolt was still menacing. Owen Glyndŵr now controlled nearly the whole of Wales and a fourth expedition against him was no more successful than its predecessors. Owen now made an alliance with the French. This was a serious menace, for Henry's government was too weak to control the Channel. He had to rely on privateers whose depredations involved him in disputes with Brittany, Flanders, and the Hanseatic League; all injurious to England's overseas trade. The French were not prevented from ravaging the south coast nor from sending an expedition to Wales in 1405 to help Owen Glyndŵr.

In the same year Northumberland, helped by his kinsman, Richard Scrope, the saintly Archbishop of York, revolted again, accusing Henry of grave misgovernment and usurpation of the throne. The archbishop was captured by treachery and promptly beheaded. This unprecedented execution of an archbishop might have had dire consequences for Henry but for the schism in the Church; the Roman pope failed to punish this gross violation of ecclesiastical rights for fear that Henry would desert to the obedience of the rival pope at Avignon. Northumberland was still at large, and it was not until 1408 that he was brought to bay and killed at Bramham Moor.

With the death of this selfish magnate, Henry's throne became more secure. His eldest son, the Prince of Wales, was already showing his military ability by slowly getting the better of Owen Glyndŵr, who could hope for no more help from France. The French king's attacks of insanity were now longer and more frequent, and in 1407 the murder of his brother, Louis, Duke of Orleans, by his cousin the Duke of Burgundy, initiated over a quarter of a century of civil war. The mutual hatred of Burgundians and Armagnacs soon reached such a pitch that both sides began to negotiate with Henry IV. Henry, for his part, was anxious for peace, but his masterful heir, without his father's leave, sent to France a small force in support of the Burgundians. The success of these twelve hundred Englishmen at St Cloud showed how weak France had become through her dissensions, but Henry, alarmed at his son's insubordination, recalled the English force. The Armagnacs now bid high for Henry's help by offering him the whole of Aquitaine in full sovereignty and Henry therefore sent a force to help them in 1412, but its complete failure through the defection of the Armagnacs brought him only fresh discredit. Since 1408 he had been in very bad health and in March, 1413, he died at the early age of forty-six.

The last five years of his life had been free from rebellions, invasions, and conspiracies, but the turbulence and power of the magnates had not been lessened. The rivalry between the Prince of Wales, assisted by his father's half-brothers, the Beaufort's, and Henry IV's second son, Thomas, and Arch-bishop Arundel, supported by the king, had given wide scope for aristocratic faction in high politics. The disorder in the country was scarcely checked, for a Crown which was chron-ically in debt and dependent for its very existence on the goodwill of the magnates was in no position to suppress it.

Henry V came to the throne a self-confident young man of twenty-five, determined to restore order and unity in his realm. He had many qualities admirably suited to these aims – leadership, organizing ability, patience, energy, and determination. The difficulties might, however, have been too great even for his talents had he not chosen the road which, though bound to be ultimately disastrous, produced for a few years wonderful dividends in order and unity – an imperialist war on French soil. The expeditions of 1411 and 1412 had revealed the weakness of France, and since then her state had grown even more deplorable as the worsening civil strife continued to drain her strength. France was in no condition to resist a foreigner and therefore, in 1413, Henry confidently asserted his right to the French throne.

In this demand Henry was not cynical. It was only natural that he should share the growing nationalism of his fellow-countrymen, who believed in the justice of English claims on France; and he was a hard and priggish man who invariably invoked divine approval for his actions in a way which his enemies found infuriating. Convinced that it was his mission to conquer France and then to lead the united forces of both realms to recover Jerusalem from the infidel, he did not take seriously the negotiations about his claims in France. Nevertheless negotiations dragged on until 1415; chiefly as a propaganda justification for the English demands and as a cloak for diplomatic and military preparations for invasion. The French were prepared in their weakness to concede a large part of Aquitaine together with the hand of their king's daughter, Catherine, and the unprecedented dowry of 850,000 crowns; their ambassadors, however, found Henry V overbearing and his demands outrageous. The negotiations lasted only until he had completed with Burgundy an understanding which permitted him to cross to Normandy in safety, and until the French refusal to concede English claims had induced a Parliament to vote large sums which enabled the military preparations to be completed. The prospects of a war on French soil were enough to arouse enthusiasm in England, but the knights of the shire in Parliament expressed misgivings and disunity still existed. This was revealed by an aristocratic plot to depose Henry, betrayed to him on the eve of his departure for France. There was not only privy conspiracy, but open lawlessness in the country, especially in the midlands, and on the Welsh and Scottish borders.

It was against this home background that we must picture Henry as he set sail from Southampton in August, 1415, with his army of about 2,000 men-at-arms and 6,000 archers. To transport these, as well as the specialist and supporting units and the stores and arms, 1,500 ships, mostly hired or impressed, were used; for Henry was a master of military organization and the expedition was most carefully planned. His first action in France was to besiege Harfleur, then the chief port on the north bank of the Seine estuary. When, after five weeks' siege, the town surrendered, Henry's army was already much reduced by dysentery, but he determined to expose the weakness of France by marching on to Calais. The French thought that he had over-reached himself, and at Agincourt blocked his progress with a host many times the size of his. Henry was, however, a consummate general enjoying the confidence of a well-trained and disciplined army; the French forces were ill-led and disorderly, their units badly co-ordinated and jealous of one another. The English employed their favourite combination of long-bow archers and dismounted men-at-arms, and won a victory even more dazzling than those of Crécy or Poitiers; the English casualties were not more than 500, whereas the French casualties numbered 7,000, including many of the highest nobles in the land. The political results of the battle were more important than the military. Henry's force was now too weak to do more than struggle on to Calais; but his gain in prestige, both at home and abroad, was enormous. To men at the time a success as brilliant as this was a proof of England's strength, her monarch's talent, and divine favour. Henry was received in England with great acclamation; and his ascendancy was sufficiently assured to prevent trouble at home for the rest of his short life.

The expedition of 1415 had shown him that large and careful military and diplomatic preparations would be essential before any systematic attempts could be made to conquer France, so that he waited until July, 1417, before invading again. For the next two years he was engaged in the conquest of Normandy, in campaigns very different from that of Agincourt or those of Edward III. It was now a matter of long, hard, unspectacular, careful sieges of town after town, culminating in the siege of the key city of Rouen, which lasted almost six months. His steady advance at last caused the two great French factions to draw together, and their leaders, the Dauphin and Duke John of Burgundy, met at the bridge of Montereau in September, 1419, for negotiations. The murder there of the duke by one of the Dauphin's followers made possible the realization of Henry's claim to the French throne. The young duke, Philip, so burned for revenge that he accepted the English terms. In this he was closely allied with the French queen (who had repudiated the Dauphin), and, through her, controlled the mad king and their daughter Catherine. By the Treaty of Troyes, concluded in May, 1420, Henry was to marry Catherine; the mad Charles VI was to remain king during his lifetime, but on his death the French crown was to belong to Henry and his heirs for ever.

This was a consummation more swift and glittering than even Henry can have hoped for; but it was largely a hollow triumph. Some historians have assumed that only Henry's early death prevented its terms from being fully carried out; but this is most improbable. None of Henry's campaigns had been paid for out of current revenue, and whereas in the first flush of enthusiasm parliaments had readily granted money, by 1420 and 1421 they were becoming restive. A statement presented by the treasurer in May, 1421, to the king's Council shows that every department was heavily in debt, and that a huge deficit was expected. Loans staved off a crisis, but the government's credit grew steadily weaker as arrears to soldiers and civilians mounted up. The war became more, not less, expensive as it went on, for not only were there campaigns to finance, but conquered territories to administer and protect. These territories were too ravaged by prolonged warfare to pay for their keep, and any attempt to make them do so would eventually induce a resistance movement which would in turn increase the costs of the occupying power. And there was no end to the war in sight. Apart from the conquered territories, and the northern and eastern parts of France which were under the domination or the influence of the Duke of Burgundy, France refused to accept the Treaty of Troyes. Frenchmen might be too dispirited and badly led to put up strong resistance, but only conquest would force them to accept Henry's claims. Consequently after his marriage to Catherine in June, 1420, he took only one day's honeymoon before beginning once more the wearisome task of sieges. In this work the remainder of his short life was spent, except for a six months' visit to England to collect, with some difficulty, fresh supplies for the war. In the winter of 1421–2 he contracted dysentery from the hardships of the six months' siege of Meaux, and this wasting disease killed him at the end of August, 1422, at the age of thirty-five. The dark days through which England was to pass made men mourn him as the ideal warrior-king, cut off at the height of success and in the flower of manhood. In reality, he was fortunate in the hour of his death, for he reaped the renown from his policy of war but not the inevitable bitter harvest of it. Like Edward III, he won unity for his realm and glory for himself at the price of immediate misery for France and eventual confusion for England.

His unfortunate son, Henry VI, succeeded to the throne at the age of nine months, and his long minority gave the magnates a golden opportunity of ruling the kingdom unopposed by the Crown. The late king's youngest brother, Humphrey, Duke of Gloucester, wished ardently to be acknowledged as regent. A patron of art and letters, his affability and bellicose patriotism made him popular with the London bourgeoisie and the mob, and he was long remembered as 'the good Duke Humphrey'. If he had become regent, however, his ambition, greed, rashness, and amorous irresponsibility would have brought disaster even quicker than it did come. It was not, however, so much for these defects of character that the magnates successfully opposed his claims but rather because they had just lost a strong master and had no wish to be saddled with such another. Gloucester had to be content with the name of Protector, and the real power was vested in an aristocratic Council which was to control all official appointments, and in fact the whole royal prerogative. The Council was irremovable; it filled its own vacancies; and as attendance at the Council meetings was not only paid but lucrative in many other ways, it is not surprising that the attendance of the magnates was better than ever before. Soon they were quarrelling over the spoils of government, and the Council was quickly divided into two factions, one headed by Duke Humphrey, the other by his uncle, Henry Beaufort, Bishop of Winchester. Beaufort was as grasping as Humphrey, but far more able and discreet; and as the bishop was also the richest man in England, to whom the government was almost perpetually in debt, he would have been altogether too strong for the duke had he been gifted with Humphrey's arts of popularity. The quarrels between these two became so violent that in 1426 Gloucester's elder brother, Bedford, had to be sent for post-haste from France to stop armed attacks on Beaufort's life.

In contrast to his brother Gloucester, John, Duke of Bedford, was tactful, conciliatory, resourceful, unselfish, a skilful soldier, and a capable administrator. On the death of Henry V Bedford assumed the arduous and ungrateful role of Regent of France and laboured ceaselessly to uphold his nephew's claim to the French throne. His military talent was shown by his victory at Cravant in 1423 and his still more notable victory at Verneuil in the following year. His statesmanship was displayed in the wise laws which he made for the occupied territories; his diplomatic skill by the fact that he held the confidence of two such very difficult men as Humphrey, Duke of Gloucester, and Philip, Duke of Burgundy. But Bedford was toiling in vain. His administration, though humane, met with passive resistance everywhere in the conquered territories. He had to use threats to obtain supplies from the Estates of Champagne or Normandy and he was constantly encountering open desertions or secret treachery. He had not only to try to hold down the occupied territories, but also to conquer the great regions of southern France still adhering to the Dauphin.

The task was too great for the resources of the English Crown. The English Parliaments were becoming increasingly reluctant to pour money into the bottomless pit of the war, and the financial deficit was becoming disastrous. It was with difficulty that in 1428 reinforcements of some 2,700 men were scraped together; and the attack on Orleans which began in October of that year was a travesty of a siege. In view of the exhaustion of the English and the precariousness of their hold on Northern France neither military genius nor divine inspiration was necessary for Joan of Arc to relieve Orleans and capture other towns. The need was to overcome the apathy caused by the fearful devastation of France and to restore the confidence of the Dauphin and his followers in their cause; and this St Joan did with miraculous speed. When, in May, 1430, she was captured by the Burgundians and handed over to the English, her real mission was already accomplished. Bedford tried to efface the impression made by the Dauphin's coronation at Rheims in 1429, by having young Henry crowned at Paris in 1431, but the manoeuvre failed completely, serving to exasperate the Parisians whom it was designed to impress.

The English were now close to the end of their resources and in 1433 Bedford had to go to England in person to seek supplies. The new treasurer tried to startle Parliament into generosity by his survey of the financial position – necessary expenditure exceeded revenue by nearly £30,000 without allowing a penny for active operations by sea or land, and the schedule of debts amounted to £164,000, or nearly thrice the normal revenue – but the Commons were weary of the chronic burden of taxes, especially for an unsuccessful war, and voted a quite inadequate grant. The yield of taxation was dropping with the decline in national prosperity, and bankruptcy was looming ahead as the last expedient of a desperate government. In 1434 Bedford was recalled to France by a general rising in Normandy against the English garrisons; more important still, Duke Philip was thinking that it was time for him to change sides. He urged the English to make concessions, and in 1435 a conference took place at Arras between the English, the Burgundians, and the French. The English clung obstinately to unrealistic demands, and refused to give up Paris or Henry's claim to the French throne. Thereupon Duke Philip abandoned them and made a profitable peace with Charles VII.

With Burgundy as an ally the English had, since 1429, barely managed to maintain their position in France; with Burgundy as an enemy the ruin of the English cause in France was only a matter of time. Bedford was spared the pain of witnessing this, for he died in 1435. His place as heir to the throne was taken by his brother Humphrey, who continued to proclaim the duty of carrying on the struggle to the end. This view was popular, for it was easy to persuade men that failure was due to mismanagement and treachery and not to the superiority of French generalship and resources. His policy also appealed to all those who had profited from the war in reputation and wealth. But the French captured town after town, and Cardinal Beaufort was gradually converted to the wise but unpopular view that England must come to terms with France. He was supported by a party which included his nephews, John and Edmund Beaufort, and William de la Pole, Earl of Suffolk. Most of the royal household officials were on the same side, for they saw the administrative difficulties of continuing the struggle in France; and, greatly aided by his peaceful nature, they helped to influence the king to the same view. Henry had grown up into a gentle and saintly scholar, lacking the determination, energy, military skill, and administrative ability essential in his position. His very virtues were a handicap to his Crown and country. Too humble to defend the interests of his house, too generous to resist solicitation, as formal head of the government he incurred the blame for the extravagance and mismanagement of the oligarchy which still governed in his name. Too kind to resist those around him, and too loyal to dismiss unpopular ministers, he supported the Beaufort party until the Crown itself was discredited.

By 1444 the war was going so badly that the king's ministers (now entirely of the Beaufort party) sought a truce with France. They were by now so anxious for peace that they arranged to marry their master to a French princess for the small recompense of a two-year truce. This princess,

Margaret of Anjou, came to England in 1445, a beautiful girl of 16, passionate, spirited, and indomitable. She was unpopular from the first, for to the mob she represented capitulation to the French, and her unpopularity might have been doubled had it been generally known at the time that very soon after her marriage she persuaded her impressionable husband to agree to the surrender of the county of Maine. Even this concession did not secure peace. The French looked eagerly for final victory, and the English foolishly displayed arrogance and bad faith. Hence when a raid was made from Normandy into Brittany during time of truce and the English refused to make reparation, Charles VII declared war in July, 1449. By June, 1450, the English had lost the whole of Normandy.

This swift disaster will not surprise us. The debts of the English Crown now amounted to nearly £400,000, whereas the king's net revenues were less than £30,000 a year and the royal household alone cost £24,000 per annum. So during the truce the garrisons of Normandy had been allowed to shrink to pitiably small numbers, and the soldiers who could be gleaned for an expeditionary force were hopelessly few. The people of Normandy rose to help the invading French armies which were, thanks to the reforms of Charles VII, large and well-trained. His care in improving the French artillery and the organization of the French army made obsolete the hitherto successful English combination of archers and men-at-arms. But, though the loss of Normandy may seem to us inevitable, to the English of the time it came as an unexpected catastrophe, which shook the position of the government. One of its members, Adam Moleyns, Bishop of Chichester, who went to Portsmouth with arrears of pay for the soldiers there, was lynched by them as a traitor. The chief minister William de la Pole, now Duke of Suffolk, had made many enemies in all classes by his greed in amassing lands and offices, by his grasping of commercial privileges for himself and his friends, and by the harshness and inefficiency of his administration. The invasion of Normandy gave his foes their chance, and he was impeached in Parliament of misgovernment, malversation, and treasonable relations with the French. With the king's connivance he tried to escape to France, but was intercepted on the way by a mutinous royal ship, and beheaded by its crew. Shortly afterwards the Kentishmen rose under Jack Cade, protesting mainly against the government's incompetence and financial oppression, and occupied London for three days.

Hardly had this rising been suppressed than Richard, Duke of York, and, since the death of Gloucester in 1447, leader of the opposition, returned without permission from his virtual exile as King's Lieutenant in Ireland. Although an advocate of continuing the French war, in which he had distinguished himself, York had originally no quarrel with the Beauforts. They were jealous of him, however, for he was heir presumptive to the throne, to which Edmund Beaufort, Duke of Somerset, himself aspired. By treating him as an enemy, the Beaufort party made him one. To his demands for reforms in the government the chief minister, Somerset, replied with evasion and trickery. York was popular with the merchants and the lower classes, but many of the magnates were jealous of his pretensions. Their class was now so divided by disputes and private wars that the adherence of one magnate to York meant the automatic devotion of his rival to Somerset. Hence the two parties were more evenly matched in strength than might have been supposed.

In July, 1453, the French artillery annihilated the last English army in Gascony at Castillon, and, except for Calais, nothing whatever was left of the English dominions in France. This crowning disaster might in any case have caused the downfall of Somerset, but in August the king's hereditary weakness became too much for his delicate and overtaxed constitution. As soon as his madness became known, York asserted his claim to be regent. In October the queen bore a son; and although York recognized him as heir to the throne, Margaret's fear of the duke as a possible rival to her son made her his implacable enemy. When the king recovered his wits, Margaret, Somerset, and their party were so obviously determined to ruin their opponents that in May, 1455, York and his friends marched on London. In the first battle of St Albans Somerset was killed, but the victorious Yorkists treated the king with respect. Margaret was, however, irreconcilable, and during the next four years the opposing factions manoeuvred for position. The government ceased to exercise authority in the country, and by 1459 both parties were ready for civil war. The middle and lower classes stood aside and were for the most part content to let the barons and their followers fight it out. The struggle rapidly became so bitter that in October, 1460, York at last claimed the throne, but just after Christmas he was defeated and killed in the battle of Wakefield. In February, 1461, Margaret marched south, and vanquished the Earl of Warwick, one of the greatest Yorkist leaders, in the second battle of St Albans, a conflict notable for the Yorkists' use of small fire-arms for the first time in English history. King Henry begged her not to enter London, as her wild Welsh and northern levies would certainly have run amok. While she hesitated, the late Duke of York's eldest son, Edward, hurried towards the city from the Welsh border; and he and Warwick entered London with their combined forces. The executions after the battles of Wakefield and St Albans, and the plundering of the queen's army, had swept away the last hesitations of the Yorkists; on 4 March, 1461, Edward seated himself on a throne in Westminster Hall and was hailed by his supporters and by the populace as king by hereditary right. Then, hastily collecting their forces, he and Warwick marched out against the Lancastrians, who retreated north, ravaging the countryside as they went. At Towton in Yorkshire they were overtaken and defeated with fearful slaughter; and Henry, Margaret, and their son fled to Scotland.

Edward IV was at this time a young man of nineteen. His tall, handsome figure and affable ways made him popular, especially with the Londoners, whose favour he was always careful to cultivate. Time was to show him a born general and a strong ruler, but he had not yet had the opportunity to display these qualities. He owed his throne largely to his cousin, Richard Neville, Earl of Warwick and Salisbury, who derived great influence not only from his vast estates but also from his membership of the mighty northern family of Nevilles, who with their connexions formed the core of the Yorkist party. Warwick had already won distinction and popularity, by his liberality and courtesy, and by his energy, courage, and military exploits as captain of Calais (1456–9) and Yorkist leader. For the first few years of Edward's reign he was the most powerful man in England. His ascendancy was strengthened by his campaigns in 1462–4 in the north of England against the indomitable Queen Margaret, campaigns which ended in 1464 with the crushing of her efforts and the capture near Clitheroe in 1465 of the fugitive Henry VI. Well might a member of the Milanese embassy write home in 1461 that the Earl of Warwick 'seems to me to be everything in this kingdom'.

By contrast Edward appeared to be merely a dissolute young soldier, caring only for fighting and, when fighting was done, for wine, women, and pageantry. Beneath this pleasure-loving exterior (which won him much popularity) was hidden the ruthlessness of a Renaissance despot and the strong-willed ability of a statesman. Gradually he asserted his independence. In 1464, when Warwick was in the midst of negotiations for a peace with France to be sealed by a royal match with a French princess, he was astounded and humiliated by the king's announcement that he was already married to a beautiful young widow, Elizabeth Wydeville. Warwick was disgusted; for the new queen's family was of no great importance, and she was the widow and daughter of Lancastrians. Moreover, Edward began to shower favours on her two sons, her five brothers, and her seven sisters, building up a group of magnates who would be a counterpoise to Warwick and the Nevilles. Gradually Warwick lost all influence at court and when once more he was negotiating for an alliance with France Edward renewed his humiliation by concluding an alliance with France's enemy, Burgundy. Edward's sister, Margaret, was betrothed to the Burgundian

duke, Charles the Bold, and Edward proposed to allay unrest in England by invading France. In retaliation the King
of France, Louis XI, stirred up rebellions in England in 1468
and 1469, revolts which were supported by Warwick. Warwick had found a tool in King Edward's weak brother,
George, Duke of Clarence, to whom in 1469 Warwick
married his elder daughter and co-heiress in defiance of
Edward's orders. In 1470 Edward declared Warwick and
Clarence traitors and they had to flee for their lives to
France. Louis XI promised them support – on condition that
they became reconciled with the exiled Queen Margaret.
Both sides found this a bitter pill to swallow; but the queen
and the earl were eventually induced to come to terms, and
an invasion of England, backed by the united strength of
Lancaster and Neville, was made possible. The alliance was
sealed by the betrothal of Warwick's younger daughter,
Anne, to Edward, Prince of Wales, Margaret's only son.

In September, 1470, Warwick, Clarence, and various
Lancastrian magnates invaded England and marched on
London. Edward could not resist and fled to the Netherlands,
to the protection of his brother-in-law, Charles the Bold.
Warwick, 'the king-maker', took Henry VI from the Tower
and set him on the throne once more, but as Henry was now
a permanent imbecile, Warwick was king in all but name.
Henry's nominal restoration lasted only from October, 1470,
to May, 1471. Warwick resumed his policy of close alliance
with France, whereupon the Duke of Burgundy fitted out and
financed an expeditionary force for King Edward, who
landed in March, 1471, at Ravenspur on the Humber – the
same place that had seen the landing of Henry IV in 1399.
Edward was soon joined by all the Yorkists not of the Neville
connexion, and by his brother, Clarence, who had realized
that his ambitions were thwarted by Warwick's alliance with
Margaret. The two armies met at Barnet on Easter Sunday,
14 April. Both sides suffered heavy losses in the thick mist,
but as the king-maker was slain on the field the battle was a
Yorkist victory. Warwick's talents were political rather than
military and Margaret was not sorry to hear of his death, but

the loss of his decision and energy, as well as of his great influence, was a grievous blow to the Lancastrian cause. Nevertheless, Margaret rallied her supporters in the west. King Edward marched rapidly in pursuit and caught up with the Lancastrians at Tewkesbury; and there on 4 May the last hopes of the Lancastrian cause were crushed. Nearly all the remaining Lancastrian leaders were killed on the field or executed afterwards, and Prince Edward, heir of the Lancastrian house, was slain. With Prince Edward dead King Edward had no need to keep Henry VI alive, and on the day after his triumphant return to London it was given out that the mad king had died in the Tower 'of pure displeasure and melancholy'.

The year 1471 not only saw the end of Lancastrian hopes and of Edward's perils; it marked the end of an era in the history of the monarchy – the end of a long period of weakness and the beginning of over a century of strength. The Wars of the Roses had thinned by battle and executions the ranks of the nobility whose power had become such a menace to the Crown. Moreover, the monarchy's chronic lack of resources was being mitigated by the wide estates of the house of York, and by the confiscations and resumptions of lands, in spite of exemptions and restorations of property to pardoned opponents. And in the coming century the vivid memory of the brutalities, disorder, and impoverishment of the civil war would be a potent aid to the monarchy; for men would now submit to great arbitrariness and oppression rather than court by rebellion a revival of the time of troubles.

## CHAPTER II

# The Government of the Realm

THE greatest problem of the Lancastrian kings was how to reconcile facts with theories. In theory the king had very wide prerogatives, which could not be alienated, and to him belonged both the right and the duty of administering his realm. An old and strong tradition laid down that the ruler should govern in accordance with divine law, with natural law (i.e. equity), and with the laws of the realm; but it was generally agreed that he had considerable powers of dispensing from, and suspending, the operations of laws and that he could make proclamations and ordinances to meet special cases or new needs. Hence in favourable circumstances the royal prerogative could be a formidable authority. And the Lancastrian kings had no wish to sacrifice that prerogative and reign as 'constitutional' or 'parliamentary' monarchs. Henry IV had not defeated Richard II's autocracy in order to submit to a parliamentarianism which was a cloak for baronial faction. He was delighted when in his first Parliament the Commons expressed the wish that he should be 'in as great royal liberty as his noble progenitors were before him'. The royal prerogative in this period was emphasized and in some ways heightened by the judges, and, given the opportunity, the Lancastrians were ever ready to act strongly. They claimed that the same divine grace was bestowed on the royal person as had descended on their predecessors; the continued faith in the sacrosanctity and miraculous powers of kingship is illustrated by the belief that the Lancastrian monarchs healed scrofula by the royal touch, as their predecessors claimed to have done, in virtue of the anointing of the royal hands with holy oil at the coronation.

For Henry IV and his grandson, however, there was a large and painful discrepancy between the theories of kingship and the facts; and the same gap might have yawned for

Henry V had he not achieved dazzling victories in France and died at the height of his success. The Lancastrian dynasty could not shake off the consequences of the usurpation of 1399. If one great noble could usurp the throne, why should not another do the same if, like Henry IV, he could plausibly claim that there had been 'oppression' and 'want of governance'? Hence by the very circumstances of its inception, the Lancastrian house was forced to be responsive to the criticism and wishes of the politically powerful classes, and, above all, of the magnates.

One of the strongest constitutional doctrines of the great magnates was that they were the natural leaders of society (as, indeed, from a conservative point of view they were). Hence they claimed that they were the king's natural councillors, and, influential as they had been in the Council of Edward III, they gained still greater authority in the governments of the Lancastrian kings. But though the Lancastrian period was the golden age of the aristocratic Council, there were variations in the degree of baronial domination. In his early years Henry IV struggled to retain control over the composition of the Council and thus came into conflict with magnates such as the Percies and with his Parliaments. But in 1406 he was forced to nominate his Council to meet parliamentary criticisms; and thenceforward the lords were increasingly prominent in the government, until, in the closing years of the reign, when the king was ill, the Council became dominated completely by one faction of magnates or the other. This aristocratic composition of the Council continued under Henry V, for not only were his connexions and outlook aristocratic, but the goodwill of the lords was essential for the successful prosecution of the war in France. Henry's personal ascendancy enabled him to maintain the unity and authority of the Council; after his death the magnates controlled it unchecked, and, free from any effective control, they split up into factions once more.

During the minority of Henry VI the magnates were all-powerful. The whole royal prerogative was in the hands of the Council, which was a self-perpetuating oligarchy; and the lords of the Council not only helped themselves to large salaries, which the royal Exchequer could not afford, but also collected enormous gifts, expenses, and bribes. It is not surprising that the Council ceased to redress grievances or repress disorder in the country. Henry's personal assumption of authority in 1437 did not make much immediate difference, for he was too weak and kindly to withstand the importunities of the nobles. With the growing ascendancy of Suffolk and the Beauforts in the forties, however, the Council faded into insignificance, for the ruling group got its way through direct contact with the king and queen. Hence the Duke of York claimed at this period to stand for 'constitutionalism' – control of the government by an oligarchical Council; and whenever the Yorkists were in power, from 1453 onwards, they ostentatiously made much use of Councils and Parliaments. By this time, however, the Council was clearly in the hands of a party to which the opposition refused to submit, and it was powerless to compel obedience or even attendance. The land was coming under the unchecked dominance of the powerful and the unscrupulous, who resorted increasingly to intimidation and private war; decisions were being transferred from the council-chamber to the battlefield.

The accession of Edward IV in 1461 inaugurated a revival of the monarchy which the events of 1471 were to confirm. He brought to the Crown the resources of the great Yorkist estates, and the confiscations of his first Parliament drew in still more. The middle and lower classes were by this time longing for a strong ruler who would restore peace and justice. Moreover, Edward's success strengthened the theoretical basis of the monarchy; for the Yorkist claim rested essentially on indefeasible hereditary right, which not even sixty years of Lancastrian rule had sufficed to extinguish. It seemed that henceforth no considerations of 'default of Governance and undoying of the gode Lawes', no election by the estates of the realm, would avail against the judgement of God, who alone could provide an heir.

The gradual revival in the power of the monarchy affected the composition of the king's Council. As Edward by degrees asserted his authority, he made more use of knights, squires, doctors of law, and clerks, and less of magnates. Indeed, the alleged lack of great lords in the Council, and its domination by mere officials, was one of the grounds of complaint of Warwick and Clarence when they rebelled in 1469. But the days of aristocratic control of the government were nearly over; and we shall see that after Edward's victories in 1471 he was the unchallenged master of his realm. Indeed, many of his acts were done by his own authority, without the formal attestation or assent of his Council at all.

Aristocratic domination of the government in the Lancastrian period was exercised not only through the Council, but through occasional assemblies of the nobility, known as Great Councils, and, much more frequently, through Parliaments. Of course, Parliament was still very much the King's Parliament – if the king was strong enough to enforce his prerogatives. He could summon, prorogue, or dismiss a Parliament at his pleasure. He could still determine the agenda of Parliament, and could veto or amend the bills it produced. He could still exercise his discretion as to which lords he summoned to Parliament, and could create new peers by letters patent. Even when the king was as feeble as Henry VI it could be a matter of anxious discussion whether Parliament could transact any business without the physical presence of the monarch.

The weakness of the Crown and the strength of the aristocracy made these royal rights more impressive in theory than in practice. The magnates asserted with growing force that their attendance at one Parliament established a hereditary right to a summons; and in the Lancastrian period practice tended more and more to conform to this view. As for the royal veto and control of parliamentary business, the Crown could have no real freedom of action while it was dominated by aristocratic factions. Henry V might have enough prestige to exercise effective leadership, but his father and his son could not stop the magnates in

Parliament saying and doing things obnoxious to the dignity and interests of the Crown. Indeed, Henry VI's government acquiesced in clear violations of royal rights. Thus, Thomas Yong, the member for Bristol, who was imprisoned for proposing in the Parliament of 1451 that the Duke of York should be declared heir to the throne, was not only released, but petitioned for compensation, and the king ordered the lords of the Council to provide a remedy; whereas the speaker of the Parliament of 1453, Thomas Thorp, was for his opposition to the duke not only put in prison but kept there, in spite of the protests of the Commons.

Their objections, even though ineffective, are a useful reminder that the Commons were not mere tools of the dominant aristocratic faction, as has sometimes been asserted. Naturally, the magnates often influenced or controlled parliamentary elections, and many members of Parliament were, if not actually on the staff of some great lord, at any rate of his affinity; and in the Wars of the Roses the Commons were usually prepared to register the triumph of the dominant faction. In 1459 they petitioned for the attainder of the Yorkist leaders, in 1460 they asked for the repeal of that attainder, and in 1461 they justified Edward IV's claim by 'Godds Lawe, Mannys Lawe, and Lawe of Nature', and dutifully attainted his enemies.

This submissiveness of the Commons in times of stress did not result only from the manipulation of elections and fear of the mighty; it was also due to a strong conviction of the knights and burgesses that, although they had a right to petition against bad or inefficient rule, and to share in the making of laws, they were not responsible for the conduct of the government. So determined were they to keep out of trouble that, after their vicissitudes of fortune in Richard II's reign, in 1399 they got Henry IV to put it on record that the judicial power of Parliament resided only in the king and the Lords. What they did feel belonged to them was the right of control over taxation. In 1407 they obtained from the king a formal recognition of their exclusive right to initiate money grants. If, in their opinion, the government

was asking for too much money, they were capable not only
of refusing but of demanding administrative reforms which
in their view would lessen or remove the need for taxation.
In 1401 they even tried (though unsuccessfully) to insist that
their petitions should be answered before they made any
grant. Their aversion to taxation, and failure to realize that
the chronic insolvency of Lancastrian kings was a national
responsibility, made the Commons inclined to look with more
favour on the authoritarian Edward IV, whose resources
were large enough for him not to trouble them so much, than
on the amenable Henry VI, whose constant indebtedness and
genuine kindliness made him responsive to their demands.

The middle classes from whom the knights and burgesses
of Parliament were drawn might disapprove of Henry VI
for his failure to keep order and provide 'good governance';
but the weakness of the Lancastrian régime – and the growing social importance of the middle classes – strengthened
the position of the Commons in several ways. First, the
government's chronic lack of money led to frequent appeals
to the Commons for grants, since the Lancastrians were
too weak to raise money by extra-parliamentary devices,
and had to pay very high interest on their loans – often
25 per cent or 33⅓ per cent. The result was to confirm
the tradition that financial resources beyond the Crown's
normal income must be granted by Parliament. Secondly,
the frequency of Parliaments increased the corporate feeling
of the Commons and their experience in the conduct of
business, which not only hastened the development of forms
of procedure, such as the successive readings of a bill, that
improved the efficiency of their work, but contributed to
their rise in prestige. Not only humbler folk but the great
now used the supplicating power of the Commons more
and more to forward their petitions. Even the king used this
device increasingly if he wished his acts to have a popular
appearance. And in the third place, this growth in the
petitioning activity of the Commons went hand in hand
with an increasing share in legislation. By 1414 they were
claiming (unhistorically) that no statute had ever been

made without their assent, and demanding that their bills should not be amended before enactment without it. This demand was unsuccessful, and the practice which arose in Henry VI's reign of introducing petitions already worded in the form of the proposed statute was probably due to the government itself. Nevertheless, the consent of the Commons to legislation became more and more usual, and an important international agreement, such as the Treaty of Troyes, was submitted to their approval. By the end of this period the judges held that no enactment could be a statute without the assent of the Commons, as well as of the king and the Lords. To the older conception of Parliament as the king's high court of justice was grafted the notion of it as composed of the three estates of the realm; and the Commons now felt that they represented not merely a number of local communities, but the commons of all the realm. Their rising importance, and the growing power of the upper middle classes, led in this period to limitations of the parliamentary franchise, and in 1430 to the famous 40s. freehold qualification for county electors. So influential had the Commons become, and so closely knit, that early in this period the invasion of borough seats by non-residents began. Already by 1472 at least half the borough representatives were not true burgesses but were either country gentlemen who had induced the electors to return them, or royal household officials and civil servants, for whom the government was anxious to find parliamentary seats.

Of increasing consequence the middle classes might be, but in the Lancastrian period the magnates were politically and socially dominant. This fact affected not only parliamentary transactions but royal administration. The Lancastrian kings were not strong enough to use the Wardrobe or the Chamber, as Edward II had done, as a royal weapon against baronial attempts to control the government. The Wardrobe still played a useful role in military affairs by organizing the king's household retinues and equipping and paying the soldiers of these, and Henry V entrusted to it the preparations for his campaigns; but it was not without political importance. The kings made little attempt to turn into an instrument of personal authority the privy seal, whose keeper had become a great officer of state, head of an office which transmitted the king's wishes to the Chancery or Exchequer. The privy seal's place as the king's personal instrument for sealing documents had been taken by the signet, whose keeper was the secretary. In the Lancastrian period the secretary was still normally only a humble household clerk, except for a few years from 1438 to 1443 when the able and energetic Thomas Beckington held the post. For those five years the signet was used to combat the influence of the baronial opposition whose influence was strong in the Chancery and Privy Seal Office; but thereafter the secretaryship sank again to the position of a confidential clerk, without political significance, until the monarchy became strong once more with Edward IV. Then the rise in the number and importance of letters under the signet became very striking, and the secretary began the ascent in importance which before the middle of the next century was to make him the most powerful servant of the Crown.

The increased activity of the secretary and the royal household under Edward IV was made easier by the discredit which aristocratic councils had brought on themselves in Lancastrian days. The corruption and inefficiency which had characterized the administration under their control may be illustrated from naval affairs. Under Henry IV the French could not be restrained from ravaging the south coast; and though in 1401 the king ordered various sea ports and other towns each to provide a ship for coastal defence, he was forced to drop this project because of the opposition of the Commons. So low had the naval power of the country fallen that in 1406 a committee of merchants undertook the duty of clearing the seas. Later in the same year John, Earl of Somerset, was appointed sole Admiral of England, the first in the regular succession of the Lord High Admirals. But, apart from the fact that the admirals' functions were largely political and legal, Henry IV's lack of money and other embarrassments prevented him from supporting them adequately in the policing of the seas. His son was in a better position to build up England's sea-power, and his war in France spurred him to do so. He, like former kings, relied on impressed merchant craft to transport his men and supplies to France, but he also bought or built several ships. The *Grace Dieu*, built at Southampton, was probably the best equipped ship yet designed in England, and a ship still under construction at Bayonne for Henry V when he died was the biggest, as far as is known, ever yet ordered by the English Crown – the over-all length being 186 feet.

This ship was never finished, however, for on the death of Henry V one of the Council's first orders was to direct the sale of most of his ships. Things grew worse instead of better when Henry VI came of age. The aristocratic government of his minority, though corrupt and inefficient, had been saved from the domination of a clique by the balance of parties in the Council; but Henry's personal rule meant the ascendancy of a single baronial group, and the machinery of the State was made to serve the private ends of the dominant party. For the two years ending 31 August, 1439, the expenditure on the king's ships was only £8 9s. 7d. Not only was a royal fleet not maintained, but letters of marque for privateering were sold more freely than at any previous time since the century began. This may have improved the seamanship of the Devon and Cornish privateers, but it alienated the merchant classes by its disruption of trade, and the attacks on alien shipping aroused the anger of foreign powers whom the government was too weak to oppose with success. No wonder the ardently nationalist author of the *Libelle of Englyshe Polycye* (*c.* 1436), written to support the claims of English commerce, laments the decay of England's navy, and reiterates the theme that the aim of English policy must be to make ourselves 'masters of the narrow sea ... that is the wall of England'. It is true that in 1442 an act was passed for the provision and maintenance of a fleet of twenty-eight ships to protect English shipping. But these ships were provided by powerful individuals closely connected with certain members of the king's Council, and became simply an instrument of semi-official privateering, thus intensifying the anarchy on the high seas. This method of raising a navy by contract not only failed to protect English traders; it left unguarded the south coast, which the French were again able to ravage. Not only the merchants but all those who lived along this coast were therefore apt to favour the Yorkists, especially as the Earl of Warwick made himself popular by his naval exploits; and when Edward IV came to the throne the policy obviously marked out for him was not only the encouragement of trade, but the recovery of the dominion of the sea.

Local government had become enfeebled too. The menace to law and order did not come from an extension of seignorial liberties and franchises; on the contrary, except on the Scottish and Welsh borders, the formal authority of the royal administration tended to become greater rather than less. It was rather that the magnates manipulated the royal forms of justice to their own advantage. The previous work of the justices of the peace not only continued, but their functions were increased; yet even if they did not actually belong to the affinity of some magnate with influence in the region, it was dangerous to oppose a great lord, especially if he was of the king's Council. The same was true of sheriffs, coroners, escheators, and other royal officials of local government; they were either nominees of some magnate with local influence, or at least took care not to offend him. Juries were still empanelled; but they could be bribed or intimidated, and he would be a bold man who ventured to bring a lawsuit against a great lord or one of his dependants – for example, against the Duke of Suffolk or one of his affinity in East Anglia in the 1440s. If the aggrieved person did appeal to the law he might find that no counsel or witnesses would dare to support him; and common-law processes often allowed long delays before a judgement was given. And if subtler methods failed, a lord might, if he were strong enough, break up the session of the court by violence. In 1439 the justices of a special commission could not hold their session in Bedford Town Hall

because Lord Fanhope came in with forty or sixty armed
men, and an uproar ensued. Fanhope was a member of the
king's Council, which subsequently condoned his action,
and recommended a pardon for him and all his followers.
But a powerful wrongdoer often obtained the favour of the
Crown at a much earlier stage in legal proceedings. When,
for example, in 1451 Lord Moleyns was indicted for an
armed attack on the Pastons' manor of Gresham, the sheriff
of Norfolk received 'writyng from the Kyng that he shall
make such a panell to aquyte the Lord Moleynes'; and
acquitted he was.

It was in vain that statute after statute was passed em-
powering the justices of the peace to take action against
riots, routs, unlawful assemblies, and forcible entries; just as
repeated enactments empowered them to proceed against
the magnates' giving of liveries of uniform, food, and badges
to their retainers. The justices were either too afraid to enforce these statutes or too much in league with the offenders.
They can hardly be blamed for lack of zeal when even royal
judges were sometimes to blame. In 1411 Sir Robert Tir-
whit, a justice of the Court of Common Pleas, with a force
of 500 men, set an ambush for Lord Roos; and when called
to account, he actually pleaded that he did not know he had
broken the law. In spite of the inability of the J.P.s to repress disorder and corruption, the strength of the land-
holding classes and the weakness of the Crown combined to
give the justices fresh powers at the expense of the sheriff.
The most important step in this direction was taken in 1461,
when the sheriff was deprived of the police jurisdiction,
which he had so far exercised in the court known as the tourn
or lawday. Henceforth he could no longer arrest but must
transfer indictments to the J.P.s of the county at their next
sessions. Such statutes hastened the decay of the sheriff's
authority, but they did not remedy the perversion and
defiance of justice.

The problem could not be solved in the Lancastrian
period by appeal to Parliament or Council, dominated as
these bodies usually were by the magnates who were the

root of the trouble. Even if Council or Parliament condemned an act of lawlessness, the decision was rarely enforced. In 1437, for example, William Pulle, or Poole, a kinsman of the rising Stanley family which was powerful in south-west Lancashire, burst into the house of Isabel, widow of Sir John Butler, near Warrington, at five o'clock one Monday morning, with a band of warlike followers, and carried her off by force. Taken to Bidston in Wirral, she was compelled, under menace of death, to go through the ceremony of marriage, so that Poole could enjoy her inheritance. For this outrage no remedy could be obtained from the courts, and when Parliament was petitioned all that it did was to summon Poole to appear before the justices to answer for his crimes. It is very doubtful whether he did so, for he was already an outlaw. As the prestige and power of Henry VI's government declined, magnates began to settle their disputes in the field rather than in the royal courts. If one side obtained the help or approval of the government, the other would declare support for the opposition, especially after the administration had clearly passed into the hands of one baronial party, that of the Beauforts. Thus in the private wars which troubled Devon in the forties and fifties the Courtenays received the support of the government, and their rivals, the Bonvilles, that of York. As the government sank to the position of a weak partisan in these local disputes, men relied increasingly on the protection of one of the great men of their neighbourhood, and less and less on the king's courts. The royal system of local government was, in fact, breaking down.

The remedy could come only from a revival in the power of the monarchy, and the accession of Edward IV was the first step towards this. The young king was alive to the problem and gave personal attention to solving it. In 1462 he even sat in the Court of King's Bench where the king had not appeared in person for generations, and, what was more important, in several years he accompanied his judges on judicial progresses through the shires to suppress disorder. But habits of lawlessness died hard; and between the fighting of 1462-4 and the renewal of civil war from 1469 to 1471 lay an interval too short and uneasy for order to be restored. The solution of the problem belongs to the next period, not to this.

It is interesting to note that during the early years of Edward's reign complaints of violence and intimidation were no longer generally made to Parliament and Council, which had become discredited through their connexion with aristocratic faction and maladministration of justice in the Lancastrian period. Suitors now addressed their petitions to the king or to the chancellor. It is easy to see why petitioners should supplicate the king; but why the chancellor?

The chancellor, who had for so long been a great administrative official, was now becoming a judge as well, owing to the inadequacies of the common law. By the fifteenth century it was conservative and inelastic, much bound by rules and precedents, and therefore unable to cope with new needs and circumstances. This tendency was fostered by the rise in the mid fourteenth or late fourteenth century of the 'Law University' in London – the four great Inns of Court and the lesser Inns of Chancery. Common-law judges and pleaders (the predecessors of the modern barristers) received their legal education in these Inns, which in many ways resembled university halls or colleges. But whereas Oxford and Cambridge taught no common law, the Inns taught no civil (i.e. Roman) or canon (i.e. ecclesiastical) law. Unlike their thirteenth-century predecessors, the common-law lawyers now knew hardly anything of other legal systems; they were proud of their own law and its antiquity, and loath to change its principles and methods. Aggrieved persons with new needs could not usually hope that the common-law courts would devise new remedies, and parliaments were either too preoccupied or too much under the influence of the common lawyers to do so by enactment. One of the greatest needs which the common law failed to meet was the protection of trusts. The device of property held in trust for the use of someone other than the legal owner had been popularized by the friars, who could legally own no property. In this troubled period it spread widely in the lay world, especially among the magnates, who might thus escape not only feudal dues, but forfeiture in case of convictions for treason. The common law gave no remedy to the person for whose benefit the land was conveyed if the trustee abused this trust. The only resource for the aggrieved party was to appeal for equitable remedy to the king and his Council. But such cases were often too subtle, too involved, too time-consuming for the Council to deal with, and they were referred to the chancellor. He was not only a prominent and constant councillor of the king, but his control of skilled clerical assistance and of the issue of writs, and his close connexion with the common-law courts, facilitated inquiry and action by him. Moreover, as a great ecclesiastic he had some acquaintance with the principles of canon and civil law, and could therefore bring to the solution of new problems a broader and deeper outlook than that of the lay common-law judges. The faithlessness engendered by the unrest of the time caused the chancellor's jurisdiction to increase enormously, in enforcing trusts, contracts, and other cases where breach of faith was alleged. During the early years of Edward IV it looked as if the entire jurisdiction of the Council, including cases of violence, corruption, and intimidation, as well as the equitable cases concerning property, would be absorbed by the Chancery. But what was wanted to suppress disorder was not the administrative and legal resources of the chancellor, or his training in ethics, but power and vigour. The appropriate weapon to deal with turbulence and the over-mighty subject proved to be, not the Chancery, but the Council, when the monarchy had become strong once more.

It has already been noted that developments in the royal government were often followed by similar developments in seignorial administration. In the fifteenth century this is seen in the importance of baronial councils. Some of their members were landholders, valuable for their influence and prestige – fellow magnates, neighbouring landholders, or a group of the chief tenants; some were important permanent officials of the estates, such as the stewards; and some were advisers learned in the law, including, for important baronial councils, an itinerant royal judge, or a justice of the peace. As for the council's functions, just as the king's Council dealt with a very wide range of matters, so the private council not only dealt with the administration of the states but made ordinances for their government and advised the lord on disputed franchises, feudal rights, or conflict of jurisdictions. The private councils also developed something like an equitable jurisdiction. This probably originated in the right of the lord to override, in the case of the unfree tenants, customs which he thought unreasonable. The more professional the councillors became, the less patience they usually had with local rules and customs, and the more eager they became to decide cases by equity and reason instead.

There was still plenty of local custom for baronial councils to supervise. During the late middle ages the extension of royal jurisdiction, especially that of the justices of the peace, began to rob private courts of some of their former importance, especially in disputes about freehold; and with the leasing of their demesnes, lords began to lose interest in the enforcement of labour services, which had been one of the functions of manorial courts. Nevertheless, many modern writers have ante-dated the decay of private courts. In the fifteenth century manorial courts, though of less consequence than they had been two hundred years earlier, still performed important functions, such as formally admitting new tenants, registering titles, sales and exchanges of land, and commutation of services, enrolling leases and rules of succession, settling boundary disputes, and regulating the village agriculture. Moreover, in many of them were exercised franchisal rights. These varied enormously, but the most common were view of frankpledge (that is, supervision of the police arrangements of the franchisal area); inspection of weights and measures, and of the quality and measurement of essential victuals such as bread and ale; the presentment and punishment of petty crimes, especially assault; encroachments on commons or roads, and diversion of watercourses. Very frequent were the presentment and punishment of failure to repair walls, ditches, roads, and bridges; of nuisances such as fouling of wells, of deceitful methods of trading, and of haunters of taverns. A lord might also have the right to hold a hundred court, still active for the collection of petty debts. None of these types of jurisdiction was limited to the Welsh or northern marcher lords, with their exceptional liberties, or to great ecclesiastics; all were to be found in every part of the country. The countless manorial courts, often meeting every three weeks, and the kind of franchises just described, mattered much more in the normal routine of great numbers of humble country folk than the operations of royal justice in legislation or administration, which are apt to seem so much more important to us. The right to hold such courts was cherished, not only because of the prestige it conferred, but because of the profits they brought in – profits which were very welcome at a time when lords were finding the revenues from the cultivation of their estates tending to decline; for the agricultural depression which had set in early in the fourteenth century continued during this period, as we shall see in the next chapter.

## CHAPTER III

# Economic and Social Developments

IT has already been noted that during the fourteenth century there developed an agricultural depression, which
resulted in a movement towards the leasing of demesne
lands. The process went forward at varying rates, according
to the state of the local market or the character of the lord.
The lands to be leased first were often those furthest from
the headquarters of the organization – the great castle or
manor-house on a lay estate, and the episcopal palace or
abbey on ecclesiastical lands; for the cost of supervising estates and transporting their produce often made direct exploitation unprofitable in this age of contraction. Monasteries
were often slower in leasing their estates than lay magnates,
since abbeys needed fairly large supplies from their estates –
at least, those near the monastery – for their sustenance. And
the leasing of the demesne depended also on the kind of crop
in cultivation. Roughly speaking, the depression was most
serious in the case of cereals, whereas the wool trade still
flourished. Export taxes on wool tended certainly to reduce
the demand for it abroad, but they acted as a tariff shelter
for the nascent English cloth industry. English clothiers
could sell cloth on very favourable terms, since the raw
material cost them so much less than the foreign cloth-
worker had to pay. Hence for a time the decline in wool exports was compensated by the increase of cloth-manufacture
in England, which, together with the smaller number of
workers needed for sheep farming, encouraged landholders
in those days of high wages and labour shortages to continue
wool production and to turn arable into pasture.

In the second quarter of the fifteenth century the prospects for English foreign trade, which had seemed favourable in the first quarter, began to cloud over; and the burden
of the French war, together with growing disorder at home,

injured domestic trade. The result was that by the fifties the market even for wool was depressed, and great landholders were leasing their flocks and sheep-runs as they had earlier leased their arable land. By the end of the Lancastrian period the magnates, ecclesiastical as well as lay, had largely ceased to produce directly for the market, and had become a rentier class. Their incomes were often smaller than they had been in the thirteenth century, the golden age of demesne farming, though for the highest lay magnates the accumulation of estates by marriage sometimes more than offset the effect of the economic depression. Not all magnates were as fortunate as the Duke of York or the Earl of Warwick; indeed, it has been conjectured that dwindling revenues, especially after the war in France ceased to provide booty and ransoms, prompted many barons to seek additional income at the expense of the much-depleted royal exchequer, or through violence and intimidation.

Certainly the leasing of the demesne had important social consequences, for the lords no longer had an interest in retaining labour services, which were generally commuted for money. Theoretically the lord could in such a case demand what rent he liked; but as there was a glut of land, he often had to be content with a fairly low rent, maintained at the same rate year after year. Men whose forefathers had been subject to labour services regarded as servile now owed merely a moderate rent instead. If such obligations hardened into custom, the difference between villeins and freeholders grew less. Careless or indulgent lords allowed descendants of bondmen to forget that in the early fourteenth century the Court of Common Pleas had adjudged all rights over a villein's lands to vest in the lord; indeed, bondmen now came to think of themselves as having a legal title to their lands, and to regard themselves as 'customary tenants', who held their lands by the custom of the manor, 'copyholders' who held by the copy of the record in the manorial court rolls. Naturally, lords were unwilling to allow appeals to the custom of the manor against their interests, but the economic situation was against them and, moreover, legal theory began to follow economic development. The earliest case in which the chancellor is known to have protected customary tenants against their lord dates from 1439. The common-law courts, jealous of the extension of the equitable jurisdiction of the Chancery, soon began to do the same, and in 1467 we find Chief Justice Danby declaring: 'If the lord ousts his (customary) tenant he does him a wrong, for his tenant is as well inheritor to have the land to him and his heirs according to the custom of the manor as any man is to have his lands at common law.'

This dictum was followed in the Yorkist period by others in the same vein but, when the economic tide turned, the protection of the law courts proved too cautious. Moreover, commutation of labour services and security of tenure did not necessarily mean the abolition of personal bondage. Lords still valued the profits of personal serfdom, such as merchet (fine paid by villeins for leave to give their sons and daughters in marriage), chevage (fine paid by a villein for leave to dwell outside the manor), and heriot (sum payable from the chattels of a deceased villein tenant); just as the king cherished the profits from his rights of wardship, marriage, and other feudal incidents long after feudal military service had become obsolete. Hence personal serfdom often long survived labour services. A mayor of Bristol was claimed as a bondsman as late as 1586, and manorial incidents lingered to irritate tenants sometimes even in the nineteenth century. Such incidents were abolished only in 1922.

Even personal bondage was waning, however, in the fifteenth century, and the Lancastrian period was, on the whole, a time of prosperity for the peasantry. The real sufferers from the agricultural slump were the great landlords, whose incomes were declining with the general fall in agrarian values, and whose cost of living was still rising. It was a time when, for the lower section of the peasantry, wages were high and prices were stationary or falling, and, for the upper section, land could be acquired. The lords were leasing their estates; there was often no market for the poorer soils, which then fell back into waste, but the better land found peasants ready to lease it. The small man, who could till his holding mainly by his own labour and that of his family, was more favourably placed than a great lord, who would not find it easy to hire labourers except at unprofitably high wages. The peasant's sheep, hens, pigs, ducks, goats, cattle, bees, and crops not only made him almost self-sufficient in foodstuffs but provided him with a diversified economy much more suited to the limited markets of the fifteenth century than the specialized, large-scale production which thirteenth-century magnates had often undertaken. This period saw an expansion in the numbers and importance of the yeomen, a term originally applied only to freeholder peasants, but by this time beginning to be used for prosperous peasants generally, whether freeholders, customary tenants, or tenants at will.

This period saw not only the rise of the yeomanry but increasing differentiation among the peasantry too. Even in the thirteenth century there had been buying and selling of land among the peasants; some had been wiser, luckier, or more unscrupulous than their fellows, and differentiation in wealth and fortune resulted, even then. But such divergences increased with the leasing-out of the demesne. In days when lords had produced direct for the market and had found it profitable to insist on labour services to till their demesne, they had naturally wished to ensure that no obstacles were placed in the way of the performing of such services. Hence they had then used their great influence to oppose division or alienation of bondmen's holdings. But once the lord had leased his demesne, he no longer had the same interest in stopping one peasant from increasing his holding and another from allowing his to shrink. On the contrary, if the tenement of a poor peasant lapsed, through poverty, into the lord's hands, it would pay him to lease it to a richer peasant; for now that the lord's income was coming to be derived from rent, it was to his interest to obtain as good a rent as possible. The full effect of this economic interest of the lord was often mitigated by conservatism, by a paternal concern for the welfare of his tenants, and also, especially in the north and west, by the political and social advantage of a numerous tenantry, to provide fighting men for their lord. Nevertheless, the leasing of the demesne tended to weaken the lord's interest in maintaining the old framework of the village community, which began to change more rapidly than before.

In such a changing society there were numerous ways in which an able or lucky peasant might rise. Often the leasing of the demesne was in itself a factor which helped him; he might turn the lease to such good advantage that it became the first rung on the ladder of his ascent. The glut of land meant that lords were only too glad to allow assarts or intakes at low rents, instead of charging dearly for them, as they had done in the thirteenth century. The scarcity of labour and the lord's desire for money instead of labour services increased the peasant's choice of occupation, not only if he ran away or arranged to pay chevage outside his village, but even in his native township. For a rudimentary specialization was going on in the villages of the fourteenth and fifteenth centuries, and brought into being the man who was half peasant, half artisan or tradesman, who could employ the money he made in his trade or craft to enlarge his husbandry. Such men were the butchers, bakers, smiths, shoemakers, tailors, turners, carpenters, chapmen, and the like, who figure so often in court rolls. And in some areas, especially the West Riding, the Lake District, the West Country, and East Anglia, the rising cloth industry, carried on in the home of the peasants, provided an additional source of income, to the womenfolk as carders and spinners, to the men as weavers, shearers, fullers, and dyers.

Although the rise of the yeomen involved the decline of some other peasants, and a greater variety in the economic status of the peasantry as a whole, the changes of this period meant, in general, an upward movement for the peasantry, more mobility, more opportunities, more scope for enterprise, and higher wages with lower prices. The disorder and civil wars brought some destruction of property and loss of life to the peasants, but very little compared with the almost indescribable miseries inflicted by the Hundred Years War on large areas of France. The prosperity of the English peasantry was noted by English and foreign contemporaries. It supplied military strength to the nation, especially as it was from the yeomanry that the famous English archers were primarily recruited; too down-trodden a peasantry would not have had the spirit, intelligence, or leisure for archery.

From the early fourteenth century the effectiveness of the English long-bow had been so obvious and so important that the government did everything it could to encourage archery. Proclamations were published insisting that every prosperous male peasant was to possess a bow and arrows, and shooting at the butts was prescribed by law. From the reign of Edward III onwards statutes had been made enacting that archery was not to be neglected in favour of tennis, football, skittles, bowls, hand-ball, club-ball, and cock-fighting, and the search for military efficiency also led to the official encouragement of wrestling, running, jumping, and fisticuffs. Notwithstanding official disapproval, however, the various games remained popular, as did dancing and singing, for which, in spite of the disapproval of ecclesiastical authorities, the churchyard was a favourite venue. The public also flocked to travelling entertainers, such as jesters, acrobats, musicians, and bear-baiters, or walked to the neighbouring town to watch a miracle play.

Fishing and hunting were also popular, but these were pleasures reserved for the nobility. In the twelfth century, when the kings had normally been so strong, they had claimed such oppressive hunting-rights that all classes had united in protest; but now that the magnates were politically dominant, they had been admitted to a share in such privileges. One of the demands of the rebels in 1381 had been that hunting and fishing should be common to all; not only was this refused, but in 1390 Parliament (dominated by landholders) enacted a penalty of one year's imprisonment for every layman not possessing landed property worth 40s. a year and every clerk with an annual income of less than £10 who should presume to keep hunting-dogs or use ferrets or snares to catch deer, hares, rabbits, or any other game. Hunting, said the statute, was the sport of gentlefolk. During the Lancastrian period the hunting-rights of the landholders increased, for the kings had not the strength to resist. On the one side were the king and the magnates, both spiritual and lay; on the other were the peasants, artisans, and lower clergy. Penalties against poachers gradually became more severe, and the road was taken towards the ferocious game laws of the eighteenth century.

Hunting as practised by the gentry was an expensive diversion. It was surrounded with costly ceremony, and the hawks and hounds were not cheap to maintain. (Trained hawks or falcons were used for hunting birds, since handguns were coming into use only in the latter half of the fifteenth century and were then still primitive and uncertain. Hounds were used for pursuing deer, rabbits, and hares, but not foxes, which were despised as vermin.) Other diversions popular among the upper classes were also costly. Chess, draughts, backgammon, and shovelboard, were often played for high stakes, and the main point of dice was, of course, the gambling. The same was true of cards, which first became popular in England in the middle of the fifteenth century (the queens and knaves of our present packs depict a stylized form of late fifteenth-century fashions). A more essentially expensive amusement which was also very popular was the tournament. By the fifteenth century plate armour covered the wearer completely from top to toe, and by that time it was so well made that, together with the splendidly strong horse needed to carry such a weight, a knight's equipment was extremely costly. Tournaments, originally a utilitarian mode of training cavalry, became more and more an occasion for pageantry and display. Kings and nobles nevertheless continued to arrange them, since they brought prestige both to the organizer and to the knights who took part; for such occasions appealed both to the contemporary delight in a sophisticated and increasingly artificial chivalry, and to the contemporary love for pomp, colour, and conviviality. (This taste for lavish display manifested itself in other forms, such as the splendid pageants arranged by the city of London on occasions of popular rejoicing, for instance the victory of Agincourt, with gorgeous robes, elaborate tableaux, costly scenery, and fountains running with wine.) The same love of show is also evident in the gorgeous and extravagant fashions of the upper classes of this time, in the cut of the garments and in the furs, velvets, silks, and other costly materials of which they were made.

The magnate had also the cost of the host of retainers necessary to him if he wished to be influential. A great lord had in his household a throng of soldiers who had to be fed and paid, and very often clothed by him as well. These wore either the uniform or 'livery' of his connexion or affinity, or at least bore his badge or cognizance – for instance, the bear and ragged staff of Neville, the rising sun of York, the silver mullet of De Vere, or the portcullis of Beaufort. These large numbers of soldiers naturally made it difficult to enforce order and economy in household administration, but they and the domestics were by no means the whole of the affinity of a great lord: lawyers, clerks, neighbouring knights and yeoman found lords anxious to obtain their services. In the twelfth century lords had secured service by grants of land; now they secured it by pay; and whereas the twelfth-century tenant could not seek another master, the fifteenth-century retainer might and often did change his employer. It is true that the indentures of retainer which a magnate made with lesser barons, knights, soldiers of fortune, and professional men often stipulated a connexion for life, but dependants were often paid retainers of one or more other lords and the loyalties might prove incompatible. Overlords tried to counter this danger by inserting in indentures and letters patent the proviso 'as long as he be not retained by anyone else'; but it has been found that retainers sometimes left the service of even the most powerful magnates, like John of Gaunt. If this could happen to a king's son, whose favour and protection could make a man's fortunes, how much more likely was it to happen to lesser lords! It is true that some retainers probably supported their master to the end –

men such as the tenants of his estates, or those who had a traditional loyalty to his house. But if a magnate wished to be in the front rank, his affinity had to comprise more than these; it had to include men who might desert him if some other lord could pay them better or help them more effectively. Thus the new social order lacked the stability of the old feudal world.

Livery, maintenance, and indentures of retainer were not new – they are to be found as early as the thirteenth century; but the Hundred Years War had immensely encouraged them. The drain on the resources of the Crown and the decline in its power to keep order, the raising of armies by contracts with the magnates, which increased their wealth and power at the expense of the monarchy and brought home eventually thousands of household retainers with nothing to do but brawl and bully – all these and other consequences of the Great War provided a soil in which this new social order, this 'bastard feudalism' as it has been called, could grow and spread. Richard II's attempt to resist its consequences had contributed to his deposition, and after Henry V's renewed invasion of France had ended in the disasters of his son's reign, the evil became unmanageable. The unstable connexions of bastard feudalism meant that magnates had for ever to be struggling to increase their wealth and authority, or their affinity would begin to crumble away; and in such troubled times the dwindling of a magnate's connexion might jeopardize not only his prestige, but his livelihood, and life itself. Lords felt that if they did not strive to keep on going up, by any means, peaceful or violent, they would start to go down – perhaps to disaster. So the competition became ever fiercer, and as the weapons – the threat of intimidation, the armed band – were so dangerous it is little wonder that the rivalry ended in civil war.

This ever-increasing competition was as burdensome an expense to magnates as an armaments race has been to governments in the twentieth century, and it reached its climax at a time of agricultural depression. It is not surprising that many baronial families went down and had to part with their estates, and that even lords of the highest rank, such as the Duke of Somerset, were reduced to borrowing money. A better relief for financial embarrassment was a marriage with the daughter of a rich merchant, or even participation in trade, and magnates of Henry VI's reign, such as the Earl of Westmorland or the Duke of Suffolk, and even members of the royal family, did not disdain to procure licences for the export of wool.

If magnates were to enter trade, they did well to choose wool, for traffic in this commodity was more prosperous and stable than in most others. In this age of contraction merchants in Western Europe tried to safeguard their livelihood by establishing a monopoly, and, especially in the reign of Henry VI, when the government was too weak and inefficient to support them, English merchants found it increasingly hard to retain their markets. In Northern Europe the Hanseatic League of North German towns had by the beginning of the fifteenth century established not only control of the Baltic but also a monopoly over trade with Poland and Russia, and with Scandinavia too, even to the detriment of Scandinavian merchants. The cod-fish which had come from the Norwegian fisheries had been an essential import, and when the English fishers and merchants were excluded by the Hanse they looked round for an alternative source of supply. Their needs may have encouraged the striking advance in shipbuilding which now, to an extent hitherto unknown, made ocean trade practicable. The single-masted ship, with its bluff, broad build, and its one square sail, which had been in use since the twelfth century, began to be replaced in the early fifteenth century by a two- or three-masted vessel with high pointed bows to resist the heavy waves of a strong head sea. The main-mast was square-rigged as before, but the mizzen had the three-cornered lateen sail, recently introduced from the Mediterranean, and this, together with the spritsail which had just been adopted, greatly facilitated the working of the ship, by making it possible to sail nearer the wind.

This progress in the arts of shipbuilding and navigation,

together with the closing of Norway to Englishmen, combined to encourage English fishermen, from 1412 onwards, to fare over the stormy seas to distant Iceland, now more isolated than at any time since Viking days. Her coasts teemed with fish, and her inhabitants were short of almost everything else; and the fishermen were soon followed by merchants, who found a market for many commodities – food, timber, iron, pitch, tar, wax, salt, and above all, cloth. But the Hanse was steadily increasing its hold over Iceland's overlord, the King of Denmark; and soon he forbade Englishmen to trade in Iceland unless they paid very heavy tolls. Merchants of Hamburg and Danzig began to reach Iceland in growing numbers, and armed clashes with the English in Icelandic waters became increasingly frequent. And the English government, far from helping the trade, became a hindrance. By 1440 rival baronial parties in England were securing the issue of licences to sail to Iceland, not on any consistent economic principle, but to gain allies among the merchants. It is no wonder that by 1450 English trade with Iceland had passed its peak.

The fifties was the blackest decade for English commerce in the fifteenth century. The weakness and lack of principle shown by the government of Henry VI with regard to the trade with Iceland was exhibited in every other field. In 1435 it had quarrelled with its powerful ally, the Duke of Burgundy, who controlled the Low Countries, England's most important market; and English anger against the 'Burgundian traitors' had led to frequent interruptions in English trade with the great marts of Flanders, Zealand, and Brabant. In 1453 England finally lost her ancient foothold in Gascony, which had long been the chief supplier of wine to England and had become a great market for English wheat and cloth. Charles VII thought that political hostility necessitated economic severance, and for the time being the flourishing English trade with Gascony almost ceased. The local trade of the south coast towns with Picardy, Normandy, and Brittany had already succumbed, and the hostility of victorious France and mounting piracy imperilled the important trade with the Iberian peninsula, which supplied iron, oil, fruit, leather and other skins, etc., and food for the numerous English pilgrims to the shrine of Santiago de Compostella, in return for English cloth and other wares. In this difficult situation a merchant of Bristol tried a bold experiment. The great sea powers of Venice and Genoa regarded the Mediterranean as their preserve; but in 1446 Robert Sturmy dared to send thither a ship laden with pilgrims for the Holy Land, and wool, tin, and cloth for Pisa, the port of Florence, now only a humble rival to Venice and Genoa. The pilgrims were landed safely at Jaffa, but on the way thence to Italy the ship was wrecked in a great storm off Greece. Undaunted, Robert Sturmy in 1457 fitted out other ships and went with them himself. He never returned, for he and his ships were sunk off Malta, where the Genoese had lain in wait for him.

Immediate reprisals were taken against the Genoese in London, but Genoa could afford to be bold, for by this time the English government was near to impotence. For the past twenty years its actions had been guided by the rivalries of baronial factions rather than by any clear policy, and its sporadic bursts of energy had been, if anything, more disastrous to trade than its more usual nerveless inactivity. For instance, it was now too poor to maintain a royal navy; so the keeping of the seas was entrusted to privateers (chiefly from West Country ports), who plundered foreign shipping for preference, but English shipping if it was tempting enough. This piracy naturally aroused anger abroad, anger which the English government was powerless either to placate or to oppose. Its idea of a remedy was to sanction in 1442 an organized system of privateering, to be conducted by a fleet of 28 ships, provided by men closely connected with the dominant Suffolk party. The result of this policy was the unprovoked capture by the English privateers in 1449 of a fleet of 110 vessels on its way from the Bay of Bourgneuf. The Flemish and Dutch ships were released, but most of the booty, which belonged to Hanseatic merchants, was kept as lawful prize. The government refused redress, for many of its members were in league with the pirates; but the greatest sufferers were the English merchants, for the Hanseatics seized all English goods in their territories as compensation for their losses. Moreover, they made Denmark close the Sound to English shipping, and forbade the passage of English cloth to the East. And this was not all. The Hundred Years War had powerfully stimulated the already considerable anti-foreign prejudices of English mobs; and in 1456 and 1457 there were particularly serious anti-Italian riots in London – attacks so severe that the Venetians, Genoese, and Florentines threatened to abandon London and settle at Winchester. The government had been too feeble to suppress these attacks, yet it subsequently annoyed the English merchants by issuing letters of pardon to numerous Italians accused of trading offences. In the spring of 1460 the government, alarmed by the prospect of invasion by Warwick, attempted, unsuccessfully, to seize the Venetian trading fleet. At the crisis of its fate the Lancastrian régime had therefore not only lost the support of the English merchants but had alienated every commercial power in Europe. No wonder English merchants looked for better things from Yorkist rule.

The accession of Edward IV was followed by a certain revival of trade, since even the first decade of his reign was not quite so troubled as the period of sharp civil war from 1459 to 1461, and this fact alone raised trade from its lowest depths. Then in 1461 Louis XI ascended the French throne. Unlike his father he did not believe that political hostility should involve economic estrangement, and he began to grant licences to English merchants to trade once more with his dominions, and especially with Gascony. An Act of 1463 forbidding the import of cloth from the Continent, though designed to encourage English cloth manufacture, annoyed the Flemings and led to reprisals; but the rapprochement of England with Burgundy in 1467 was accompanied by guaranteed facilities for English trade with the very important Netherlands market. Unfortunately, this made the government less careful to remain on good terms with the Hanse. Edward IV was so anxious to promote the interests

The chantry of William of Wykeham, *c.* 1400, Winchester Cathedral, ants. (*Herbert Felton*)

**2.** The porch and tower, Cirencester Church, Glos. (*A. F. Kersting*)
**3.** The south choir aisle of Bristol Cathedral (*Herbert Felton*)

**4.** The fan vault of
Sherborne Abbey
Dorset (*F. H. Crossley*)

**5.** The double
hammer-beam roof of
St Wendreda, March,
Cambs.
(*Professor G. F. Webb*)

**6.** 15th century screen,
Kenton, Devon
(*National Buildings
Record, Photo F. Pitcher*)

**7.** The Divinity
School, Oxford
(*Dr Weaver*)

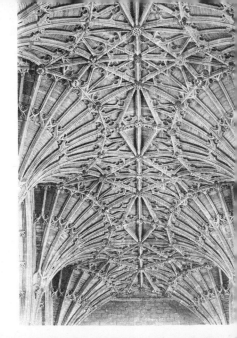

**8.** Stratford-on-Avon Grammar School and Old Guild Chapel, Warwicks. (*Reece Winstone*)

**9.** Bodiam Castle, Sussex (*Leonard and Marjorie Gayton*)

**10.** Tattershall Castle, Lincs. (*Country Life*)

Ockwells Manor (Berks.) : Hall interior (*Country Life*)
Much Wenlock (Salop) : The Prior's Lodging (*Country Life*)
William Grevel's House, Chipping Campden, Glos.
*T. Batsford. Photo B. Clayton*)

**14.** Didbrook (Glos.): Cottage Cruck construction
(*National Buildings Record. Photo W. A. Clark*)

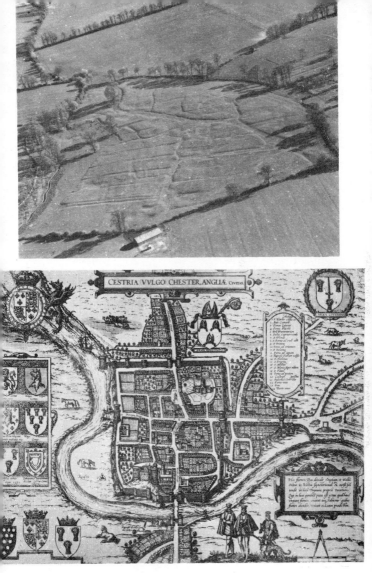

**15.** Burston (Bucks.): a village depopulated in the late fifteenth century
(*Reproduced by permission of the Air Ministry*)
**16.** Chester about 1580, according to Braun

**17.** Massingham's sculpture of Richard Beauchamp, Earl of Warwick, St Mary's, Warwick
(*Photo F. H. Crossley*)

**18.** Alabaster group of the Father and Son (perhaps originally of the Trinity), *c.* 1410
(*Courtesy Museum of Fine Arts, Boston, Mass.*)

**19.** Head of alabaster effigy of Edward II, Gloucester Cathedral
(*H. Gernsheim*)

Gloucester Cathedral: Angel from the Choir Vault
(*The Courtauld Institute*)
St Christopher, Haddon Hall Chapel, Derby (*Hallam Ashley*)
Richard II (portrait), Westminster Abbey (*W. A. Clark*)

23. Holograph letter of Henry V (British Museum)

Furthremore I wold that ye comeend with my brothre, with the chanceller, with my cosin of Northumbrelond, and my cosin of Westmerland, and that ye set a gode ordinance for my north marches, and specialy for the Duc of Orlians and for alle the remanant of my prisoners of France, and also for the K[ing] of Scotelond; for as I am secrely enfourmed by a man of ryght notable estate in this lond that there hath ben a man of the Ducs of Orliance in Scotland and accorded with the Duc of Albany, that this next somer he schal bryng in the maumet of Scotlond [the pretended Richard II] to sturre what he may, and also that ther schold be founden weys to the havyng awey specialy of the Duc of Orlians, and also of the K[ing] as welle as of the remanant of my forsayd prysoners, that God do defende. Wherfore I wolde that the Duc of Orliance be kept stille within the castil of Pomfret with owte going to Robertis place or to any othre disport, for it is bettre he lak his disport then we were disceyved. Of all the remanant dothe as ye thenketh. (?A.D. 1419)

RICHARD CV MN

RICHARD ꝺNOꝺ ꝼꝺꝼꝛꝛ

**24.** Panel showing detail of bell-founding, from the Bell-Founders Window, York Minster (*The Yorkshire Philosophical Society*)

**25.** York School. Last Supper, from window in Priory Church, Great Malvern, Worcs. (*National Buildings Record. Photo S. Pitcher*)

**26.** The geese and the fox; bench-end, Brent Knoll Church, Som. (*A. F. Kersting*)

**27.** Sir John Cassy in judge's robes, and Lady Cassy, at Deerhurst, Glos. (*National Buildings Record. Photo S. Pitcher*)

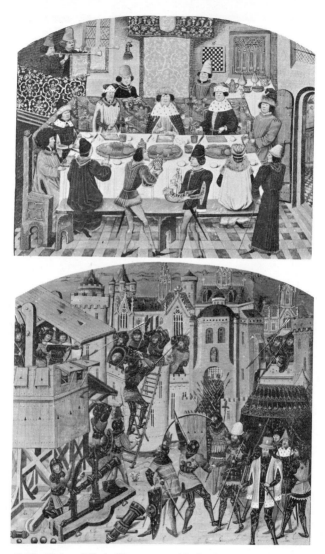

**28.** The Dukes of York, Gloucester and Ireland dine with Richard II
(*British Museum, Royal MS.* 14 *E IV*)
**29.** The Taking of Ribodane (*British Museum, Royal MS.* 14 *E IV*)

**50.** John, Duke of Bedford, prays to St George
*British Museum, Add. MS. 18, 150)*

**31.** Birth of St Edmund (*British Museum, Harl. MS.* 2278)

of English merchants that when in June, 1468, an English fleet bound for the Baltic was captured by the King of Denmark off the Sound, Hanseatic goods in London were seized as compensation for the English losses. This led to the outbreak of a naval war with the Hanse. Inevitably the war injured trade, though at first not so much as might have been expected; for the export of English cloth to Northern and Eastern Europe and the import of timber, pitch, tar, potash (for cloth-dyeing), and furs from the Baltic countries was carried on indirectly through the neutral markets of Zealand and Brabant. In fact, England might have made peace on not unfavourable terms, but for the turn of political events. In 1470 Edward had to flee to the Netherlands; and in 1471 he returned – in Hanseatic ships. For this invaluable help he had to promise to satisfy all the Hanseatic demands, including the reinstatement of the Hanseatic merchants in full possession of their ancient privileges in England; and English attempts at direct relations with the markets of Central and Eastern Europe received a blow from which they did not recover until Elizabeth's reign. Nevertheless, as we shall see, the latter part of Edward IV's reign saw a marked revival of English commerce, which after 1475 was more prosperous than at any previous time in the century.

The trade depression of the mid-century had had an adverse effect on most of the towns, some of which, such as Nottingham, Leicester, Northampton, and Lincoln, even contracted in area. Many towns were so impoverished that they had to be granted tax reliefs.* We read, too, of the decay of fairs, including even such famous ones as St Botolph's at Boston and St Giles at Winchester. But the picture is not a simple one of universal decline. Some of the old fairs, such as St Bartholomew's, London, and Stourbridge, near Cambridge, continued to flourish, and new ones were started. One or two regions, such as Devon, found it a time of opportunity. And three ports continued to prosper and expand.

*Research has recently shown that these claims of impoverishment were often exaggerated; Coventry even throve while it pleaded poverty to the Exchequer.

Bristol's trade with Ireland and the Iberian peninsula suffered less than the traffic of the east coast ports with Northern Europe, and her important trade with France revived after 1461. She benefited from the fact that the wool production of the Cotswolds and the Welsh border, the cloth manufacture of the West Country, and the lead and tin mining of the southwest were all flourishing; she was immune from foreign invasion or attack by pirates, and was becoming the chief port for the West of England, Wales, and the Midlands. Her merchants were numerous, thriving and adventurous; and a shipowner like William Canynges (d. 1474), with a fleet of ships manned by almost 800 men, had wealth and piety enough to build St Mary Redcliffe, as nearly faultless an example of late-Perpendicular as exists in England.

Southampton, too, continued to flourish.* It benefited from the resilience of the Italian trade for which it became during this period the chief port. The decay of the fairs of Champagne, with the devastations of the Hundred Years War, had led to the development of the sea-route through the Straits of Gibraltar. Every year came fleets of Italian galleys, first from Genoa, then between 1425 and 1477 from Florence, and, after the anti-alien riots in London in 1456 and 1457, a great Venetian fleet, owned by the Republic and hired out to its merchants. Laden with silks, satins, cloth of gold, damask, furred gowns, fruit, spices, sugar, and gems, they stayed for sixty days at Southampton on their way to Sluys, and exchanged some of their costly freight for the products of England, especially her wool, cloth, hides, and metals. The commercial revival of Edward IV's reign saw the zenith of Italian trade in England, and with it of Southampton's medieval prosperity.

But the most prosperous town of all was London. Well situated for trade with the Low Countries, which by the end of this period were more than ever England's most impor-

---

*Miss Olive Coleman has shown (*Econ. History Review*, 2nd series, Vol. 16, 1963–4) that Southampton's commercial activity benefited mainly merchants from outside the town – Italians, Londoners, and traders from other English towns.

ECONOMIC AND SOCIAL DEVELOPMENTS

tant market, her activities were, moreover, so diversified that
she could bear fluctuations in trade better than east coast
ports whose trade was principally with Northern Europe.
Whereas the merchants of Newcastle were interested chiefly
in coal and those of Lynn in corn, London's traders were
concerned with every branch of commerce. Her trade was
now on such a large scale that increasing specialization was
worth while – the differentiation of the merchant from the
manufacturer, the shipper from the merchant, the concen-
tration of the merchant on a single commodity or market;
more than any other English town she could develop commercial and financial techniques, from the extensive use of
credit and sleeping partners to bills of exchange and speculation in futures. The great wealth of London's merchants
caused the government to turn to them for loans; and loans
could open the door to fresh commercial advantages, for
example, in the Company of the Staple.* Moreover, government departments, growing ever bigger, tended to settle
down at Westminster and London; and as this area became
the capital of England and the centre of affairs, it became
increasingly fashionable for the great ones of the land to
have houses in or near London. This was now true not only
of all the important lay magnates, but also of the greater
abbots and all the bishops; from Temple Bar the bishops'
inns stretched all along the south side of the Strand, except
at the Savoy, as far as Charing Cross. The presence of all
these brought trade to London, for such great persons were
attended by hundreds of servants and followers. And so
London merchants were important enough to be wooed and
knighted by Edward IV. We see them controlling rural
cloth-workers, lending to country dealers and chapmen,
entering into partnerships with gentlemen wool-growers.
Many merchants were wealthy enough to endow their towns
with churches and amenities – like Dick Whittington; and
some, more ambitious, were leading a most important
social development – they were buying country estates, and,

*In 1334 London had 2% of the taxable lay wealth of the country; by
1515 it enjoyed nearly 9%.

like the Wottons or the Boleyns, turning themselves into gentry. These successful merchants might, like the Russells, increase their wealth by exploiting their newly-acquired country estates on shrewd business lines; or they might make themselves useful to the king, as did so many of the gentry who prospered in the service of the Crown – the Leventhorpes or the Oldhalls, the Hungerfords or the Stanleys. It was with these rising merchants, with the gentry, and the yeomen, that the future of England was to lie.

## CHAPTER IV

# Religious and Educational Movements

WE have seen how the economic changes of the time were bringing forward men of the middle classes – city merchants and country clothiers, knights and yeomen. Personal initiative, receptivity to new ideas, and industry helped such men to rise; and they were often inclined to grow out of sympathy with a Church which laid stress on obedience to authority and tradition, and contained in the higher ranks many clerics who did not justify their wealth and power. Literacy was spreading through the middle class, and many of its members were tempted to read and judge for themselves, even in matters of faith. Jealousy of clerical wealth and privilege encouraged anti-clericalism, and nationalism, especially strong among the middle classes, fostered anti-papalism. It is therefore not surprising that Lollardy found much support among the middle classes.

In the reign of Henry IV it was mainly Lollards of the 'lower middle class' who were hunted down – priests, craftsmen, artisans, and the like. Henry IV backed Archbishop Arundel in a persecution of Lollardy more vigorous and determined than that of Richard II's day, for not only was the new king very orthodox but his weak position necessitated a close alliance with the Church. The burning of heretics had previously had only common-law authority; but in 1401 it was enacted by statute. Henry also supported Arundel in his suppression of Lollardy in its birthplace and intellectual centre, Oxford University; this cut the movement's intellectual roots, and from then onwards scarcely any men of learning in England adhered to Lollardy. Not everyone of influence had yet deserted the movement, however. Henry's position was so weak that he could not afford to alienate men of rank if he could avoid it, and they were handled gently by the bishops or left alone. There were many Lollards among the country gentry, and in the Parliament of 1404 there were enough Lollard knights of the shire for a vigorous attack to be made on the wealth of the Church. In the Parliament of 1410 the Lollard party petitioned for the disendowment of the Church and asked that any Lollard arrested by the bishops should be admitted to bail. One prominent Lollard knight, Sir John Oldcastle, was actually a friend of the Prince of Wales. The persecution was enough to harass and exasperate the Lollards, but not enough to eradicate them, and in this respect, as in others, Henry V found a dangerous situation on his accession.

The young king, sternly and narrowly orthodox, had no doubt as to the policy to be pursued. He made it clear at once that he would resolutely support the bishops in suppressing Lollardy, even if it meant attacking an old friend as influential as Sir John Oldcastle; the result of this policy was a formidable Lollard rising under Oldcastle in January, 1414. The plot was, however, betrayed to the king, who took prompt action to crush it. Although Oldcastle escaped to Wales, and evaded capture until 1417, Henry had no more danger to fear from Lollardy. Men of rank, such as knights and merchants, not only found it dangerous to cling to Lollardy if they valued their lives and possessions, but also were alienated from it by the political and social radicalism to which persecution had helped to drive many Lollards.

Lollardy retained many adherents, however, among craftsmen, artisans, and poor priests. As they were deprived of organization, and as one essential of Lollardy was the claim to private judgement, Lollards varied considerably in their beliefs. Nevertheless, all were in some degree anti-sacerdotal, and all believed that they should have unhindered access to the Scriptures, from which, they held, could be deduced by individual interpretation the rules of faith and salvation. Those who were illiterate found some kindred spirit who could read, and in secret listened to the reading of the Bible, or some Lollard work such as *The Wycket* or *The Lantern of Life*. The size of the movement continued to alarm the orthodox and the secular prisons were crowded with prisoners awaiting trial. As for the bishops' prisons, their accommodation was so severely taxed that in 1428 the bishops had to ask the monastic Orders to receive heretics into their prisons. In 1431 the government was much alarmed by a formidable conspiracy, which revived the scheme of 1410 for the confiscation of the temporalities of the higher clergy, and the diversion of these endowments to the maintenance of the poor and more parish priests. And this was not the end of Lollardy. Recent research has shown that the late Dr Gairdner was wrong in supposing that after 1431 Lollardy was negligible. Lollards continued to be numerous, especially in towns associated with industry, and a source of spasmodic anxiety to the authorities until the Reformation. Besides, there were probably more heretics than the written evidence indicates. Unorganized and without notable leaders, Lollards were mostly obscure persons who might escape detection for long periods in towns. Moreover, except at times of scare, persecution was not very thorough; there was no Inquisition as in France or Spain. In the middle decades of the century the Lollards seemed to Bishop Reginald Pecock to be growing in numbers so much that he wrote many books to confute and convert them.

Pecock was a prolific writer, who wrote seven works which have survived, and over forty which have not. He believed that if what the Church taught was the only true faith, it should be possible to subdue heresy not by threats and burnings, but by the much better method of teaching and persuasion. He was not only a bishop but very much an Oxford graduate, with a respect for the intellect which inspired his whole philosophy. It was his aim to refute the Lollard emphasis on faith in Scripture alone, and to uphold an intellectual method of approach to Christianity. His books were too academic and unemotional in style to appeal to humble Lollards, but his effort to reach them made him write in English, and it was the first time that theological treatises had appeared in English since Anglo-Saxon times. The most gifted theologian of fifteenth-century England, and a man who defended even the abuses of the Church, he was nevertheless tried and condemned for heresy in 1457, made to resign his bishopric, and sentenced to a comfortable but life-long imprisonment in the Fenland Abbey of Thorney.

There were several reasons for this disastrous end to his career. Although honest, kindly, and devout, he was disliked for his intellectual vanity. He was a determined and indiscreet supporter of the Beaufort faction, to whom he owed his rise; and in the increasingly envenomed atmosphere of the fifties the Yorkists determined to weaken the tottering Lancastrian government by striking at one of its most outspoken supporters. Moreover, Pecock's views alienated two very different parties in the Church. Those who, like Gascoigne, the Oxford theologian, bewailed the abuses which afflicted the Church, felt that Pecock was attempting, as has been said, to defend the indefensible. He had, for example, made himself unpopular with the reformers as early as 1447 by a sermon in which he argued that bishops were not bound to preach or reside in their dioceses because they had more important work to do, and defended their appointment by papal provision and their payment of first-fruits or annates for their sees. A much more influential party in the Church, concerned, not with reform, but with the maintenance of the existing order, thought Pecock's views dangerous, for though he always declared his obedience to authority, his emphasis on reason rather than revelation could be held to involve a denial of all authority and faith. Both parties were angered by what they deemed the presumption of 'this peacock' – his critical attitude towards great doctors of the Church, such as Jerome or Augustine, his scepticism about the Apostles' authorship of the creed which bears their name, or his proposals for amendments in the church services, to enable both clergy and laity to understand them better. His willingness to argue against the Lollards on their own ground was as resented as his use of the English tongue for the discussion of theological questions. Nevertheless it was only by wrenching his words from their context and giving them a different meaning from what he had intended that it was possible to prove charges of heresy against him. And so he was made to recant doctrines which he never taught, and two propositions which the Council of Trent later declared to be true. Pecock appealed to Rome, and Pope Calixtus III not only sympathized with him but ordered him to be restored to his see. The Yorkists could not allow this blow to their prestige, and the tottering Lancastrian government feared that it would be weakened still further if Pecock's appeal were allowed by Rome. The upright Calixtus died in 1458 and his wily successor, Pius II, thought it inexpedient to interfere in the matter; so Pecock died in prison.

His suppression was a great misfortune to the Church in England. His teaching may have laid too much stress on reason; but it was the only large-scale attempt in the fifteenth century to harmonize reason and faith, increasingly divergent since the Thomist synthesis had been repudiated by the followers of Duns and Ockham, and such a harmonizing was one of the vital needs of religion in the late middle ages. The condemnation of Pecock and his works meant that faith was once more driven back on revelation and authority as its sole support, and that philosophy was encouraged to be merely an increasingly subtle intellectual exercise which, if it had any bearing on religion, tended by its agnosticism to undermine the faith. Soon intelligent men of Renaissance sympathies were to despise the scholars of the old learning as obscurantist logic-choppers, and the prestige of the Church supported by those scholars suffered, too.

The condemnation of Pecock also demonstrated the weakness of papal authority in England by this time. With the growth of nationalist feeling the royal control over the Church had been strengthened, and in spite of the weakness of his position and his need for the support of the Church, Henry IV was able, because of the Schism in the Church, to maintain the claims of the English Crown in relation to the Papacy. His successor was in a stronger position, and, although severely orthodox, Henry V vigorously upheld the royal authority. In 1417 Bishop Beaufort of Winchester persuaded the newly-elected pope, Martin V, to make him a cardinal, in recognition of his services in helping to end the Schism and secure Martin's election. Beaufort was the king's uncle and his wealthiest subject; yet as soon as Henry heard of the new honour, on which he had not been consulted, he privately but firmly ordered Beaufort to resign the cardinal's hat, or be deprived of his see and all his possessions in England under the terms of the Statute of Praemunire of 1393. The ambitious and powerful bishop was forced to obey. The Statute of Praemunire had been aimed only against those who appealed to Rome for a papal provision to a benefice in derogation of the king's rights; but now the act was used to strike at any appeal to Rome which might be held to diminish the royal prerogative and jurisdiction in any way. It was not until 1427, when Henry V was in his grave, that Beaufort finally obtained the coveted cardinal's hat. His elevation aroused great hostility in England, however, and it was decided that he was to take no part in the proceedings of the king's Council when the relations of England to the Apostolic See were in question.

Other English prelates were created cardinals later in the century without friction, but only because in each case the appointment was made with the consent, or even at the request, of the government. After the twenties the royal control over ecclesiastical appointments was unchallenged. In 1426 Martin V, encouraged by the apparent weakness of the English government after the death of Henry V, and hoping to rehabilitate the Papacy after the Schism, tried to secure the repeal of the obnoxious Statutes of Provisors and Praemunire. Finding the king's Council adamant, he turned to Archbishop Chichele, who was threatened with suspension if he did not act. Chichele dutifully urged Parliament to comply with the papal demands, and was supported by the Archbishop of York, four bishops, and two abbots. Parliament would not hear of it, however; and there, to the great discontent of the pope, the matter had to rest. For the rest of the century relations between England and the Papacy ran fairly smoothly, for the popes recognized that it was useless to struggle against the claims of the Crown.

There was, indeed, much truth in Martin V's bitter exclamation, 'It is not the Pope but the King of England that governs the Church in his dominions'. Bishops were now habitually royal nominees, and the papal power was normally limited to confirmation and provision of the royal candidate (unless, as in the case of the adult Henry VI, the government was so weak that its nominations sometimes lacked force, or even clarity). Indeed, in the latter part of the century papal consent to the king's nominee came to be taken for granted, and the Crown usually bestowed the temporalities of the see on its candidate without awaiting papal confirmation or translation. The role of the cathedral chapter had long become an unimportant formality, and bishops were in fact chosen by the king with the assent of the pope. Elections of abbots were usually allowed to proceed freely; but the Crown had by now established that the heads of all the important monasteries and of many of the lesser ones needed royal approval before their election could be deemed valid.

Many lesser benefices were by this time in the king's gift, for this was a principal means of providing a livelihood for servants of the Crown. Bishoprics often went to the higher civil servants – royal ministers, diplomats, jurists, confessors. Lesser benefices in the very extensive royal patronage were bestowed on the lower grades of the civil service. A regular system had been evolved whereby a certain living would be reserved, so far as possible, for the holder of a particular royal office; thus the deanery of the London church of St Martin-le-Grand had been for generations the preserve of the Wardrobe clerks. The king's resources, especially under the impoverished Lancastrians, were not large enough to enable him to pay his servants adequate salaries, and so in the circumstances such a system was inevitable. Moreover, it can be said in defence of the system that whereas in many other parts of Western Europe at this time bishoprics had become the almost hereditary preserves of noble families, in England many bishops were men of humbler birth who had risen by their talents. Even though the magnates were so politically and socially powerful under the Lancastrians, we find in the Lancastrian period important prelates who were sons of yeomen or traders. And the English bishops of this period were, on the whole, much more respectable than those of many other provinces of the Roman Church.

Nevertheless, the bishops were very far from being the inspiration to holiness which, according to St Thomas Aquinas, the holders of episcopal office should be. Even if they had been saints, their dioceses were often much too large for effective supervision – the diocese of Lincoln, for example, stretched from the Humber to the Thames. But no fifteenth-century English bishop has been put forward for canonization; prelates were usually chosen for their administrative or diplomatic talents, or their aristocratic connexions, rather than for piety, zeal, or learning. There were some, like Alnwick of Lincoln, who tried to look after their dioceses conscientiously; but in this century the absence of bishops from their sees became more frequent and their residence in London more permanent. One of the most important prelates of Henry VI's reign was John Kemp, several times chancellor of England, Archbishop of York from 1426 to 1452, a cardinal and Archbishop of Canterbury from 1452 to 1454. Yet he visited his diocese, Gascoigne tells us, for only two or three weeks at intervals of ten or twelve years during all his long tenure of the see of York. Such a prelate appeared to his flock not as a pastor and father in God but as a distant judge and master, whose most frequently encountered activities were the exercise of his jurisdiction and the protection of his rights.

The absence of a bishop from his see did not mean that diocesan routine broke down. His spiritual functions – for instance, ordination, confirmations, and consecrations – were performed by a suffragan bishop, often a friar who had been provided to a titular see *in partibus infidelium* or to the equally hollow dignity of an Irish diocese, and his other duties were delegated to a vicar-general, who in the fifteenth century became more and more of a permanent official. But neither suffragan bishops nor vicars-general had the power or authority to arouse the fervour of their flock as a St Hugh

or a Grosseteste had done, and the spiritual life of the diocese
suffered accordingly.

It would, however, be over-simplifying the matter to say
that the bishops' neglect of their sees was a chief cause of the
abuses which existed in the church. By the fifteenth century
the Church in England was so old and complex, and its
constitution so minutely regulated by law and custom that
if a reforming bishop did appear on the scene, he ran up
against entrenched privilege at almost every turn. Even if he
had the great determination, the zeal, and the skill necessary
to overcome such formidable obstacles, he might be dis-
heartened by the ill-will and friction which such clashes
inevitably caused. It might, for instance, be supposed that,
with so much complaint about absentee bishops, a prelate
who visited his flock would be welcomed joyfully. In fact,
however, law and custom, accumulated during the past three
centuries, had encrusted episcopal visitations with such a
burden of hospitality and fees that to a poor region the
bishop's visit might prove a financial disaster. Thus Kemp
may well have been confirmed in his absenteeism by his
experience in 1428. In that year he set out to visit the archdeaconry of Richmond, to whose most remote part in north
Lancashire, Cumberland, and Westmorland no archbishop
seems to have penetrated for a century and a half. But on his
way thither he was met by a deputation which told him on
behalf of the clergy of the archdeaconry that the countryside
was so impoverished by failure of crops, murrain, and other
causes that it could not bear the cost of his visit. He was persuaded to accept a composition fee instead; and soon afterwards he began his career of almost permanent absenteeism.

Worthier and more persistent bishops than Kemp found
their well-meant efforts at reform wrecked when they came
up against privilege. For instance, in the early part of the
fifteenth century there was a long-standing dispute at Lincoln between the dean and chapter. In 1412 Prince Henry's
chancellor, John Macworth, was appointed dean. Haughty,
uncompromising, persistently absent yet claiming all the

advantages of a residentiary, he quarrelled with the chapter so violently that in 1435 he entered the cathedral with a band of armed men while vespers were going on in the choir. The chancellor was dragged about by his vestments and maltreated and menaced. In 1437 Bishop Alnwick, one of the worthiest prelates of the century, carried out an official investigation and tried hard to settle the dispute. He realized that part of the trouble was due to the confused and contradictory customs of the cathedral church, and by 1440, after much labour, he had prepared an admirable code of reformed statutes. But so old and strong was the tradition of the autonomy of the cathedral chapter in relation to the bishop that dean and canons, in spite of their quarrels, united to oppose the new statutes; and when Alnwick died in 1449 the dispute was still unsettled.

The tissue of legal rights and vested interests in the Church was the quite understandable growth of centuries of development; but it was undoubtedly sapping her vitality. By this time perhaps the only treatments which could be effective were the stimulus of a threat to the Church or the painful method of a surgical operation. The danger from Lollardy was both too great, and not great enough; it was not great enough to force the Church to set her house in order, but was enough to scare most of the clergy into a defence of the established order. The result was a strengthening of the *status quo*, with all its abuses, for, like the Old Tories of the early nineteenth century, the ecclesiastical authorities believed that if one began to tamper with the fabric of the constitution, however convincing the arguments for such action, the whole edifice might eventually crash. It is easier for us than for them to see that such a die-hard attitude might produce the very revolution which was feared.

In any case, reform by legislation could not be effective without some spiritual revival on which to build, and, after the suppression of the Lollard ferment and the failure of the conciliar movement, there seemed to be no effective force for spiritual regeneration in England. In the past monks and friars had supplied it; but they were now in no condition to initiate such a movement, for they themselves had become too much part of the established order.

The friars were, perhaps, more alive to the needs of the times than the monks, and were still expert and popular preachers; yet their moral influence was diminished by the contrast between their professions of poverty and their practice, and there was now less enthusiasm to become a friar. The decline in their numbers has often been ascribed to the Black Death; but if so, it was a case of delayed action. Immediately after the first attack of the plague there was a successful campaign to fill the gaps, and in some friaries the numbers reached their highest point about 1370. In the fifteenth century the recovery in numbers from the lowest point of 1350 continued for the orders of friars as a whole; but even by 1500 they were only about 60 per cent as numerous as they had been before the Black Death began.

Nevertheless, they still performed notable services to the Church, not only as preachers, but as confessors, suffragan bishops, and theologians. The monks of this period had, generally speaking, no comparable record to show. As we have already noted, the Carthusians formed a noble exception to the general laxity; and one or two other houses of pious intensity were founded in this period. Such was Sion Abbey in Middlesex, the richest nunnery in England, founded in 1414 by Henry V for Bridgetine nuns. But the ardour of the Carthusians and Bridgetines was unusual and the foundations of monasteries had almost ceased. In the twelfth century, as has already been noted, the laity had venerated the monasteries, had eagerly sought their prayers, and had showered endowments on them. Now an increasingly critical laity was talking of the unworthiness of the monks; and pious benefactors were giving wealth, not so much to monasteries, but to parish churches, chantries,* and educational institutions. Hence, as income declined and expenses grew, religious houses were often in financial difficulties and some of the

---

*Miss K. L. Wood-Legh has shown in *Perpetual Chantries in Britain* (1965) that founders of chantries often entrusted the administration of them to monasteries.

devices often employed to make ends meet increased the tendency to worldliness. Thus monasteries frequently obtained ready money from lay men and women by promising in return an annuity for life of food, drink, and lodging. Apart from the loss incurred by the abbey if the pensioner lived longer than had been calculated, the presence of layfolk within the precincts was not conducive to the observance of the Rule. When Bishop Alnwick visited Langley Priory, he was told how an aristocratic pensioner, Lady Audley, would bring into church her twelve dogs, which competed with the singing and terrified the nuns. Bishops frowned on corrodies, as such speculative life annuities were called, but needy communities found them too useful to be abandoned.

In this period the recovery in the number of the monks from the minimum of 1350 continued, though more slowly than in the fourteenth century; and on a small scale dissolution now began. The piety of the twelfth century had provided many French monasteries with English manors, supervised by two or three monks, who acted as land-agents and transmitted the revenues. The growing anti-French feeling stimulated by the Hundred Years War caused these alien priories to be repeatedly taken into the king's hand; and in 1414 they were confiscated by the Crown. Some of these endowments went to Carthusian houses. Shene Priory, the greatest and most richly endowed of the Carthusian houses in England, founded by Henry V in 1414, benefited greatly by them. Most of their resources were, however, used by the Crown to endow educational colleges like those of All Souls Oxford, King's College Cambridge, Eton and Winchester, and many chantry colleges.

The founding of chantries continued to be popular, and in educational and monastic foundations one of the foremost aims was usually to provide for masses to be said or sung for the founder and his kin. The idea of intercession for the dead as well as the living lay at the basis of all medieval pious foundations, so the principle behind chantries was centuries old. It was, however, not until the late middle ages that it became common to provide especially for masses for the repose of the souls of the founder and his family. Chantry chapels became numerous not only in parish churches, but in cathedrals (e.g. Winchester), abbeys (e.g. Tewkesbury), and friary churches (e.g. Grey Friars', Newgate). The very wealthy might endow a whole college of chantry priests to say masses in perpetuity for the souls of the founder and his kin, either in a chapel built especially for the purpose, or in a parish church turned into a collegiate one. Those who were too poor to found a separate chantry combined with others in a gild. Such religious gilds abounded all over the country, and, like the craft gilds, tried to provide for their deceased members an obit, a mass said on the anniversaries of their deaths; if this was too costly, a candle or a mortar-light was lit on the anniversary of death before the rood, or the image of a patron saint.

There were many reasons for the immense popularity of chantries. It was to some extent a sign of the growing individualism and specialization of the times, and, paradoxically, was due partly to the increasing attraction of this world, which made death seem the more terrible. The prevalence of war and pestilence impressed on men a sense of the transitoriness of life and the need to prepare for death:

> Unto the Death gois all Estates,
> Princis, Prelatis, and Potestatis,
> Baith rich and poor of all degree:
> Timor Mortis conturbat me.
>
> Since for the Death remeid is none,
> Best is that we for Death dispone,
> After our death that live may we:
> Timor Mortis conturbat me.*

or

> Remember that thou shal dye,
> For this world in certentee
> Hath nothyng save deth truele.
> Therfore yn thy mynde use this lessone:
> Liffe so that deth take the yn sesone.†

*William of Dunbar (1465–1520?) Timor mortis conturbat me – The fear of Death doth trouble me.

†From an anonymous poem printed for the first time by Carleton Brown in his *Religious Lyrics of the Fifteenth Century*.

Moreover, the Church in this age was laying stress on free will, the efficacy of good works, and the Last Judgement. No wonder men made increasing efforts to mitigate the punishment they might expect by what was thought to be the best of all good works, the offering of as many masses as possible for the souls in Purgatory.

The idea of Christ as a terrible Judge was partly responsible for another late medieval development – the increasing cult of Mary and the saints who might intercede with Him for sinful men. Another reason for this cult was the increasing tendency in the Western Church to think in concrete images; hence the increasing desire to characterize the Virgin and the saints and to dwell on their attributes and physical appearance. This attitude of mind fostered a more intense religious emotion (as in the cult of the Five Wounds of Christ or the Stations of the Cross), and helped to bring religious elements into the most common aspects of everyday life. But this involved the risk that holy things would become too commonplace to be reverenced; it was in this period that the great French artist, Foucquet, painted the most sensual Madonna of the middle ages, dressed in the height of fashion, with the seductive, thoughtless features of Agnes Sorel, the royal mistress. Theologians feared lest the luxuriant growth in the number of saints and observances should obscure the central truths of the faith, and lest the popular attachment to corporeal concepts and material relics of the saints should sink into superstition and idolatry. It was this popular attitude that helped to produce the multiplication of identical relics which many intelligent men of the time found embarrassing.

These abuses, resulting from a very natural human trait, eventually necessitated vigorous attention from both the Reformers and the Council of Trent, but there was at work in England another tendency which in quite another way was undermining the old order. This was the drift towards a less sacramental, less sacerdotal religion, fostered by the continued popularity of the English mystics, who, though orthodox, stressed personal rather than corporate religion, the inner life rather than ecclesiastical practice, and the possibility of an immediate approach to God. Their influence was reinforced by that of the contemporary mystics of the Devotio Moderna in the Netherlands and the Rhineland, whose works were popular in England, especially the *De Imitatione Christi* attributed to Thomas à Kempis (*c.* 1379–1471). Wearying of the quibbling and hair-splitting into which the university philosophers, the 'schoolmen', had fallen, this brotherhood cultivated a piety that did not stress theological learning and produced a literature 'undenominational' in character. The unrealized but important effect produced by such works, especially among the urban middle classes who read them so much, was not checked by the preaching of the day. Understandably anxious to move their hearers to moral endeavour, and conscious that to expound theology was an increasingly difficult and dangerous matter, preachers tended to aim, through the emotions, at stirring the will to goodness, and rarely attempted to make the people understand their religion. This influence coincided with that of many of the manuals of devotion which were becoming increasingly popular (since more and more laymen could read), for use at mass. These manuals did not translate the liturgy; they provided parallel yet separate devotions which often unconsciously encouraged the layman to retreat into himself and to leave the service to the celebrant. It was thus possible to slip into a devotional life in which the mass had, except at the elevation of the Host, little part; this was all the more possible as lay communion had normally become very infrequent and as too little effort was made officially to ensure that humble laymen understood the order and ritual of the mass.

All these tendencies were preparing the way for the development of Protestantism in the next century; but they were as yet unnoticed currents below the surface. Even among the middle classes, where there was much grumbling at wealthy prelates, idle monks, or papal commands, the great majority feared and disliked Lollardy as much as they do Communism today.

In education, too, there was the same lack of any apparent challenge to the established order. A growing proportion of schools were founded by merchants, but on conventional lines. An anti-sacerdotal tendency does appear in the first known school established by a citizen of London, William Sevenoaks, grocer, who laid down in his will of 1432 that the master in his proposed school at Sevenoaks was to be 'expert in the science of grammar and a Bachelor of Arts, but not in holy orders'. But this is a rare case. No such novel tendencies appear in most of the numerous schools founded in this period, even those which town gilds began to establish, such as Stratford-on-Avon grammar school (1426–7). In the case of the most famous educational foundation of the period, the King's College of Our Lady of Eton, for which Henry VI issued letters patent in 1440, one of the chief reasons ascribed was the salvation of the King's soul, and the chapel of Eton was intended to be larger than Salisbury cathedral. The colleges founded in the Universities – Lincoln (1429), All Souls (1438), and Magdalen (1448) at Oxford, King's (1441), Godshouse (1441–2), and Queens' (1448) at Cambridge – were all established for conventional reasons. Godshouse broke new ground as the first known institution in England founded specifically for the education of those intending to teach; but its founder aimed to train the old type of grammar-school masters in the accepted dialectical methods.

Neither university nor school curricula were as yet affected by the humanism which was beginning to make its way into England. The Italian humanist Poggio spent over three years in England (1418–22) at Bishop Beaufort's invitation, but left no mark at all. Beaufort's rival, Humphrey, Duke of Gloucester, was much more genuinely interested in classical learning. He became well known in Italy as a patron of scholars, and invited Italian humanists to England, among them Tito Livio Frulovisi who at the duke's command wrote a life of Henry V in Latin. Humphrey built up a large collection of books, which show his classical tastes, and his bequests to the University of Oxford formed the basis of its library. He encouraged various Englishmen in classical studies, such as Thomas Beckington, who rose to be king's secretary (1439) and Bishop of Bath and Wells (1443). By the middle of the century Englishmen were beginning to go to Italy to study under classical scholars; William Grey, later Bishop of Ely, was soon followed by Richard Flemmyng, later Dean of Lincoln, the first Englishman of this century to learn Greek. Then that revolutionary figure, the Renaissance nobleman, comes on the scene; John Tiptoft, Earl of Worcester, from 1458 to 1461 paid a visit to Italy which gave him many of the qualities of Italian princes of the Renaissance – their classical culture, their patronage of scholars, and their ruthlessness and cruelty.

By the end of the century classical studies in England were important enough to challenge the old order; and even before Duke Humphrey died (1447) the Latin Renaissance was beginning to make its mark on the curriculum at Oxford. For neither Oxford nor Cambridge was this a fruitful period, however. Cambridge increased in numbers and importance, but only because some parents were now loath to send their sons to Oxford, recently notorious for its heresy. Oxford, once so distinguished, had declined both in intellect and in numbers (which by the mid-fifteenth century probably did not exceed six hundred), in part because of the blow to intellectual activity with the suppression of Wyclifism there, in part owing to the condemnation of Bishop Pecock. Another cause was probably the Statute of Provisors of 1390. Designed to stop the pope bestowing English benefices on foreigners, it also prevented him from providing livings for impecunious English scholars who had no wealthy patron to help them. Careers for university graduates in England were therefore reduced. Instead of entering the university, and, subsequently, holy orders, many gifted youths took advantage of the growing opportunities for educated men in the common law, administration, or trade.

## CHAPTER V

# The Arts

THE decline in intellectual activity was paralleled by a decline in the quality of courtly verse and art. It is difficult to account for the creation or lack of great literature in any particular age, but it is not enough to say that it is simply because there were no great writers. Genius is born, not made; but environment will help or hinder its development. The almost constant preoccupation with war of Crown and aristocracy, the traditional patrons of courtly art and letters, was not compensated by any patronage of painters and writers from the prelates, comparable to that offered by some of the popes of this period. The dearth of intellectual stimulus and great issues to strike the imagination helped to create a climate unfavourable to courtly art. And when more orderly and prosperous times returned, some spheres of art were dominated by Flanders and France, whose products almost monopolized the attention of the king and other great patrons at the expense of English work.

One reason sometimes advanced for the decay of courtly poetry, in spite of Chaucer's inspiration, turns on the change in pronunciation which occurred shortly after his death. The final e was becoming mute, and this, together with bad transcription of his poetry, made his lines seem rugged and variable. His disciples thought that this authorized them to lapse into irregular and clumsy versification – a fact which contributed to a decline in courtly verse-form from which it did not really recover until the sonnets of the Earl of Surrey (1517?–47).

This explanation will not suffice for two of the most prominent versifiers of the fifteenth century, John Lydgate (c. 1370–1450) and Thomas Hoccleve (c. 1368–c. 1454). Both had known Chaucer and both called him master; yet neither was capable of continuing his work. Lydgate's insensitivity to verbal music cannot be blamed on the vagaries of copyists, for he admits that he 'toke none hede nouther of shorte nor longe'. Some modern apologists say that his verses are to be read in terms of stresses, not of syllables; but he often accents unimportant words. His loose grasp of syntax, his verbose use of synonyms and pleonasms, his stale epithets and hackneyed phrases, make his verses far removed from those of Chaucer. Perhaps his worst fault is his prosaic long-windedness; about 140,000 lines of his verse are extant. He was not unduly distracted by the turbulence of the times, for his life from boyhood to death was passed in the quiet of a monastery. Indeed, this seclusion probably fostered his sterile dependence on books for his descriptions. The most lively poem formerly attributed to Lydgate, *London Lickpenny*, a satire on London and the law, is now denied to him. A few of his shorter poems, on religious and didactic themes, show true lyricism and satire, however, and it should be remembered that he was very popular, both in his own day and for several generations afterwards. His longest poem, *The Fall of Princes* of 36,000 lines, composed for Humphrey, Duke of Gloucester, remained a favourite until the end of the sixteenth century. An age less feverish and sophisticated than ours did not view long-windedness and moral platitudes as defects. Lydgate never lacked distinguished clients, and had a pension from the Crown. His second longest work, *The Troy Book* (30,000 lines), was commissioned by Henry V when Prince of Wales.

Hoccleve was less fortunate. He was a clerk in the Privy Seal Office with a small income and expensive tastes; and he ruined by marriage his chances of a lucrative benefice. He hoped for financial salvation by securing a wealthy patron, and was constantly writing verses with that end in view. His chief work, the *De Regimine Principum*, written in 1411–12 to win the favour of the Prince of Wales, afterwards Henry V, was a series of lessons on conduct, translated from the Latin of Giles of Rome. His writing was clearer, more succinct and more spontaneous than Lydgate's, but lacked the monk's occasional touches of poetic feeling. The chief interest of

Hoccleve's verses is, in fact, not poetic; his egotistic out-pourings throw much light on the social history of his time, for they show how dependent was the versifier on the favour of wealthy patrons.

A much better poet than either of these prolific writers was James I, King of Scots. It is now once more generally accepted that he was the author of *The Kingis Quair*, written in Chaucerian seven-line stanzas, a verse-form which derives its name of 'rime royal' from this poem. Captive in England for eighteen years, he tells how, looking from his prison window, he saw and fell in love with Lady Jane Beaufort, niece to Henry IV, whom he married in 1424. Many of the conventions he employed – for instance a dream leading to an allegorical vision – are derived from Chaucer, Lydgate, and perhaps Gower. But because the king had lived through some of the scenes he describes, there is in his poem a freshness and a personal emotion all too rare in the courtly verses of this century. It is likely that the poem was originally composed in the courtly English with which the king became thoroughly familiar during his long captivity; but in its vitality it belongs rather to the Scottish poetry of the fifteenth century, which with men like Robert Henryson (*c.* 1429–*c.* 1508) and William Dunbar (*c.* 1460–*c.* 1530) showed a wonderful efflorescence markedly lacking in England. Not that this country produced no pleasing courtly verses in this period. Some of them, such as *The Cuckoo and the Nightingale* or *The Flower and the Leaf*, are charming enough to have been ascribed until recently to Chaucer. Though conventional in theme and construction, they describe nature with an exceptional freshness. The exquisite *Flower and the Leaf* is also interesting for its morality, which does not conform to the older ecclesiastical or artificial courtly standards, but is imbued instead with the new and more secular common sense.

The most attractive poetry of this time, however, is not that which was written in the artificial courtly tradition, with its 'aureate' language and conventional machinery for aristocratic delectation, but poetry which appealed to lower strata of society as well. This is a great age of carols. The

carol had originally been a song for a round-dance in which
the general body of dancers sang the refrain; and although
by the fifteenth century the connexion with dancing had
gone, the carol still kept the refrain and the lyrical, singing
mood. But it now had a strong infusion of religious feeling,
possibly through Franciscan influence (much as the Salvation Army in our time has turned popular, rhythmical
tunes to religious purposes). Though a few quite secular
carols are extant, most of them are apparently intended for a
great Christian festival, and especially for Christmas. The
mood is often joyous; but laments are not infrequent, especially, as one would expect, in connexion with the Crucifixion,
and the theme 'Timor mortis conturbat me' often appears.
The cult of the Virgin is prominent, for this age found the
tender, sorrowful 'Mother and maid' particularly appealing.
But although carols suited popular taste, they are too elaborate in form and materials to have been created by peasants
or artisans; and they were probably often set to music by professional musicians connected with the choirs of the royal
chapels. The usual form, a traditional one, is of four-line
stanzas, the first three verses of which are four-stressed lines
in a single rhyme, while the last line rhymes with the refrain.
It is wrong to imagine that carols were always clear and
simple; a carol which is haunting in its beauty is also one of
the most obscure (though it may be a poem of the Holy
Grail type). In partly modernized spelling it runs as follows:

> Lully, lulley, lully, lulley;
> The falcon hath borne my mate away.
>
> He bore him up, he bore him down,
> He bore him into an orchard brown.
>
> In that orchard there was a hall
> That was hangèd with purple and pall.
>
> And in that hall there was a bed
> It was hangèd with gold so red.
>
> And in that bed there lieth a knight
> His woundès bleeding day and night.

By that bedside there kneeleth a may [i.e. maid]
And she weepeth both night and day.

And by that bedside there standeth a stone,
'Corpus Christi' written thereon.

Besides carols this period produced a wealth of other forms
of the lyric, including religious songs such as the lovely 'I sing
of a mayden that is makeles'. And it was a great age, not only
of lyrics, but of the predominantly narrative ballad. Ballads
are now no longer believed to have been communal in
origin, spontaneously created in choric dances, but are
thought to have been composed by individuals, though their
form was often changed and worn down by the repetition of
countless voices. Written for the most part in four-stress
rhyming couplets or in quatrains with alternate four-stress
and three-stress lines, of which only the three-stress lines
rhyme, ballads were usually, though not always, meant to
be sung, and were simple and vigorous in style. Their vogue
was helped by the growth of national consciousness and the
victory of the English tongue; and their essentially oral
vitality was not yet doomed by the invention of printing and
the later spread of literacy among the common people. The
Scottish border, with its epic tales of heroic conflicts, was
especially prolific in ballads, of which the finest is the *Ballad of
Chevy Chase*. This lyrical epic, of which several versions exist,
seems to commemorate the battle of Otterburn (1388), but
probably took shape in the early fifteenth century. Ballads
were, however, composed elsewhere in England, and it is
possible that some of the extant ballads of Robin Hood and
his Sherwood band were composed at this time. Many features of the social life of this age are discernible in these – the
disorder and lack of just governance in the land, the popular
hatred of oppressive sheriffs and wealthy prelates, the general
respect for noble rank and also for the rising yeoman class,
the faith that the king will do justice and set all right.

There were other forms of verse in which politics featured
more directly; for in an age when illiteracy was still widespread

it was natural that events, like the battle of Agincourt or the siege of Rouen (1418), which struck the popular imagination, should be recorded in the more easily memorable form of verse. One of the finest early fifteenth-century carols was the Agincourt song; and there are many political carols (mainly Yorkist) connected with the Wars of the Roses. The period also produced many political songs besides carols, on events ranging from the coronation of Henry VI in Paris to the restoration of Edward IV.

The town miracle plays were also at their height. In addition to the other great cycles the Wakefield plays began about 1425. The history of Wakefield is a useful check on sweeping generalizations about the decadence of towns in the Lancastrian period, for though the older industry of York was declining, Wakefield prospered as a centre of the West Riding woollen industry. Its gilds and wealth became great enough to maintain a cycle of plays, some of them borrowed from York, but some composed especially for Wakefield; the latter were written by an unknown master who showed himself a realist and satirist with a saving sense of humour. This is used to good effect in the scuffles and recriminations of Noah and his wife, and still more in a broad comedy of the shepherds of the Nativity. Here a sheep-stealer pretends that the stolen sheep is a new-born baby, and his wife tucks it up in a cradle. His house is searched in vain, until the shepherds, leaving in despair, return to give the child a sixpence. When the baby proves to have a sheep's snout, they toss its 'father' in a canvas. Noah and the shepherds also introduce humour into the York cycle, completed in this period. By this time there were 48 plays in this cycle, which could be crowded into Corpus Christi day only by starting at 4.30 in the morning and continuing until nightfall. The vitality and popularity of these cycles is shown by the long opposition against having them acted by professionals and the eager competition of the various gilds of the town to produce the best play. And there were in this age not only miracle plays, which told the leading incidents of the Bible, but morality plays, which, developed from the homily, pointed a moral by means of allegory. Whereas the interest of the miracle play is essentially in its story, that of the morality play lies in the speeches, the disputation between abstract vices or virtues. One of the most effective moralities is *The Castell of Perseverance* (*c.* 1405), which tells of the fortunes of the human soul.

Just as English verse shows increasing variety in this age, so does English prose. Now that English had become the everyday speech of even the highest classes of society, the language was employed in an increasing number of ways. Especially after Henry V had set an example by using it in his correspondence, men took to writing English as well as speaking it, and it was employed for purposes as varied as letters and wills, recipes and legal proceedings, religious works and didactic treatises. There was as yet no tradition of English prose except in devotional works, and scholars often tried to infuse into the unfamiliar language the Latin syntax and vocabulary to which they were accustomed. Such self-conscious prose is often obscure, turgid, and pompous; and, as in verse, the best work is normally to be found at less pretentious levels. The language was so far scarcely adequate as a vehicle for the philosophical, religious, didactic, historical, and even scientific themes for which men now began to use it. Bishop Pecock, for example, ventured on to new ground when he wrote theological and philosophical treatises in English, and to do so he had to grope for a new style and an extended vocabulary. Some of the best prose which the age produced was the simple, homely language of plain men and women with no pretensions to style. In this class are some of the letters of the Pastons and Stonors, the outpourings of mystics such as Margery Kempe, and the statements of some of the Lollards, such as William Thorpe, when on trial for their lives. The workaday English of the fifteenth century has until recently been held of small account in the development of English prose, but it was probably of some importance in the evolution of a conversational style. Its straightforward manner sometimes gives it a vividness and charm which greater artifice missed.

It was not only in literature that some of the best work was created for the enjoyment of less exalted patrons than in the past. The Lancastrian kings were too poor to encourage the arts on the scale that Richard II had done; and if they did commission work it often had to proceed slowly, for lack of funds. Thus Henry V's chantry in Westminster Abbey took nearly 25 years to build, and King's College, Cambridge, begun in 1446, was not very far advanced by 1461 when the deposition of its founder, Henry VI, stopped all work on it. Edward IV had greater resources than his luckless rival had enjoyed; but until 1471 he was too precariously seated on his throne to pay much attention to the arts.

The enfeeblement of royal patronage did not involve all other great patrons. Henry V's brothers, the Dukes of Bedford and Gloucester, encouraged painting and letters; Archbishop Chichele organized the building of All Souls College (1438–43); and the memorial chapel and tomb of Richard Beauchamp, Earl of Warwick, begun in 1443, are worthy of comparison with anything produced in contemporary Europe, including Italy. But the commissions of great magnates were comparatively few and small; castles such as Warkworth, Tattershall or Hurstmonceaux, the last two being examples of the revived use of brick, and moated manor-houses like Great Chalfield or South Wraxall, were exceptional. The troubled times and the economic depression prevented the aristocracy from building on the lavish scale of the following age – unless, like the owners of Tattershall and Hurstmonceaux, they had done well out of the French war. Of great ecclesiastical buildings, only two or three new abbeys were founded, though there were some additions to existing monasteries, such as the nave at Crowland or the cloisters of Durham or Hereford. Cathedrals and minsters had for the most part been reared by the piety of earlier generations. Efforts of the men of this period in cathedral building were less than appear at first sight; the nave of Winchester Cathedral, for example, is rightly regarded as a particularly beautiful composition in Perpendicular Gothic, but actually it is a remodelling of Norman work.

Genuine new building on a large scale, such as the splendid west front of Beverley Minster, was rare.

The greatest building activity of this age, before most construction was checked by the disorders of the fifties and sixties, was to be found, not in cathedrals, abbeys, or palaces, but in parish churches or civic buildings. To this period belong the London Guildhall (though it has been greatly altered since then) and the fine Guildhall of York, burnt down in the Second World War. The parish churches of this age are fairly numerous. This great production was possible even in a time of economic difficulty because generally speaking, the middle classes did not suffer as much as the aristocracy, and the wool and cloth trades suffered least of all. Hence the legacy of fine churches in areas such as East Anglia, the West Riding, or the Cotswolds – parish churches like those of Worsted or Wakefield or Northleach. Hence, too, the number of splendid churches built in Devon even in the forties and fifties when trade in many other regions was depressed. Of course, not all parish churches were due to the wealth and piety of a clothier or woolman. Many were built, extended, or enriched by the exertions of the parishioners and by means of church rates, bequests, church ales, and even manual labour. Additional revenue could sometimes be obtained from the grant of indulgences by bishops or pope to anyone visiting the church at stated times and festivals.

The building of parish churches began, indeed, to replace the erection of monasteries and cathedrals, which in turn began to be affected in their alterations by parish church design, as can be seen in the west fronts of Winchester and Gloucester cathedrals. The towerless west ends of these must not, however, be taken as typical of fifteenth-century parish churches, of which the towers – most commonly in the peculiarly English form of a square tower crowned with a battlemented parapet with pinnacles at the angles – are a particularly frequent and splendid feature. The uniquely English character of the Perpendicular style, corresponding to the increasing nationalism of the country at that time, became more pronounced in other ways. Porches became larger and more splendid than in preceding centuries, and the fifteenth-century porches of East Anglia, like its towers, are especially famous. They not only served liturgical ends, such as parts of the rites of baptism and matrimony, but were increasingly used for secular purposes. The room (if any) above the porch was used for the administration of justice or sometimes as a treasury or armoury, and in the lower part business was transacted by the parishioners.

Another peculiarly English characteristic in these fifteenth-century parish churches was the prominence and splendour of their woodwork. From about 1370 onwards woodworkers had become fully conscious of the potentialities and limitations of their material. In Richard II's reign began, for example, the series of splendid timber roofs which continued for two centuries, the best of which are to be seen in Norfolk and Suffolk, though good specimens are found in many parts of England. Wood was also used with great effect for rood-screens – another differentiation from contemporary Gothic on the Continent. In East Anglia there was evolved in this period the type of parish church with chancel and nave of the same height, and a rich wooden screen to mark the division. Many of these screens are very beautiful, sometimes with fine painted panelling, and East Anglian screens are rivalled only by the richly-carved screens of Somerset and Devon. The use of splendidly carved wood was not limited to roofs and rood screens but extended to choir stalls and to those new phenomena, chantry-chapels, pulpits, and pews. The finest choir-stalls of this time were usually made by Northern carvers, with their strong and restrained designs, as at Lincoln, Chester, Carlisle, Ripon, Manchester, and Beverley, and their misericord seats, carved with grotesque and delicate foliage.

The devotion of this age found expression not only in the building or adornment of parish churches but in the foundation of chantries. Manchester Cathedral is a reminder that the largest chantries took the forms of colleges, with a staff of priests. Sometimes these colleges had grammar schools attached to them, as at Tattershall, founded by Lord

Cromwell, treasurer to Henry VI, or both a school and a hospital, as at Ewelme, established by the Duke of Suffolk. Less costly and more numerous than chantry colleges were chantry chapels, erected inside an existing church; some of these are imposing structures, for example those of Bishop William of Wykeham and Cardinal Beaufort in Winchester Cathedral.

Some have said that the design and detail of these fifteenth-century chantry chapels, and indeed of most work of this period, cannot compare with the spiritual vision of thirteenth-century art, since much of fifteenth-century construction is shop-work, bought ready-made. Yet no one can deny that the technical level of craftsmanship had improved to a very high level; and even the most unoriginal of fifteenth-century churches has usually a quiet, spacious dignity. The builders employed the rational and economic means of construction of an age which had grown more worldly and scientific than the one before it, and yet achieved in their churches a sense of richness, and even of mystery. The profuse decoration of Perpendicular Gothic has been criticized as ostentatious and as covering dullness of design. But simple plans were what the patrons of the age demanded, and, moreover, they represent a fine mastery of skill over material; while in their use of ornamentation English craftsmen nearly always showed a sense of restraint and proportion. Their work is usually pure when compared with the extravagant riot of ornament in contemporary German or Spanish Gothic and strong compared with the wiriness of French Flamboyant. If work was done specially to order, the English craftsmen of this age could achieve a great work of art, as happened with the effigy of Richard Beauchamp in the Warwick chapel. This figure, carved by John Massingham, shows the realism of the time at its best, and the Wardens of the Worshipful Company of Barber-Surgeons had advised on the anatomical details.

The same sculptor was probably also responsible for part of the figure-sculpture in the chapel of All Souls College (1438–42), a building which illustrates the skill in plan-

ning of this period. The idea of the closed quadrangle
appeared in New College Oxford, and was taken up in the
fifteenth century in All Souls Oxford, and Queens' College
Cambridge (founded in 1448 by Margaret of Anjou, and
refounded by Elizabeth Wydeville, queen of Edward IV).
The plan seems to combine that of the hall and offices of an
ordinary large house with that of a Carthusian monastery,
with its cells grouped round a cloister. The idea was partly
adopted in the Hospitals of St Cross, Winchester (1445) and
Ewelme (1436), and more completely at Hurstmonceaux
Castle (1440), and it spread rapidly, for it was not only
adaptable but very suited to the troubled state of the
country.

It is easier for us today to grasp the plan of a fifteenth-
century church than it is to imagine what it would have
looked like when first built; for the stained glass which was
one of its chief glories has by now for the most part disappeared. One of the aims of builders in northern countries
like England had for centuries been to make great windows
without endangering the structure of the building. By the
fifteenth century the system of dynamic equilibrium which
was the heart of Gothic construction had been brought to
such perfection that churches could have almost as much
glass as green-houses. The increased amount of glass needed
was made chiefly in London and York, though the contract
for the great east window of York Minster (1405–8) was
given to John Thornton of Coventry. The later choir windows of the Minster, with their more finely proportioned
and better drawn figures, and their lighter effect, are more
typical of fifteenth-century work than the east window. The
desire for more light was so keen that the colours were often
paler than they had been in the past (though with touches
of deep blue and ruby), and there was more use of grisaille
and white glass. Canopies were no longer the brassy yellow
of early fourteenth-century work, but a combination of
white and yellow stain, which gave a silvery effect. Sometimes windows were now made with only a single figure or
an heraldic shield on a background of 'quarries' or lozenges

of clear glass. The glowing dimness of two centuries earlier has given place to a spacious clarity; there is a loss in brilliance of colour but a gain in unity of conception and skill in drawing and execution. Whereas the thirteenth-century designer was primarily a glazier, his fifteenth-century successor was primarily a painter, who relied less on leading and more on shading. His greatly improved technique enabled him to express the earthy realism of the age, in close delineation of donors, increased characterization of the figures, and subtle details of dress, architecture, and nature.

Realism is also evident in the sculpture of the period. Fifteenth-century statues are often stereotyped, for many were stock shop models, but carving could still display great power, as is shown in the splendid heads now preserved in Winchester Cathedral. By now there is always life-like detail, so that the changing fashions in dress and armour of this century can be traced minutely from memorial effigies and brasses. Bronze was a suitable medium for rendering fine details, such as the veins of the hand, and Richard Beauchamp's famous tomb is in this medium; but a more popular medium, for indoor work, was alabaster, which was easy to work and could take both fine detail and colour. Alabaster therefore continued to be used a great deal both for retables and for tombs. The latter were now stereotyped in form, consisting of a chest, surmounted by the recumbent effigy of the deceased; for the increasing egoism of the time and the growing popularity of chantry tombs had caused the effigy to be raised from its earlier, humbler position on the floor. If the dead man was a knight, his head rests on a helm and his feet on a lion (symbolizing courage); his lady's head reposes on a cushion and her feet on a dog (typifying fidelity). Before about 1440 bare-headed knights are as rare as are helmeted ones after 1455. The sides of the chest were usually divided into canopied niches, filled with mourners or 'weepers'. That it is possible to generalize so much shows how conventional tombs had become; gone were the romantic and varied forms of previous centuries. These tombs were, in fact, made in large numbers by the London shops for stock, and, except for the effigies, were often ordered ready-made. This commercialization enabled a far wider range of patrons to enjoy technically skilled work but it hindered the production of great works of art. It was one of the factors which led to a decline in alabaster work in the latter half of the century.

A similar decline took place in English illumination. At the beginning of the century the German influence, introduced in Richard II's day, still lingered and helped to produce such fine works as the Hours of Henry Beauchamp, Earl of Warwick, and his wife, now known as the *Hours of Elizabeth the Queen*, since the volume was later owned by the wife of Henry VII. Other outstanding works showing German influence are the *Grandison Book of Hours*, and the gorgeous *Psalter and Hours of John, Duke of Bedford*, illuminated for him between 1414 and 1435 by Herman Scheere. Besides these London works we have two manuscripts finely painted by John Siferwas, monk of Sherborne Abbey, who had a wonderful eye for birds and other naturalistic detail. One is the gigantic and splendid *Sherborne Missal*, and the other a *Lectionary* ordered by his patron, Lord Lovel, for Salisbury Cathedral; and John Siferwas is probably also responsible for the sketch-book of birds now in the Pepysian Library at Cambridge. But these are almost the last outstanding English illuminated manuscripts. Henry V's invasion of France introduced a taste for French illumination, then at its peak; and most of the decorated volumes done in the next two generations for wealthy patrons were either the work of French artists or of English imitators who copied the foreign methods as closely as they could. It was not that English production dried up; on the contrary, there had never been so many Books of Hours and other works produced, for the reading public was growing, and every country gentleman and merchant now felt that his position demanded the possession of a few books, preferably illustrated. But such works were commercial products, produced for customers who were satisfied if the illumination was effective, expensive-looking, and fashionable. When the French influence waned, it was replaced, not by a revival of native art, but by a vogue for Flemish illumination. The best English work of the middle of the century, the *Liber Apologeticus* of Thomas Chaundler, Chancellor of Oxford, shows this Flemish influence in its realistic manner, its full heavy draperies, with their sharply broken folds, and its grisaille technique.

The developments in illumination are paralleled by those in wall- and panel-painting. Paintings on the walls and rood-screens are more numerous in fifteenth-century churches than in those of earlier centuries, but such work was the commercial product of firms of lay craftsmen who were by this time established in every large town. The idealistic inspiration and freshness of line of an earlier day have gone, but there is a certain charm in the realistic detail and in the interest in everyday life. These traits are to be seen in the many paintings of St Christopher, very popular because of the superstition that whoever looked on his painting would be safe from death that day. The preoccupation with death led to frequent paintings of the Last Judgement and of the Three Living and the Three Dead Kings, the moral of which was the fleeting quality of human life. Paintings of the Virgin and her miracles also increased in popularity. Some of the best work is to be found on East Anglian rood screens; the saints on the panels of the screens in Ranworth church may be worldly, but their elegance and liveliness give them great charm. Some of the painting of this period displays the contemporary interest in the pathetic or the macabre, but English work was usually too restrained to exhibit the tortured, surcharged emotion and morbid, gruesome detail of some fifteenth-century German work.

The tendency towards accepting commercial work did not strike the contemporary world as unfavourably as it has done some modern critics. By this time, for example, the decoration for ecclesiastical vestment had become standardized; it usually consisted of a few motifs such as seraphim, thistles, crowns, bells, etc., cut out and sewn on a plain velvet ground. If figures of saints were used, they had become stereotyped, and the work cannot compare with the 'opus anglicanum' of about 1300. Yet the effect was sumptuous, for the subjects were padded and much gold was used. English embroidery, like English alabasters, was still prized highly abroad as well as at home, and considerable quantities were exported.

In music England in this period displayed much creative power. Henry IV had an ear for music, and Dr Frank Harrison has recently suggested that it was he who composed three competent pieces – a Sanctus, a Benedictus, and a Gloria in Excelsis – formerly ascribed to his son or grandson. The centre of the musical revival which Henry IV sponsored was the Chapel Royal; the fine collection of music in the Old Hall manuscript was written for it, and its composer-singers may have been responsible for many of the carols of this period. Some of the musical fertility of the time may have sprung from contact with French musicians. Henry V's invasion brought English musicians to France in the trains of the king and of the English lords. The great French composers Guillaume Dufay and Gilles Binchois lived in Paris under English rule. Whether by this or by other means, English musical influence became strong on the Continent in the early fifteenth century, particularly in the development of fauxbourdon proper, or pieces in a progression of $\frac{6}{3}$ chords, with the *cantus firmus* in the highest voice. In John Dunstable, who died in 1453 and was buried in the Church of St Stephen Walbrook, London, England produced a genius who seems to have been the first composer aware of harmonic sequences as such. Not only did he lead the advance towards functional harmony but he also showed a remarkable gift for creating lovely melodies in each voice-part, thus developing greatly the art of counterpoint and paving the way for the madrigal. Most of his life seems to have been spent abroad, and his influence was apparently felt on the Continent sooner than in England. Nevertheless, the musical productivity of Henry IV's reign continued into that of his son and grandson, and produced many beautiful songs, such as 'Alas departynge is ground of woo' and 'Go hert (heart) hurt with adversite', and the first known solo song with accompaniment, 'I rede [advise] that thou be jolly and glad'. The civil war checked musical as well as other artistic activities, and not until after 1471 was Edward IV free to encourage music through his Chapel Royal. For music, as for the other arts, the fifties and sixties were depressing periods for the courtlier forms, though popular work still flourished.

CHAPTER I

## God Save The Kynge!

THE battles of Barnet and Tewkesbury not only ensured the safety of Edward's throne for the rest of his life; they opened a new period in the history of the English monarchy. Warwick's death relieved Edward of the menace of a 'Mayor of the Palace' and of the great Neville connexion; and though Edward soon endowed his brothers Clarence and Gloucester, husbands of the co-heiresses of the Kingmaker, with most of Warwick's vast estates, the Crown was solvent for the first time for generations. Edward's victories were followed by a fresh wave of confiscations; and there were now no costly French wars to drain away the Crown's resources. And not only did the healthy state of the royal finances increase the king's independence, but many of the 'over-mighty subjects' had died on the scaffold or the battle-field. Moreover, the Wars of the Roses, though not so destructive as was once believed, had caused enough violence and injury to trade to make the middle classes in town and country turn to the Crown as the one hope for the restoration of order.

It has often been emphasized that Edward's indolence and love of pleasure prevented him from displaying the zeal which Henry VII was to show in putting down disorder and intimidation. The contrast is true but often exaggerated; and in any case the character of the two kings was not the only cause of difference between their reigns. The social evils which had become the habit of generations were not to be stamped out in a year or two. It was not until the last decade of Henry's twenty-four years of rule that he began to achieve success in giving the country peace and quietness; after

Tewkesbury Edward IV had less than twelve years to live. He was well aware of the need to restore the authority of the Crown and its courts of law, and made personal efforts to achieve that end. The Yorkists achieved much, in spite of their brief rule, especially on the Welsh and Scottish borders, the most turbulent regions of all. Edward's accession brought to the Crown the great Mortimer inheritance, the most important of the Welsh marcher lordships. The Council appointed in 1471 to administer these and other royal estates in Wales and the Welsh marches, assigned to the Prince of Wales, received by royal commission wide judicial and military powers in those regions; and the foundations were laid for the great Council in the marches of Wales by which the Tudors were to crush disorder there. As for the north, Edward's method was to heap lands and offices in that region on his faithful brother Richard, until in 1482 he was made sole 'King's Lieutenant in the North'. Richard began to enforce the royal authority in that wild area, and when he became king he established the 'King's Council in the North'. So soundly did he do this that the Tudors had no need to alter either its jurisdiction or procedure when they used it for the pacification of the north.

Old habits died hard, however, though Edward IV showed that he could turn inconvenient traditions to the Crown's advantage. There was, for example, still a strong feeling that the king should assert his claims to the French throne and French territory. Edward therefore made great preparations in 1474 and obtained a large grant from Parliament. He then invaded France, in alliance with his brother-in-law, the Duke of Burgundy. When, however, Louis XI offered to buy him out, he showed no hesitation in accepting the offer; and by the Treaty of Picquigny (1475) Louis promised him a lump sum of 75,000 gold crowns, and an annual pension of 50,000 more for the rest of his life. This financial help, combined with other means of raising money, freed Edward from dependence on parliamentary grants for the rest of his life. And though the treaty may have been humiliating to English pride, it did not displease the middle classes; for after the treaties with France and the Hanseatic League in 1475, and with increasing peacefulness at home, there was a great revival of trade and prosperity. Edward kept in close touch with the increasingly powerful London merchants, with whom he made himself very popular by his affable ways. He himself made money out of trade, and became so ingeniously avaricious that he ended his days worth a fortune – the first English king to do so since the twelfth century. When he died in 1483 at the age of 40, perhaps worn out by his dissolute living, his throne seemed firmly established. If he had been succeeded by an able, grown-up son, England might have taken the road towards an absolute monarchy, wealthy enough to dispense with parliamentary rights, strong enough to keep order, and basing its claims on the indefeasible divine right of hereditary kingship.

But Edward's successor was a boy of twelve. His youth seemed to open up a depressing prospect of a minority during which the new-found strength of the monarchy would be dissipated in quarrels between the boy's maternal relatives, the Wydevilles and Greys, and his paternal uncle, Richard, Duke of Gloucester. Most Englishmen were, however, heartily tired of weak government and civil war; and this helps to account for Richard's easy triumph. He had always (in marked contrast to Clarence) been faithful to his brother, and he was known to be a good soldier and a capable administrator. Later Tudor propaganda represented him as a monster from birth who had not only killed Henry VI and his son in cold blood, but was responsible for the death of his own brother, Clarence, in 1478. The men of 1483, however, knew nothing of this, and accounted him an upright and pious prince. He therefore aroused no suspicion, but rather gained support, when he struck at the unpopular Wydevilles and Greys, and had himself made Protector. Even when he shut up the king and his younger brother in the Tower, and had them and their sisters declared bastards, thus making himself the legitimate heir to the Crown, there was no opposition. This was partly because men were cowed, but also because they dreaded a renewal of civil war, and a grown and capable man seemed likely to give the realm firmer government that a child could do. But when to secure his position the new king probably had his two young nephews murdered in the Tower there was, except in the north, a general revulsion of feeling against him. The disappearance of these innocent boys broke up the Yorkist party, thus making Richard's position precarious and giving the Lancastrians renewed hope. One of his chief supporters, the Duke of Buckingham, rebelled against him in October, 1483; and although this rebellion was suppressed, Richard did not feel safe. In vain he strove to make himself popular by acts of parliament to stop the practice of benevolences, or forced gifts, which Edward IV had extorted, to encourage English traders, and to suppress intimidation and corruption in justice. Had he come to the throne in a normal way, his ability as a soldier and administrator, his courage, generosity, culture, and intelligence might have given him a long and successful reign. As it was, all these qualities were not enough to overcome the formidable hostility to him; and to make matters worse, his only son died in April, 1484. The narrow basis of his power was still further weakened by forced loans which he had to raise in the spring of 1485 to finance defences against an invasion threatened by the Lancastrian claimant, Henry Tudor. When Henry landed at Milford Haven in August, 1485, he was able to collect soldiers in his native Wales, and march to meet Richard in battle at Bosworth, in Leicestershire. Richard had the larger army and was an able soldier, but the disaffection of a large part of his forces cost him the victory. He refused to flee, and died, fighting manfully, on the field.

The battle of Bosworth is usually endowed with great significance, as marking the foundation of a new dynasty and the end of medieval England. It is, however, difficult to see why Henry VII should be regarded as the first of the modern kings of England; for neither in outlook, aims, nor methods did he make any important innovation, and no break with the medieval past occurred in his reign. His accession in 1485 appeared to contemporaries of less significance than the changes of 1461 and 1399 had done in their time. By 1485 there had been so many upheavals within living memory that men were very dubious whether Henry could keep the throne for long. He was generally accepted because Richard was dead, and because the country was weary of civil war, but his claim to the throne was very weak, and there seemed at first no reason why some rebel with a better claim should not dispossess him. It is true that he married the person with the strongest hereditary right – Elizabeth of York, eldest daughter of Edward IV – but Henry refused to rule merely as king consort. His most effective claim was at first the fact that he was in possession – a claim which any successful pretender would acquire. Richard III had been popular in the north, as was the Yorkist cause in Ireland; the spirit of rebellion was not easily exorcised; no foreign power believed in Henry's survival, and Edward IV's sister, the Dowager Duchess of Burgundy, longed to overthrow him. It is therefore not surprising that one rising followed another – that of Lord Lovell in 1486, the imposture of Lambert Simnel as Clarence's son, the captive Earl of Warwick, in 1487, and the more dangerous imposture of Perkin Warbeck, as the younger of the murdered sons of Edward IV, from 1491 to 1497. As late as 1495 Henry was still so insecure that an act was passed exonerating any person who assisted the reigning monarch from subsequent impeachment or attainder. Two years later ill-armed Cornish peasants and miners who had rebelled against heavy taxes were able to advance within sight of London before they were defeated. It was not until 1499, when Warbeck and Warwick were executed, that Henry could feel at all secure. Even then the conspiracies and rebellions had not ended; in the last decade of his life Henry had to cope with the plotting of Edmund de la Pole, Earl of Suffolk, and his brother Richard, nephews of Edward IV. It is doubtful whether the Tudor dynasty appeared more firmly established in 1509 than the Lancastrian had seemed to be in 1422. Only if we realize the fear, still alive in Henry VIII's day, that the battle of Bosworth might not have been permanently decisive shall we understand some of that monarch's important traits – his severity to actual and even potential claimants to the throne, and his ardent and genuine longing for a male heir to ensure an undisputed succession. The same fear helps to explain why, although he had no standing army to enforce his wishes, the great majority of his subjects submitted to his most arbitrary acts, and why his victims usually protested their loyalty even on the scaffold. The memory of the Wars of the Roses was not dead, and most men felt it better to submit to Henry's most ruthless deeds than risk another breakdown of government. Not until Henry VIII's later years was it universally recognized that the verdict of Bosworth Field was final.

As for the modernity of Henry VII, his methods were in no sense revolutionary, and the Yorkists in particular had tried, though with less persistence or clear-sightedness, to accomplish many of the things which he achieved. For example, Henry tried to secure the stability of his throne by gaining the recognition of foreign powers; but this was an obvious necessity which usurpers had long realized. The long medieval tradition of hostility to France was, however, still so strong that, in spite of the help which Charles VIII had given to Henry, he was soon drawn into a war with France over her acquisition of Brittany. Henry's wisdom in preferring lucrative peace (1492) to ruinous war had a precedent in Edward IV's treaty of Picquigny, and the commercial effects of the treaty of Étaples recall those of 1475. The treaty of 1492 did not end old English claims on France, which were revived once more by Henry VIII. Again, Henry's famous alliance with Spain was no radical departure in English foreign policy, for it arose simply from common hostility to France. Since at least the days of King John, English kings had tried to encircle France with allied states, just as France had for two centuries maintained her alliance with Scotland to threaten England on two sides at once. As for marriage alliances, they had been used since Anglo-Saxon days as an instrument of policy. The most important marriage alliance of all, that with Spain, was as much a recognition of Henry's success as a means of ensuring it. Negotiations were

begun in 1488, but the Spanish monarchs waited to see
whether Henry would make good his position in England
before coming to a final agreement; and not until 1501
was the fateful marriage celebrated between Catherine of
Aragon and Henry's eldest son, Arthur. The wedding in
1503 of Henry's daughter Margaret and James IV of Scotland came only after the King of Scots had been impressed
by Henry's power.

Henry showed statesmanship in trying to promote trade
by agreements with foreign powers – with Denmark and
Florence in 1490, with France in 1492, and, above all, in
1496 and 1506 with the Archduke Philip, ruler of England's
most important market, the Low Countries. But the foster-
ing of trade had been an increasingly important function of
the Crown since the merchant class had become so influential in the fourteenth century, and Edward IV had
taken a special interest in this matter. Luck and skill brought
Henry VII more success, though, like Edward IV, he could
not master the Hanseatic League, whose privileges in England he had to confirm in 1486 and 1504. Henry's other
measures for the promotion of English trade all had their
precedents; for example, the Navigation Acts of 1485 and
1490 to encourage English shipping had had forerunners as
far back as Henry II's time.

Similarly the means which Henry used to restore law
and order in the land were not new; they had been employed by the Yorkists, though with less persistence and
ability than Henry showed. The famous Court of Star
Chamber was nothing more than the king's Council sitting
in a judicial capacity, as it had done for generations. Edward
IV had tried to fill his Council with trusted servants instead
of powerful nobles, and Sir John Fortescue had warned him
of the danger of over-mighty subjects and councillors, and of
the importance of financial solvency. Richard III had made
special arrangements for poor men to have their complaints
heard speedily and cheaply. The Yorkist kings had, like
Henry, increased the Crown lands by attainders and their
revenues by ingenious devices not unlike his. They, too,

had seen the desirability of financial independence, had tried to economize by improving organization, and had realized, too, the need to impress their subjects by magnificence and state. As for ecclesiastical affairs, both Yorkist and Lancastrian kings had, like Henry, perceived the value of obtaining the approval and support of the Church while upholding what they considered their rights. Orthodox yet independent in spirit – this was not a novel trait of Henry VII; it was a tradition which went back to William the Conqueror.

In 1509 Henry died, worn out by his labours and anxieties. His handsome, talented, masterful son ascended the throne at the age of eighteen. By this time the signs of change were increasing. Renaissance scholarship and art were becoming better known in England. Civil war, sterility, and mortality had so thinned the ranks of the older peerage that by 1509 only one duke and one marquis were left in England. The revival of commerce was helping the rise of new men who could be used by the Crown as a counterpoise to what was left of the old aristocracy, and as a more reliable instrument of government. The disappearance of over-mighty subjects was leaving the king in lonely eminence, which was fostered by an ostentatious display of his power and wealth and an increased reverence for his person. But what is usually not stressed enough is the predominance of conservative forces in the early years of Henry VIII's reign. In spite of Renaissance elements in his education, the young king was a traditionalist in outlook. He was conspicuously devout in an orthodox way, and showed marked respect towards the Papacy. It is well known how in 1521 he dedicated to the pope a book denouncing Luther, and was rewarded with the title of Defender of the Faith. It is true that in 1515 he showed signs of hostility to clerical pretensions. In that year the Bishop of London's chancellor was accused of the murder of Richard Hunne, a London citizen who had been found dead in the bishop's prison. In the commotion that followed, and the popular hostility to the pretensions of the clergy then revealed, Henry openly favoured the argument of the friar and

court preacher, Dr Standish, who denied that clerics were
exempt from the jurisdiction of lay courts, and that a papal
decree bound a country where continuous usage was against
it. But anti-clericalism and royal apprehensions about clerical immunities and the exercise of papal power were now
centuries old in England. In this affair Henry did no more
than protect Standish from clerical vengeance and make him
Bishop of St Asaph shortly afterwards.

In the general conduct of domestic affairs there was also
no radical breach with the past in the early years of the
reign; but in foreign policy a fundamental change is often
said to have taken place at this time. Instead of continuing
the medieval hostility to France, Wolsey introduced, we are
told, 'the modern principle of the balance of power'. But
Henry VIII shared with his people the age-long antipathy
to France, and he waged no wars on the continent except
against France. The English people were imperialist in
sympathy, partly by tradition, partly because Charles V
controlled the great Netherlands market. Far from maintaining a balance of power, England repeatedly supported the
Emperor Charles V against the French, although Charles's
power was the greater of the two. The phrase 'the balance
of power' belongs to a later age; and the aim of a balance of
power, with the corollary of alliances and counter-alliances,
had, in fact, existed for at least four centuries in Western
Europe. In so far as a consistent principle may be discerned
in Wolsey's foreign policy it is rather a desire to stand well
with the Papacy, to further his own ambitions.

But although Wolsey's foreign policy was less novel than
is often supposed, his career as a whole was without precedent. The forces which were undermining the old order in
England had been gathering strength for generations; but if
there was a break with the past, and if that break was initiated by any one man, that man was Wolsey. It was ironical
that a great churchman should have been the unconscious
instrument of revolution; but there were several ways in
which Wolsey's career filled this role. He concentrated power
in the hands of one man – himself – to an extent unheard of

before. By 1515 he was the chancellor and the most important minister of the Crown; and control of the Council combined with that of the great seal gave him complete authority
over the jurisdictions derived from these, including the Star
Chamber, Chancery, Court of Requests, and Court of
Admiralty. He also wielded unprecedented authority in the
Church. In 1515 he was already a cardinal and Archbishop
of York, and the holder of various other benefices, to which
he eventually added the abbey of St Albans and the wealthy
bishopric of Winchester; and in 1518 he was created papal
legate, with sweeping powers over the English Church. And
this extraordinary power in both Church and State was not
only exercised by one man, but exercised in a way which was
without precedent. As chancellor he interfered increasingly
with the jurisdiction of other courts and talked of replacing
common law by Roman; and as papal legate he superseded
episcopal order to a great extent. He overrode Convocation
as he attempted to override Parliament; and if Archbishop
Warham had died earlier, Wolsey intended to have had the
see of Canterbury too. He asserted his authority over the religious as well as the secular clergy, including the Orders subject only to Rome; indeed, his declared aim was to exercise
the full papal authority in England. He dissolved a score of
monasteries without their consent to finance his schemes,
nominated abbots and priors, and usurped ecclesiastical
patronage. He controlled not only the administration of the
Church in England, but all its courts. In fact, he superseded
the medieval constitution of the English Church, and established an unprecedented autocracy instead. Henry VIII
began to feel that if such enormous authority could be exercised by an Ipswich butcher's son, who owed everything to
the royal favour, why should not these powers be exercised
by the king himself? The Cardinal's ruthless vigour as papal
legate had intensified English dislike of papal authority. The
Duke of Suffolk voiced a popular view when he exclaimed
'It was never merry in England when we had cardinals
among us'; while Lord Darcy, a staunch conservative who
later took part in the Pilgrimage of Grace, proposed a law

that henceforth no legate should be allowed in England. Moreover, Wolsey's dissolutions of monasteries showed Henry how the exhausted Exchequer might be refilled by plundering the Church.

Thus Wolsey unwittingly paved the way for the breach with Rome. It is an absurdity to assert that the breach was due to Henry's lust for Anne Boleyn. Catherine of Aragon's failure to produce a male heir would have raised a divorce question even if Anne had never existed. In any case the divorce question was merely the occasion, not the cause, of the English Reformation. The factors which made it possible, such as nationalism, anti-clericalism, individualism, the education of the laity, and the corruption of the Church, had been growing for generations. Lutheranism had been seeping in during the past decade. The power of the Crown over the Church was already considerable and Wolsey had not only aggravated some of the abuses in the Church but had shown how authority could be concentrated in one hand.

Nevertheless, although events had long been moving in the direction of radical change, it was the fourth decade of the sixteenth century which saw the close of medieval England, as far as the character of a civilization can be said to have been altered in one decade. Royal influence in the Church had been strong since the tenth century, and for over a hundred years the Crown had nominated its bishops without opposition; but no medieval king had ever claimed to be supreme head of the Church. Henry intended to be conservative, and aimed to do no more than subject the clergy to the Crown, much as Francis I, King of France, had done in 1516 by the Concordat of Bologna. Once the breach with Rome had occurred, however, there were bound to be, in spite of Henry's intentions, doctrinal, institutional, and liturgical changes of a speed and extent which the middle ages had never known. There had been suppressions of a few religious houses since the middle of the fifteenth century, but the complete dissolution of all the monasteries between 1536 and 1539 obliterated what had been one of the prominent strands of English life for nearly a thousand years. Changes in the Church of such magnitude and abruptness as these naturally accelerated or set in motion very important alterations in other spheres of life besides the ecclesiastical, as the following chapters will try to show. All history, and especially English history, shows, of course, a certain continuity. Not only did the Church of England claim continuity with the medieval Church but its organization remained largely medieval. Many medieval forms lingered for generations and some medieval institutions acquired fresh vitality. Gothic architecture survived as a living tradition in Oxford and elsewhere until the Civil War; Dr Tillyard has recently reminded us that Shakespeare's world picture was still largely medieval, and, indeed, the mechanical view of the Universe did not become influential until the Restoration period; between 1529 and 1536 Parliament was used to such purpose as to give it new authority and vigour. Examples might be multiplied. But henceforth medieval ideas and forms and institutions were either relics or legacies; the way of life which had given them birth was dead. If an Englishman of the thirteenth century could have visited England in 1520, he would have found much to excite his wonder, yet all the old landmarks would still have been there. Fifty years later he would have encountered many familiar features, but they would now have been mere survivals in a world beyond his comprehension, a way of life separated from his by a revolution.

## CHAPTER II

# The Government of the Realm

Two things in this period are of most interest: the increasing strength of the monarchy, and the limitations to its power. From 1471 Edward IV's position had a strength which the monarchy had lacked since the days of Edward I. Many over-mighty subjects were dead or weakened, and after 1475 the king was more financially independent than any king had been since Henry II. Only one Parliament was held between 1475 and 1482, and it was asked for no grants. By the time Edward died the government seemed so strong that, although few supported Richard's usurpation, none at first dared to oppose him. Henry VII came to the throne with a weak title; yet people were so weary of war, the peerage had been so enfeebled, and the Crown was now so strongly supported by the rising classes of gentry and merchants that Henry with his wise caution was able to overcome all difficulties. He realized the power afforded to the Crown by financial independence, and was the first king of England to leave a fortune of several million pounds to his successor. Parsimonious he may have been, but he knew the value of pomp in encouraging obedience. Both Yorkists and early Tudors consciously cultivated regal magnificence and dignity; and with the growth of royal power the king ascended to a peak of lonely grandeur. For example, marriages between royal children and English magnates had until now been not at all rare; but by 1515 some thought the Duke of Suffolk worthy of death for his presumption in marrying the sister of Henry VIII. Then the breach with Rome brought out the unmedieval idea that the king was supreme in every sphere of life, and that England was a self-sufficient empire, with Henry its emperor, subject to no other authority on earth. Henceforth the king would be addressed, not as 'Your Grace', a form of address which he had shared with archbishops and dukes, but as 'Your Majesty', a unique being exalted above all others in both Church and State.

Until the Reformation Parliament, however, the strength of the monarchy was not augmented by novel assertions of royal power. Both Yorkists and Henry VII asserted themselves by exercising to the full prerogatives which the Crown had long claimed rather than by formally extending the frontiers of their authority. This can be seen clearly in the matter of the king's Council. The kings had always claimed the right to choose their councillors; but whereas the Lancastrians had often been forced to fill their Councils with magnates, the Yorkists and early Tudors were increasingly able to summon whom they liked. From Edward IV's time the majority of councillors were men who owed their importance to the royal service; if grandees were admitted to the Council, it was more and more at the king's pleasure in fact as well as in form. The few who were summoned were kept in check and increasingly excluded from office and power.

The fact that the Council had greater prominence in the government of Henry VIII than it had had in that of his father or grandfather did not mean that the royal control had in any way weakened, but rather the contrary. Edward IV and Henry VII had to beware of being dominated by their councillors, as Henry IV and Henry VI had been; whereas Henry VIII felt strong enough to give his Council great authority and latitude while he still remained in complete command of affairs. Indeed, so powerful and active had the government become by his day that one royal Council could not cope with all the work; political affairs were increasingly dealt with by the members of the Council, known as the Privy Council, who accompanied the king, while judicial matters were more and more the business of the members of the Council who sat in the Star Chamber in the Palace of Westminster. But in all the activities of either branch of the Council – political, administrative, legislative, judicial – until the breach with Rome it was not so much that the councillors exercised new powers as that the traditional powers of the Council were revived and enforced by men who acted solely in accordance with the king's wishes.

This is clear in the case of the Council's judicial activities, once thought to be a novelty of Henry VII's reign. Since at least the reign of Edward I the king's Council had claimed to do justice where fear or favour hindered the common-law courts from providing a remedy. The Yorkists and early Tudors did not create a new jurisdiction in such matters, but rather put existing powers to effective use against even the greatest of magnates, whose offences a Lancastrian Council, dominated by fellow-magnates, would have condoned. The Court of Star Chamber was not a creation of Henry VII's reign; it was the royal Council which had often sat in the Star Chamber since the fourteenth century. The difference was that with a strong king to back it, and composed of men devoted to his service, the Council could be an effective weapon in crushing, by fines and by imprisonment, such serious social ills as intimidation, livery, and violence. The same methods were used to suppress disorder in the most turbulent areas, the Welsh and Scottish marches; and the Council of Wales and the marches, and the Council of the North, begun by the Yorkists, were maintained and strengthened by the Tudors. And in the restriction of livery and maintenance Henry VII was even more of a traditionalist than was formerly thought; for Professor Dunham has recently shown that what was accomplished in these spheres during his reign was done rather by the Court of King's Bench than by the Council.

The idea of a court for poor men's causes was not new, either. The Court of Requests took shape in Henry VII's reign, but the Council had since the fourteenth century made special arrangements to expedite the supplications of the poor. But whereas in Lancastrian days a humble suitor had little chance of justice if his request went against the interests of a great magnate, now he could look for redress with more confidence. Here again, what was new was not the prerogative which was invoked, but the vigour and thoroughness with which it was exercised. Similarly,

Edward IV's use of the Court of the Constable to suppress opponents was not a novel idea – Richard II had aroused opposition by relying on the prerogative courts for this purpose; but Edward's constable, John Tiptoft, was so ruthless that he earned the nickname 'the butcher of England'.

Another office which already existed but was now made a more prominent and effective instrument of royal power was that of the king's secretary. This institution had existed since the reign of Richard II, but had not become of real importance until the reign of Edward IV. By the end of his reign the secretary was sufficiently established as part of the machinery of government to remain at work in spite of the minority of Edward V. His duties were always vague and uncertain, but he was essentially a confidential clerk who kept the king's most private seal, the signet, and was frequently sent by the Yorkists and Henry VII on important embassies. By 1492 he was important enough to merit a bishopric, and he had the advantage of living in the royal household at a time when nearness to the king's person was of increasing political value. In 1526 the secretary was officially recognized as one of the inner council of the monarch.

So far, however, there had still been no epoch-making innovation. No secretary had yet been the king's chief minister, and the centuries-old tradition that the chancellor was the highest servant of the Crown had never known a more dazzling embodiment than Cardinal Wolsey. Here again, the decade of the Reformation Parliament was the watershed between medieval and modern England. The brilliance of the chancellorship in Wolsey's time proved to be a sunset glory; he was the last of the long line of great clerical chancellors who had been prime ministers of the realm. Anticlericalism, developing since the days of Edward III, now burst out, and the cardinal-archbishop-chancellor was succeeded in authority by the layman-secretary, Thomas Cromwell. For the first time there appeared a secretary who was not merely the king's private servant or an administrative official, but the chief minister of the Crown, feared and obeyed by the noblest in the realm. Cromwell's spheres of action and method are much closer to those of Walsingham and the Cecils than to those of previous secretaries; while the increasingly legal character of the chancellor's duties and his waning political importance made him less and less like his medieval predecessors.

This period also saw important developments in financial affairs. The Exchequer was too slow and independent to suit the methods of the Yorkists and the Tudors, and more and more revenues were paid at their command into the king's Chamber, which was unhampered by a prescribed routine, and, unlike the dignified and conservative Exchequer, completely subservient to the king. This development had precedents, such as Edward III's use of the Chamber as a financial department; but, whereas he had been forced to give up his policy to placate the Exchequer officials and the magnates, the Tudors overrode all opposition, and even set up a Court of General Surveyors to supplant the Exchequer of Account and audit more expeditiously. When the immense wealth of the monasteries poured into the hands of Henry VIII he did not entrust the Exchequer with its management, but set up a special Court of Augmentations for the purpose. Hitherto the revival of royal finances had been contrived mainly by the exploitation of traditional royal claims; now the spoils of the abbeys provided a revolutionary source of revenue.

The effect of the Henrician Reformation on Parliament was more profound. In the Parliaments of the thirteenth and fourteenth centuries the kings had at times the most public and dangerous opposition to fear. It is not surprising, therefore, that the Yorkists, Henry VII, and the young Henry VIII summoned them as rarely as possible, and tried to control their activities as much as they could. In Lancastrian days the upper house of Parliament had been formidable because in it were concentrated the magnates who dominated the Crown. From 1471 onwards the Crown was increasingly the legatee of these great baronial houses and, moreover, the king had not yet lost all control over the right of summons, which a strong ruler did not need to send to obnoxious or impoverished lords. The nobility became so weak and the sessions so infrequent that some of Parliament's previous judicial functions fell into disuse. Such were, for instance, impeachment, which no one dared to invoke against the ministers of a powerful king, or jurisdiction in error over the common-law courts, a function not much needed when the Chancery and the Council were so active. Yorkist and Tudor kings had no trouble from the upper house of Parliament in which sat the chancellor and many devoted royal officials.

The lower house was not always so amenable. It is true that a refortified monarchy found many ways to influence elections, and that the speaker was as much the king's agent for managing the Commons as the Common's spokesman to the king and Lords in Parliament. Furthermore the knights and burgesses were still glad to avoid responsibility for the conduct of affairs, still anxious to please their prince so long as he kept law and order in the land, redressed their grievances, and maintained the country's prestige and prosperity without excessive demands for money. But the threat of heavy general taxation could still kindle formidable opposition to the government, even to the government of Henry VIII. Well might Sir Thomas More declare that 'the gatherynge of money' was 'the onelye thinge that withdraweth the heartes of Englyshmenne fro the Prynce'. Even Wolsey had to admit defeat at the hands of the Commons on this point. Yet, apart from this question of taxes, the Commons were usually manageable enough. An acute observer in the early sixteenth century might have thought Parliament a mere legacy from a troubled past that had become a hindrance to efficient government and would eventually be reduced to insignificance by the attrition of a powerful monarchy.

The prospect was dramatically altered by the history of the Reformation Parliament. It was natural that in breaking with Rome Henry should have called on the cooperation of Lords and Commons in Parliament, for by so doing he secured the confidence of the politically powerful classes and advertised to the outside world the extent of the support he enjoyed in his realm. Once he had sought parliamentary assistance to assert his supremacy over the Church, he continued to use Parliament for the exercise of that supremacy in the suppression of the monasteries, and for declarations of doctrine and the like. By so doing he increased the competence of Parliament to a vast and unprecedented extent. In 1543 he himself declared to the Commons: 'We at no time stand so highly in our estate royal as in the time of Parliament.' These great changes shook men out of their acceptance of the traditional limitations of Parliament's functions. Henry had united spiritual to temporal authority; before a century had passed the claim would be made—inconceivable in medieval England – that both could be exercised through Parliament alone.

Assertions of parliamentary authority were to trouble Elizabeth, but they did not trouble her father. The Reformation Parliament bestowed on him not only the royal supremacy but the annates and the spoils of the monasteries, and arranged the succession to the throne according to his varying wishes. And having given him an unmedieval control over the Church, it gave him an unmedieval degree of authority in the State. The Statute of Wales of 1536 abolished by far the most important and extensive sphere still outside the Crown's normal jurisdiction – the franchises of the marcher lords – and the whole of Wales was thus brought fully under royal authority. Another Act of the same year laid down that all writs, even in the greatest franchises, should run in the king's name.

These developments did not, however, mean that Henry VIII was a dictator, for even he could not rely on Parliament to be docile if it disliked a measure, as can be seen from the difficult passage of the bill against uses (i.e. trusteeships) in the Reformation Parliament. That he never came to grief was due, not to unlimited power, but to his neverfailing sense of how far he could safely go. He knew that although public opinion could often be swayed, it had always to be respected. He never attempted to override Parliament and the law, and was always careful to provide his most immoral acts with the cloak of legality; and so, except in the less important north and west, and in spite of his growing ruthlessness, he retained to the end the loyalty of his people. It would have been dangerous had it been otherwise; for he had no great armed forces, no well-organized police, and no extensive servile bureaucracy to enforce his will.

Though by the late fifteenth century the great European monarchies were establishing permanent military forces, England had no standing army. The nearest approach to it was the Yeomen of the Guard and the Gentlemen-at-Arms, bodies formed by Henry VII, but these forces were little more than palace guards; they would have been absurdly inadequate to put down a national rising, especially in an age when artillery was still inefficient and rebel bowmen might be better than those of the government. The king could call out the shire militias by commissions of array: but if most people chose to disobey the summons or the nobles and knights who mustered them were disaffected, he had no weapon with which to coerce them, and even the troops thus raised were often inefficient (for reasons which Shakespeare shows in *Henry IV, Part 2*). The Yorkists and early Tudors, though trying with increasing success to suppress the evils of livery, still continued to raise troops (usually for foreign war) by contracts with some nobles or gentlemen. But here again, if they had refused to serve the king, he would have been impotent, and he needed not only their passive obedience but their active loyalty. Even after Edward IV established a relay system of mounted messengers from the Scottish Border to London, news of a rebellion in the turbulent north or west might take several days to reach the government. By that time the revolt could become formidable if the local magnates and gentry were not zealous in suppressing it.

In naval matters, too, the king still relied greatly on the loyalty of his subjects. Edward IV inaugurated a revival of English sea-power which Henry VII and Henry VIII continued. This involved the building of special royal ships, a policy which was continued and accentuated in Henry VIII's reign, when heavier guns were mounted, capable of sinking ships instead of merely killing men. This caused increasing divergence in design between merchant vessels and warships; gun-ports, for example, were now fitted in the hull of a warship as it was built. But even in Henry VIII's day merchant vessels could be, and still were, easily employed as men-of-war when need arose. The government saved money by relying mainly on merchant ships to form its fleet, and on merchant officers and crews to man them. Royal encouragement of the navy meant to a large degree encouragement of the merchant service and of trade. The kings gave bounties for the construction of large merchant vessels which might also be used as warships, and royal ships were in peace-time hired out to traders. If, therefore, even a Tudor king was to be sure of protection against foreign invasion, the loyalty of merchant shipowners and master mariners was essential to him.

For their police, too, Yorkist and Tudor monarchs were dependent on the loyalty of their subjects, especially those of the upper and middle classes. Disaffection was a particularly serious matter in London, which was becoming steadily more important politically and socially as well as economically. Yet when serious anti-foreign riots occurred in London in 1517 the best that the mighty Wolsey could do to anticipate disorder was to instruct all householders to keep their servants indoors; and the government could suppress the disturbance only by inviting the Earls of Shrewsbury and Surrey and the Inns of Court to march in their men. This lack not only of a standing army but also of an adequate police helps to explain why a king like Edward IV or a minister like Cromwell maintained a spy service and encouraged delation, and why there was no popular outcry against arrests and searches of houses without judicial warrant. The means for the suppression of disorder were so inefficient that the government must be allowed to be highhanded if the dreaded anarchy was to be averted. It is true that each hundred had a high constable and each parish a petty constable. But these posts were quite inadequately remunerated by fees, and their occupants devoted only their spare time and energy to their duties. If they needed help in the pursuit or arrest of criminals, they could get the justices of the peace to swear in neighbours as unpaid special constables and, if necessary, they could call out the whole neighbourhood; but all this assumed the cooperation of the local population.

The system of justice and administration also depended for its effectiveness on public support. It is true that the judges depended for their promotion and pay on the king, who could dismiss them at will, but they were eminent members of a profession proud of its traditions and principles. Occasionally judges who displeased the king, such as Fortescue or Markham, were dismissed, but their very opposition shows their lack of servility. At the beginning of this period two judges wrote great treatises on English law – Sir Thomas Littleton on land-law in his *Tenures*, and Sir John Fortescue on constitutional law in his *Governance of England* and parts of his *De Laudibus Legum Angliae* and *De Natura Legis Naturae*. The latter stressed the need for strong government, but neither of them suggests that the king has arbitrary power over the making or administration of law; indeed, Fortescue expressly holds that the king of England cannot change the laws of the realm at his pleasure, and that statutes are made not merely by the prince's will, but with the 'assent of the whole kingdom'. He draws a favourable contrast between England, which he describes as a limited monarchy (*dominium politicum et regale*), and France, which he calls an absolute monarchy (*dominium regale*). The works of Littleton and Fortescue fostered a pride in English common law that stiffened its judges to defend its principles and to resist the inroads of Roman law, which would have favoured the establishment of an absolute monarchy.

A large and growing sphere of law was, however, in the hands of the justices of the peace. These officials were appointed by the king, but they were unpaid gentlemen of standing in their shire, who could be led but not driven. The well-to-do were naturally inclined to support law and order; the Council, aided by Chancery and the Courts of Common Law, was vigilant in supervising the J.P.s and punishing them if necessary. Nevertheless, the government had no effective means of coercing J.P.s if it ordered them to enforce something of which they all disapproved strongly. It is no accident that many of the measures which the Yorkists and early Tudors commanded the justices to carry out were measures highly approved by the country gentry and merchants – the re-establishment of law and order, the encouragement of trade, the protection of English merchants, the regulation of weights, measures, and coinage, the enforcement of minimum hours of labour and maximum rates of wages, the suppression of vagrancy. This in the circumstances was not only the cheapest, but the most satisfactory, way of organizing local government. To entrust it to great lords would have been to invite civil war and a weakening of the monarchy; and to commit local administration and justice to officials like the sheriff, dependent on fees and tax-farming for a livelihood, would have opened the door to endless corruption and oppression and dangerous unrest. To confide the task to salaried officials like modern civil servants was impossible, for the Crown, though better off than in Lancastrian times, had not the money to do it. Taxation was unpopular, and the collection of taxes was supervised by men drawn from the very classes of country gentry and merchants which supplied the J.P.s. For all these reasons the monarchs of this period found the justices of the peace very satisfactory and heaped on them fresh powers and new duties.

It will thus be seen how greatly the Yorkists and early Tudors, for all their increasing might, relied on upper- and middle-class support in their central administration, and, still more, in their local government. And they also needed the obedience of the lower classes; for the J.P.s themselves lacked a police force and a local bureaucracy to enforce their orders if the countryside should resist *en masse*. Hence 'Tudor despotism' necessitated not only the cooperation of the propertied classes but the acquiescence of the masses. The limitations on royal authority were even greater in the case of jurisdictions either partially or wholly outside the Crown's authority. Franchises and private jurisdiction, from the palatine bishopric of Durham or the marcher lordships of Wales to leets and manorial courts, had passed the zenith of their vigour; but their decline was slower than is often supposed, and many of these courts and administrations lingered on until the nineteenth century. And until the Reformation Parliament there was one great sphere of jurisdiction entirely outside the royal authority, and sometimes clashing with it – the sphere of the Church. There were not only many ecclesiastical courts in England – archidiaconal, diocesan, provincial, and others – but appeals were freely made from them to Rome; and the pope was not only head on earth of the Western Church but a great international power who could greatly affect the king's policy. By modern standards the Church's jurisdiction was wide. It had jurisdiction over all men in matters not only of faith, but of morals in a very wide sense, including, for example, defamation and usury; it dealt with all matters relating to wills and marriages. It tried all criminous clerks, except those accused of high treason and one or two other offences, and this privilege (for ecclesiastical courts could not impose a death penalty) extended in practice to nearly all literates. Disputes over the boundaries between the jurisdictions of the ecclesiastical and the royal courts had been frequent; but by Yorkist and early Tudor days the latter were able to put the Church courts on the defensive by imposing the severe penalties of praemunire on anyone who had brought in a Church court any action held to belong to the royal authority. There was increasing royal jealousy and popular criticism of many aspects of ecclesiastical jurisdiction, and in the reign of Henry VII the first restriction was imposed on benefit of clergy. But until the Reformation Parliament it was only the frontiers of the two jurisdictions which were disputed; by subjecting all ecclesiastical jurisdiction in England to the royal authority that Parliament closed an era which had begun with William the Conqueror's creation of ecclesiastical courts. In this respect, as in so many others, the fifteen-thirties saw the end of the medieval order in England.

## CHAPTER III

# Economic and Social Developments

FOR the merchant class this was, on the whole, a time of swelling prosperity (in spite of the commercial distress caused at times by Henry VIII's foreign policies in the fifteen-twenties and thirties); and the rise of the traders, not only economically but socially, was far more pronounced than ever before. A development of such importance had many causes. The Yorkists and early Tudors gradually restored the law and order which were so necessary for the prosperity of trade, and encouraged commerce as much as possible according to their lights. The few short wars of their reigns were a less serious check to trade than the Hundred Years War and the Wars of the Roses had been. There was an expansion of the continental markets, which were freer from war between 1453 and 1494 than they had been for a century and a half, or were to be again for two hundred years to come. The population was at last increasing again appreciably, giving a stimulus to production. With the new century came the impetus of rising prices, as the gold and silver of the New World poured into the coffers of the Old.

The revival of foreign trade became pronounced soon after 1475, when the French and Hanseatic treaties opened up important markets once more, and Edward IV had been firmly on the throne for a few years. The Hanseatic League benefited from this revival, for Edward was forced to confirm its privileges, but the role of other aliens declined. By the end of his reign the total trade of aliens was equivalent to less than two-thirds of that of the English Merchant Adventurers, who dealt in various commodities, especially cloth. Its export developed enormously. In 1354 (when the customs accounts for cloth began) it had amounted to only 4,774½ pieces and in 1461–2 to 38,492; but it rose to 66,955 in 1481–2, to an average of 84,789 a year in the period 1509 to 1523, and to 102,647 a year in the quinquennium 1534–9.

Within the country, too, the new-found peace encouraged trade, and the power of the merchants became greater than ever. This period saw, for example, a tightening of control by wealthy traders over town gilds. We have seen the beginnings of this in London as early as the fourteenth century, and the rich master-traders were already creating oligarchical livery companies to dominate the crafts. But London's trade far surpassed that of any other English town, in both scale and organization, and it was not until the fifteenth century that in other towns merchant oligarchies began to establish control over the crafts, forbidding combinations of workmen, or organizing them in subordinate 'fraternities' or 'yeomen gilds', as had happened in London. To ensure the permanency and completeness of their control the ruling circles of many towns bought from the Yorkist and early Tudor kings new charters which put the oligarchy's control of the town on a legal and more impregnable basis.

The wealthier traders were now less concerned with the welfare and amenities of their town than their fathers had been. They were often acquiring wider interests, and the town's affairs occupied a dwindling part of their attention. This, together with the heavier burden of taxation on the corporate boroughs, the restrictive policies of the gilds, which hindered adaptation to changing needs, and the desire of enterprising craftsmen and journeymen to escape from gild control, contributed to the continued decline of many of the older towns, even in a time of trade expansion. We find many complaints in early Tudor days of dirt and dilapidation in the older towns, and the decline of civic order; though the pageants and miracle plays, which had flourished when the craft gilds were vigorous and urban society was more closely knit, usually continued until after the Reformation. Industry was moving from the corporate towns to the countryside, either for technical reasons, such as the availability of water-power, or because the capitalist entrepreneurs could pay lower wages to village workers, and control them more effectively than they could urban craftsmen banded together into gilds. The newer towns, such as Wakefield and Halifax, continued to flourish with the cloth trade; Durham Priory started to buy its cloth from Halifax instead of York. Places destined to become cities – such as Manchester with its textile manufactures and Birmingham with its forges and ironworks – first came into notice in this period as rising villages.

Some of the older towns were prosperous, however, and none more so than London, with its growing importance as the capital, the diversity of its trade and the increasing prominence of the Netherlands market, the flexibility of its commercial organization, and the specialization and skill of its merchants and financiers. The interests of London traders extended very widely. In home trade they controlled rural cloth-workers, bought wool from the growers, gave credit to country dealers and chapmen, and distributed goods over wide areas. London now dominated England's commercial life to such a degree that in this period London capitalists invaded Southampton and gradually established control of its overseas trade, until its vitality was sapped and its business transferred to London. In overseas trade London merchants were increasingly influential not only in the Company of the Staple but in that of the Merchant Adventurers – so called because they 'adventured' abroad, in contrast to the Staplers whose route to Calais was prescribed by the government. The Adventurers could export any commodity except wool, and trade in any region which would admit them; but by this period their chief export was cloth and their chief market the Low Countries. The Company's overseas headquarters were there, moving from Bruges to Antwerp in Edward IV's reign, and it aimed to protect especially English merchants trading in the Netherlands, exercising in return the usual authority of a gild over its members. It had emerged in the late fourteenth century, but first became powerful in Yorkist days, when the trade with the Low Countries was becoming so predominant in England's commerce. The Company had sprung from the Mercers of London; and although it included traders of many towns, its most important and wealthy members were Londoners. Indeed in the late fifteenth century the provincial merchants complained bitterly that the Company was dominated by the Londoners, who monopolized its offices, excluded other traders by raising the entrance fees, and yet subjected non-members to increasingly heavy dues. Henry VII tried to settle these disputes by his charter of 1505, which reduced the entrance fees, but confirmed its authority over all Englishmen trading with the Low Countries in all commodities except wool. The membership was to be open to all who would pay its fees and submit to its control; but the tendency to domination by wealthy Londoners still continued, and various deterrent rules were enforced. One ordinance, for example, ran 'No person of this fellowship shall sell . . . by retail . . . nor shall keep open shop.' The wealthy traders who were thus trying to draw away from the mere retail shopkeeper were aspiring to become gentry.

As early as the fourteenth century successful merchants such as the de la Poles had made their way into the aristocracy; but such cases had then been few. During the fifteenth century they had gradually become more numerous, until in this period the investment of merchants in landed estates assumed the proportions of a class movement. To doff the merchant's robe and don the gentleman's armour was not a hard task, for there was now no gulf between the wealthy merchant and the country gentleman; and contemporary books of courtesy, so useful for their advice on manners and etiquette to the numerous 'bourgeois gentilhommes', ranked the merchant with the squire. London wool-merchants could be in partnership with or act for the country gentlemen from whose estates the wool came; and men like Sir William Stonor did not disdain to take an active part in commerce, and call themselves merchants of the staple. The Cely family, graduating from Mark Lane to their estate in Essex, is typical of many another merchant family of the time. All that remained to complete the transition from counting-house to manor-house was a title and coats-of-arms, and these could be obtained from Yorkist and Tudor monarchs who valued the support of the middle classes and of 'new men', whose sons and grandsons were to provide the aristocracy and leaders of later Tudor society. It has often been remarked that Anne Boleyn was the great-granddaughter of a London merchant. But it is equally important to note that in no previous generation would a marriage between such a woman and the king have been possible. By 1533, however, the monarchy was so strong and so many merchants had turned themselves into gentlemen, and even nobles, that the old aristocracy had to accept the fact, though with disgust.

The old aristocracy had by this time become enfeebled. Viewed with suspicion by a 'new monarchy' it was increasingly excluded from the inner councils of government. Even more important, perhaps, was the fact that its economic and social foundations were crumbling away. The Wars of the Roses had destroyed some noble houses and impoverished many more. Estates had been diminished by forfeitures and crown resumptions. Huge fines had often to be paid, in order to recover even a part of the family estates, and further exactions were made on various pretexts by Henry VII and his son. The Crown was now strong enough to press financial claims such as wardship and marriage and, eager for financial solvency, it pressed them to the uttermost. Yet despite these heavy burdens it was hard for the old aristocracy to reduce its expenditure. Retainers might now be useless and even a reason for a heavy mulct by the Crown, but the old tradition insisted that the true magnate must be waited upon by a host of servants, and must never appear in public without a train of attendants, all splendidly clothed and equipped. A genuine grandee must have castles and houses fit for a king, and stables big enough for a regiment of cavalry. He was expected to keep open house and to entertain on a princely scale. Six thousand guests are said to have come to the feast of the aristocratic George Neville at his installation as Archbishop of York in 1467; and men long remembered the bounty of his brother, the great Earl of Warwick:

'The whiche Erle was evyr hadd In gret ffavour of the comonys of thys land, by reson of the excedyng howsold whych he dayly kepid In alle Cuntrees where evyr he sojournyd or laye, and when he cam to London he held such an howse that vj Oxyn were etyn at a Brekeffast, and every tavern was full of his mete, ffor who that had any acquayntaunce in that hows he shuld have hadd as much sodyn and Rost as he mygth cary upon a long daggar.'

All this made it inevitable that the old aristocratic houses would go down to disaster unless they acquired fresh sources of income; and fresh sources of income were difficult to find. The tide had turned, and once more the land could be made to yield large profits – if one knew how to manage it. But the great magnates had lost touch with estate management; since at least their grandfathers' days their lands had been leased, and as *rentiers* they often knew little more than a modern shareholder of the actual working of the concerns from which they drew their money. Besides, capital was usually necessary to reconstruct estates – for the purchase of flocks of sheep, for example – and capital was something which the needy magnate lacked.

And so many of the old aristocratic families were sinking while traders were rising – London merchants like the Boleyns, clothiers like the Springs of Lavenham or Thomas Paycocke of Coggeshall, woolmen like the Tames of Fairford, generous patrons of beautiful churches, proud builders of gracious, half-timbered houses, successful speculators in landed estates. Even kings now sought their friendship; Edward IV amused himself in the houses of London merchants, and the half-legendary clothier, Jack of Newbury, is said to have entertained Henry VII and his queen to dinner. Going up in the world at the same time were many knights and yeomen, some of them so closely in touch with commerce that the same man might be both merchant and yeoman or knight. The previous depression had trained these well-to-do commoners in habits of thrift and efficiency, enterprise and versatility, and had given them their start. Their expenditure was not comparable to that of great lords, for no one expected a mere knight or yeoman to maintain the pomp of a magnate. The expansion of the cloth trade enlarged the demand for wool, and the increase in the population provided an expanding market for food, especially for farmers situated near growing towns like London. Unlike the agrarian boom of the eighteenth century, this expansion was marked by no striking use of capital by great proprietors on arable land. In this earlier period what improvements were made in the raising of crops could be effected by the small farmer, so that even a peasant, favourably situated, might prosper, could he but keep his lands.

There lay the difficulty for many peasants. Keen-witted merchants saw that good profits were once more to be made from the countryside, especially from wool, and more of them than ever before wished to turn themselves into country gentlemen. The hope of profit and social ambition combined to make them invest enthusiastically in land. Even in the depression many merchants had been eagerly buying land to turn it into sheep-farms, to the extent of depopulating some villages entirely. Their expenses would be comparatively low, for, even more than the country gentry, they lacked a tradition of ostentation, which they regarded as wasteful. So they bought up the estates of impecunious heirs; and the old landlords began to see that the only alternative to sinking into ruin was to come to terms with the 'new men' and their methods. Many aristocrats began to dabble in commerce, to angle for special trading privileges, even to intermarry with merchant families wealthier than themselves. And they learnt from their new merchant partners and kinsmen how to squeeze the last penny out of their property. Why, said the businessman, should the landlord content himself with rents arranged in the days of the great slump? Why, indeed, should he not evict his tenants if he could, and convert their tenements into great sheep-runs, much more profitable than the rents from a clutter of peasants' small holdings? The old landlords must either accept this ruthless efficiency or go under; and now that private armies were no longer the political and social asset they had been in Lancastrian days, one powerful reason for the maintenance of a numerous tenantry had disappeared.

Of course, the pace of these developments varied greatly

in various parts of England. In the far north, which was scarcely affected by the new influences, the menace of Scottish forays continued the lawlessness of Lancastrian days. In a region where no one knew at what hour of the day or night Scottish raiders might attack, a holding meant not only grain and wool, but a horseman with axe and armour, bill and bow. Not until the union of the two Crowns under James I was the anarchy on the Border ended; and not until then did widespread eviction of Border tenants begin. But in the south and east the improvement in order and in trade already had its effect in Yorkist and early Tudor days. It is significant that the chancellor denounced evictions of tenants in the Parliament of 1484 and that the first statute against enclosures, because of the depopulation which normally ensued, was passed in 1489, when the trade revival which had begun in the seventies had just had time to make its consequences felt. It has been calculated that between 1485 and 1500 nearly 16,000 acres of land were enclosed in the counties of Northampton, Warwick, Oxford, Buckingham, and Berkshire, of which over 13,000 acres were devoted to pasture. Unlike the enclosures which took place in the eighteenth century, those of this period took place at a time when the Crown was strong; and the early Tudors and their ministers tried to stem the tide of enclosure and eviction. The suppression of liveries, necessary though it might be for the peace of the realm, caused a serious unemployment problem for the government without further aggravation; and to swell the throngs of vagrants with swarms of evicted peasants might create a revolutionary situation. Moreover, depopulation of the countryside lessened the effective fighting force of the realm, and was dangerous in regions like the Isle of Wight. The government therefore did a great deal, by statutes, proclamations, commissions, Chancery and common-law rulings, to check evictions.

There were limits to this policy. For one thing, not all enclosure was opposed to the national welfare; rearrangement of holdings, leading to compact tenements, and carried out by mutual agreement, had been going on in many parts of the country for generations. And even in the case of the new, injurious kind of enclosures, where a great proprietor or his agent consolidated small holdings into one estate, and evicted the tenants to make way for sheep, the government had to tread warily. The men usually most eager for such enclosures were merchant-landlords and country gentry; and these were the very classes on which the Yorkists and early Tudors relied most. To act severely against enclosures, as Wolsey did, was to rouse the determined hostility of the most influential sections of the landholders; and Protector Somerset's strong measures against enclosures contributed largely to his ruin. Moreover, without introducing revolutionary ideas of property the Crown could not give more than a certain legal protection to the peasantry. Where tenants held at the lord's will, or were lessees for a short term of years, they could be evicted with ease. It is true that many of the peasants seem to have been copyholders, that is, tenants by copy of court roll, according to the custom of the manor, but if the peasant was a copyholder for one life or more the lord had only to be patient to get his land. As for the numerous copyholders with an estate of inheritance, the lord might press them to accept leases, or charge enormous fines for admission when the heir succeeded. Whether the lord could use such devices depended on the custom of the manor; the king's courts would protect a tenant only when that custom could be shown to be clearly in his favour. Hence, only freeholders and a minority of the copyholders were secure against eviction.

For a prosperous peasant, secure in his holding, the opportunities now unfolding for the able and enterprising man might carry him into the gentry, or even higher; there were examples like the Russells to spur him on. The mass of the peasantry was, however, too poor, uninfluential and insecure to withstand the tightening pressure of the new landlords. The old type of magnate might at his worst have been a tyrant, but he had generally looked after his tenants, since they were the force on which his livelihood and his very existence depended. The new lords were businessmen, determined, with the instincts of traders and the methods of bailiffs, to exploit their estates. They did not always concentrate on sheep-farming, though that, with its expanding market and its low costs of production, could be very profitable. If, for example, their land was rich in minerals they mined for iron, copper, or coal. But in any case they were ruthless towards customary rights which conflicted with their own, and peasants were lucky if their dues were merely increased. Often they were deprived of their holdings altogether, and had to join the swelling stream of homeless vagabonds, the 'sturdy beggars' who by Henry VIII's day had become a serious social and administrative problem.

Tragic as these developments were for the peasantry, they had one redeeming feature: there was no revival of serfdom. In Eastern Germany and in Russia it was at this very time that a great movement towards serfdom set in, serfdom which did not disappear until the nineteenth century, and made a profound mark on the political and social structure of those regions. There the agrarian expansion was not in wool but in grain production, for which many hands were needed. The junkers and boyars were politically and socially strong, and, like many thirteenth-century English magnates, found that the cheapest and most effective way of getting the numerous labourers they required was to enforce labour dues and tie the peasant to the soil. To the many peasants of Tudor England who lost everything – land, homes, and livelihood – their eviction must have been an unmitigated disaster; but for their descendants, and for the nation as a whole it was preferable to a revival of serfdom. By Elizabeth's reign personal bondage was already an anomaly.

Traders, as we have seen, prospered in this period. Their overseas markets were still the medieval ones. Bristol merchants financed in 1480 a fruitless voyage of discovery across the Atlantic to open up fresh markets; and for the same reason supported John Cabot's expeditions of 1497 and 1498 to Newfoundland and the North American coast.* The dis-

*According to a letter of 1497 or 1498, preserved in the archives at Simancas and published by Dr L. A. Vigneras in 1956, the men of Bristol had found 'Brasil', part of the mainland of America, some years before.

covery of the New World did not, until after 1550, greatly affect English trade, which still ran along the Atlantic coasts of Europe, with some ventures into the Mediterranean. But the revival of commerce with Europe, and especially with the Netherlands, was enough to inaugurate an era of prosperity. The merchants profited also from the fact that they were lightly taxed. The tax on moveables, originally intended to tap commercial wealth especially, had become a fixed sum which was ludicrously small compared with the merchants' real incomes. So for the trading class this was a time when standards of living were rising. The newly-found peace and order enabled them to build town or country houses in which the emphasis was no longer on defence but on comfort. There was no pomp of the old kind, with throngs of dependants and little privacy, but a more secluded luxury. Even members of the old aristocracy were sometimes infected by this new style of living; and by Henry VIII's day the more enterprising of them began to feel that if, in this age of rising prices and inadequate means, something had to be dropped, it had better be the old lavish open hospitality. Such a decision was a fresh blow to the small man. The great houses had provided shelter and sustenance for their numerous inhabitants, and alms and entertainments to tenants and even strangers. The dwindling of the custom of 'open house', and the break-up of great households, hastened the decay of the old structure of society. But in the circumstances it was inevitable; now even some of the monasteries began to find that to make ends meet they were forced to cut down the old hospitality, as well as raise rents, convert arable into pasture, and even evict tenants.

These economic and social changes were violently hastened by the dissolution of the monasteries. It was not that the monks had always been easy landlords. (They might have been in the slow-moving north, but in the south and east financial stringency had often led them to follow the fashion. Besides, their estates had in most cases been leased to laymen and the monks in such cases needed to know as little about the management of the lands of their house as the fellows of an Oxford or Cambridge college nowadays know about theirs.) It was rather that a complete redistribution of perhaps one-sixth of all the land in the country greatly accelerated the pace of economic and social change. The king gave away or sold in a few years such huge quantities of abbey lands that a furious land speculation arose. When land changed hands two or three times in as many years or even months, the buyer had to extort high profits to recoup himself for the inflated purchase-price, and such speculation would alone have caused a rapid rise in prices. But it came at a time when the silver of Mexico and the gold of Peru were beginning to drive up prices in Western Europe at an unexpected rate, and when Henry was striving to relieve his financial position by debasing the coinage – a policy which could lead only to sharp inflation. By the fourth decade of the century prices of most commodities were at least double what they had been when the century opened, and some, like the price of oxen, were over four times as high. Proprietors now had to extract a higher income from their estates if they were to escape impoverishment. The inflation therefore tended to drag down still further the standard of living of most of the peasantry; but the same phenomenon favoured ruthless and enterprising lords, for prices rose faster than wages.

It has often been observed that the 'new men', usually individualists and anti-clerical in spirit, were won over to the cause of the Reformation by their acquisition of abbey lands; but we must not therefore identify religious and economic outlooks. Families which subsequently adhered to Rome, such as the Dukes of Norfolk, shared in the spoils of monastic lands; and one of the most important recusants of Elizabeth's day, Sir Thomas Tresham, was a notorious rackrenter. A truer conclusion is that the events of the thirties and forties completed the disappearance of the medieval social order. Many of the monastic lands were given to or bought by 'new men' – either ambitious middle-class men such as knights, squires, yeomen, merchants, lawyers, physicians, or peers of recent prosperity. This redistribution of land with the dissolution of the monasteries and then of the gilds and chantries, and the changes in social structure, personnel, methods, and outlook which accompanied it, amounted to a revolution which had had no parallel since the Norman Conquest. In the ruling classes of society the old names, like those of the Anglo-Saxon landholders after 1066, mostly disappeared and new leaders of society – Cecils, Russells, Sidneys, Cavendishes, Herberts, and Sackvilles – took their place. Very few indeed of our present peerages date back further than the early Tudor period. The monasteries had for a thousand years been a powerful force in English life. Now they were swiftly reduced to ruins and a memory, and the country house became the centre of English social life and culture for the next three centuries and more. In economic and social affairs the fifteen-thirties, more than any other time, mark the close of medieval England.

## CHAPTER IV

# Religious and Educational Changes

THE choice of the year 1485 as marking the division between medieval and modern England is nowhere more patently absurd than in the matter of religion. Not only at the beginning of Henry VII's reign but at the end the old order in the Church still seemed as strong as ever. No one who attended his imposing funeral, conducted with all the traditional rites in the gorgeous chapel he had founded, can have dreamt that in less than thirty years his plate would be confiscated and his relics lost, or that his granddaughter would sit in his chapel under a canopy made out of his Florentine vestments. In 1509 the Church in England was still part of an international body and still in possession of its traditional privileges and immunities. Edward IV had even made some extension of benefit of clergy (i.e. clerical exemption from secular jurisdiction); and though Henry VII had curtailed it, his restrictions were comparatively slight. Henry also reduced somewhat the right of sanctuary, which had been abused by criminals as a cover for their misdeeds; but he had done so by getting Pope Innocent VIII to issue a bull. The Church had not yet lost any of its great wealth. It owned at least a fifth of the land of England and its treasures were still increasing in the early sixteenth century as men endowed, built, and adorned churches and chantries. And devotion to the Church manifested itself not only in gifts but in observances. Men still kissed the pax at Mass, still lit candles to their patron saints, still obtained indulgences for their sins, still went on pilgrimage, especially to the shrine of Our Lady of Walsingham or of St Thomas of Canterbury. Congregations still carried candles round the church at Candlemas, received ashes on Ash Wednesday, crept to the Cross on Good Friday, kindled their fires from the Easter Candle, watched the dove descending from the roof of the church at Whitsuntide, joined in processions at Corpus Christi, offered loaves at Lammas, remembered the dead at All Hallows, and listened to the sermon of the Boy Bishop on St Nicholas' or Holy Innocents' Day. A Venetian who visited England at the end of the fifteenth century was struck, not only by the wealth of the churches, but by the devotion of the people. Parish churches were the centres of the social life of the community, and the clergy controlled education, hospitals, and poor relief. Economic organizations, such as the gilds, participated in a variety of religious activities, from masses to miracle plays. The towns were dominated, not by factories and warehouses, shops and civic buildings, but by a forest of church towers and steeples. Their bells were constantly tolling to call men to devotions within the churches, and friars frequently harangued the people outside. In short, the Church was everywhere in evidence and seemed to be all-powerful. Lollards might be numerous in London, Bristol, and other towns; but these heretics were obscure and humble folk. The king now constantly nominated the bishops, besides exercising many other important rights over the Church; but a *modus vivendi* had been established, and there seemed no reason why it should break down. After all, the kings of France claimed considerable powers over ecclesiastical appointments, and their claims were officially confirmed by the Papacy in the concordat of 1516.

Yet though the old order in the English Church might seem as strong as ever when Henry VIII ascended the throne, we know that before he died the Church had been humbled and despoiled and the medieval scene had vanished. What accounted for this revolutionary change?

Clearly it was not simply the result of the divorce of Catherine of Aragon; for Henry VIII had no standing army or well-trained police to impose his wishes on a rebellious people. The breach with Rome or the dissolution of the monasteries would have imperilled his throne if there had been widespread and organized resistance. Henry's almost unopposed success must have been due to something deeper than his own will for a change. At one time most Englishmen would have agreed that the corruption of the Church, which made it unpopular and incapable of resistance, was the reason for his success. Such a view contained much truth, but it was too simple, sweeping, and prejudiced. It is true that there were many abuses and superstitions which needed reform. Non-residence and pluralism were growing rather worse in the early sixteenth century. Cardinal Bainbridge, for example, never resided in his see of York; and Cardinal Wolsey held the archbishopric of York in *commendam* with the bishopric of Winchester, the wealthiest see in England, and the wealthiest abbey, that of St Albans, neglecting them all. Besides this, he secured for his bastard son, Thomas Wynter, while the lad was still in his teens, the deanery of Wells, the archdeaconries of York and Richmond, the chancellorship of Salisbury, the provostship of Beverley Minster, prebends of Wells, York, Salisbury, Lincoln, and Southwell, and rectories in Yorkshire and Suffolk. Such a state of affairs at the top not only set a bad example to subordinate clerics but contributed to poverty and inadequate education among the parochial clergy. Poverty in turn stimulated the clerical exactions, such as tithes and mortuaries (a kind of ecclesiastical death duty), so much resented by the laity, though the high fees charged in ecclesiastical courts – for probate of wills, for instance – were due rather to the excessive number of officials involved. The number of the clergy was too great for the available resources, especially as bishops ordained a hundred or two hundred priests at a time, with too little inquiry into their spiritual qualifications or their future means of livelihood. Such priests might be ill qualified to give sound instruction in either morals or doctrine. The cupidity of some led to a virtual sale of the sacraments, just as the ignorance of many laymen led them to buy for a few pence indulgences for the remission of sin.

Other superstitions offended reformers, conservative as well as radical. Popular religion had permeated every sphere of life so much that the spiritual and the material had become confused. Men had interpreted spiritual things in concrete images and human qualities, so that the saints were thought of as beings active in everyday affairs, who could be bargained with and propitiated, who could reward those who prayed to them and punish those who disregarded them. Faith had become too much divorced from reason, and the popular mind created saints who had never existed, like St Uncumber, the bearded virgin who rid women of their husbands if offerings of oats were made to her. Some of the disproportionate prominence and adoration of the saints was fostered by the stress laid on the awful majesty and justice of the Saviour, e.g. in the frequent wall-paintings of the Last Judgement; for this made men turn for mediation to the saints. The same motive helped to increase the cult of the Virgin Mary, until in the minds of many she overshadowed her Son, and His stern justice was contrasted unfavourably with Our Lady's mercy. A similar lack of proportion had deformed the rites of the Church, which had often been over-elaborated until their meaning was obscured or even forgotten. Erasmus, for example, tells how on a certain day a rabble blowing on horns and behaving as if possessed by a frenzy used to bring a stag's head on the point of a spear into St Paul's Cathedral and carry it up to the high altar; but everyone had forgotten what the custom meant. Relics and miracles had often assumed such an undue importance that people thought less of the holiness of the saint than of his wonder-working bones. Pilgrimages remained very popular, but for many they had become simply an excuse for a holiday.

But abuses and superstitions might not by themselves have been enough to produce the Reformation. There had been grave corruption in the Church before without causing disruption, and many evils were dealt with by the Council of Trent. It is easy to exaggerate the defects at this time, and they were, on the whole, much less serious in the English Church, which broke away from Rome, than in the Italian Church, which did not. They provided the Reformers with very effective arguments, but other causes of the Reformation were equally important.

One powerful factor was the nationalism which had developed so strongly in late medieval England, and fostered hostility to the Papacy. By the early sixteenth century Christendom was for most Englishmen an abstract idea, a literary expression, or a legal fiction. There were many like Bishop Gardiner who, when the break with Rome took place, thought it possible and desirable to be independent of the Papacy, and yet entirely Catholic and conservative. None of the popes from Sixtus IV to Clement VII seemed much like a Vicar of Christ and spiritual head of Christendom; even Sir Thomas More declared shortly before his execution, 'Yet never thought I the pope above the general council.' To many Englishmen of his generation the pope seemed in reality an Italian prince who drained English resources, from annates and tenths to fees for indulgences and dispensations, for purposes which were of no concern to England – the maintenance of an excessive and corrupt bureaucracy, the artistic extravagance of a Renaissance despot, and the secular wars of an Italian ruler. It is significant that the first act of the Reformation Parliament against the Papacy was the Act of Annates, and that Henry VIII had no difficulty in getting it passed. Indeed, as with the other Acts against financial claims of the clergy in the first three years of this Parliament, all that was needed was to give the Commons their head.

This anti-papal feeling was dangerous for the monasteries. They valued their independence of episcopal control and their direct connexion with Rome; but this made the ordinary man in the south of England feel that, even though monks were usually Englishmen, the monasteries represented an alien element. And it was not only growing nationalism which threatened the monasteries, but a new outlook on life. Except for the Charterhouses, and one or two other convents, the monasteries had lost their religious fervour, and were lax in the observance of their rule; but whereas in the past this would have caused only a demand for the reform of the abbeys or the foundation of new Orders, now quite orthodox people were questioning whether monasteries should continue to exist at all. In 1514, for example, when Bishop Foxe of Winchester founded Corpus Christi College, Oxford, he at first intended a house for monks; but his friend Bishop Oldham of Exeter, the founder of Manchester Grammar School, expostulated, 'What, my lord, shall we build houses and provide livelihood for a company of bussing monks, whose end and fall we may live to see? No, no, it is more meet a great deal that we should have care to provide for the increase of learning, and for such as who by their learning shall do good in the Church and commonwealth.' Over a hundred years of determined royal and episcopal efforts at reform had failed to achieve results. Cardinal Pole was soon to declare that, except for the Bridgetine nuns, the Carthusian monks, and the Observant friars, the Orders were utterly degenerate, and, with other cardinals, to recommend to the Pope that most of the Orders be abolished and a fresh start made. A man's duty to the world was now thought more important than the personal sanctity he might gain by renouncing it; and the world, too, was now more attractive than it had been in the earlier middle ages. The number of monks was less than three-quarters of what it had been in the thirteenth century, even before the marked drop in the decade before the dissolution. They were often now thought to be failing in the holiness and devotion for which pious benefactors had in past ages endowed their houses; yet the Orders remained great landowners, and a critical generation thought that their resources could be better used in other hands. Idealists like Bishop Latimer proposed to spare two or three houses in each diocese, and devote the wealth of the rest to educational and charitable purposes; but rising families hoped to acquire the abbey lands of which they were often the stewards or tenants.

The rise of the middle classes threatened other institutions of the old order. The merchants were becoming conscious of their importance in the State, and had confidence in themselves and in their methods. Their belief in individualism, progress, self-reliance, thrift, and industry was out of harmony with the ethos of the Church, whose economic teaching seemed to them out of date; the struggles of the towns for three centuries against the ecclesiastical authorities had given the merchants an anti-clerical bias. The Hunne case in 1515 revealed how anti-clerical London was, especially in the matter of ecclesiastical exactions and jurisdiction. For many townsmen anti-clericalism was beginning to widen into anti-sacerdotalism. Many laymen were now better educated than their poorly-paid parish priests; by the early sixteenth century no one above the rank of labourer seems to have been entirely illiterate in the towns, and in the countryside of the south and east. The invention of printing meant that there was far more reading matter than ever before; and though it was not at first unorthodox it helped to form a lay public opinion not dependent for its information on pulpit and cloister. Printing gave the lay moralists and satirists their opportunity; and their attacks on clerical shortcomings weakened clerical pretensions in the eyes of laymen conscious of their education and their abilities, and of new standards. Middle-class talent and industry was creating homes of an unprecedented comfort and privacy, which were replacing the church as the centres of social life; middle-class people were coming to value family life more than celibacy, and the improving of conditions more than the practice of asceticism. Neither the hut of the peasant nor the travelling household of the noble had been favourable to home life; this was created by the middle-classes in town and country, whose new ideal of the home was conducive to a personal religion, centred less on the sacraments and on corporate worship. This personal tendency in religion may have been fostered by the very popular works of the late medieval mystics of England and the Netherlands who, though orthodox, had little to say about institutional religion.

It was English merchants in the Netherlands and Germany who were largely responsible for the spread of Lutheran opinions in London and other English towns in the fifteen-twenties, and for the diffusion of Tyndale's translations of the Bible. The medieval Church tolerated translations of the Bible in principle, but frowned on them in practice as likely to lead the uninstructed layman astray. Times had changed, however, and unless the ecclesiastical authorities issued an authorized version, unauthorized translations would be made and produce just the upheaval which was feared. Unfortunately, the bishops were too slow-moving and too afraid that the authority of the clergy would be undermined. As Canon Maynard Smith has said, 'The theologians no more encouraged the laity to study the Bible than a solicitor today encourages a man to study *Every Man his Own Lawyer.*' Hence Tyndale's version appeared, and was condemned as unlicensed, and heretical in presentation and influence. The result was that Bible-reading came to be associated with heresy.

The New Learning in England underwent a parallel development. Humanism, like Bible-reading, was not necessarily unorthodox; indeed the early humanists in England had not attacked scholasticism at all, except in the matter of Latin style. But in the early sixteenth century the men of the Old Learning, instead of assimilating the new knowledge, adopted a die-hard position. They despised the new emphasis on Greek, they opposed textual criticism of the Scriptures and the Fathers, they detested the humanist preference for the classics and the early Fathers over the medieval schoolmen; and they were indignant when the moralist Colet denounced abuses and the satirist Erasmus ridiculed superstitions. By treating humanism as an enemy they made it one. Contempt for medieval scholasticism and interest in the early Fathers was transmuted into a repudiation of the developments of the medieval Church and a call to return to primitive Christianity; and by the fifteen-thirties most younger men of the New Learning in England were scornful critics of the old order in both education and religion. This critical outlook spread widely among the younger generation of the clergy; it affected not only secular priests but some monks and many friars, who produced a number of learned supporters of the reformed doctrines, such as Robert Barnes, Miles Coverdale, and John Bale. This was of some importance, for the friars were still very influential with the people; and if they had been resolutely united in defence of the old order Henry might have found them hard to suppress. But by the end of our period not only the friars, but all the clergy, were hopelessly disunited, and resolute clerical opposition to Henry VIII was limited to a handful of men. The radicals were as yet in a small minority; but the English clergy were so accustomed to a great measure of royal control in ecclesiastical affairs that they could not think of resistance. And many of the clergy were as unsettled by the onslaughts of the humanists on the traditional learning and religion as by the discovery of the New World.

With so many influences battering and undermining the old order in England, the question is not why any changes occurred but why they did not assume the drastic character of the Scottish Reformation. The contrast was partly because the Church in Scotland was more corrupt than in England and because Knox was so strong and able a leader, but chiefly because the Scottish monarchy was so weak. It was impotent to check the greed of the nobles (who seized the lands of the Church, which had supported the monarchy) or the destructive violence of a people intoxicated by the sermons of fearless and devoted preachers. But in England it was inconceivable that changes should take place without the approval of a Crown which had long been strong, and had for centuries wielded great influence over the Church – especially when the wearer of that Crown was Henry VIII. As a complete egoist, he wished to destroy papal authority in England, and as a man of the New Learning he despised superstition and scholasticism; but as a shrewd monarch he saw that great upheavals in the Church might lead to revolution in the State, and as a traditionalist and trained theologian he was anxious to preserve the old faith and the old system of Church life and worship. These aims suited most of his subjects, who were insular and anti-clerical, but had a strong sense of continuity and a respect for tradition. Even those who wanted further change, from high-minded radicals to grabbers of abbey lands, usually had a strong sense of order and a great respect for the royal authority.

Henry's ecclesiastical changes, therefore, were the most

conservative in Western Christendom outside the Roman communion, and to the last he thought of himself as merely having abolished a few abuses, and remaining an orthodox defender of the Catholic Faith. Nevertheless the abolition of papal authority and of the religious Orders were revolutionary acts, and were bound to open the door for others. In religion the fifteen-thirties mark the close of medieval England.

This is true, too, of education, where the founding of the Royal Society in Charles II's reign may seem at first sight a more significant landmark, and where medieval influences lingered on until the nineteenth century. At the beginning of our period the signs of change in education were still very few. Humanism in England has an earlier beginning and a more continuous history than was formerly realized; but in 1471 only a handful of Englishmen were interested in Renaissance learning, and even they did not see any fundamental difference between scholasticism and humanism. Nor had the growing importance of the urban middle classes yet affected the subjects and methods of the schools. But there was in the fifteenth century a striking increase in the number of schools founded by town gilds or wealthy merchants; and by 1489 so many men could read that for the purposes of benefit of clergy a distinction was drawn between literate laymen and bona fide clergymen. Margaret Paston, writing to her husband in 1484, assumes the ability to write in any man who could be put in charge of the household's bread and beer. The rapid spread of printing seems to point to a large number of readers, and a generation later Sir Thomas More estimated that more than half the population could read. During this century many private elementary schools were started in towns by priests and scriveners; and some of the latter opened commercial schools, in which were taught reading and writing in English, accounting, French, and, perhaps, a smattering of legal knowledge. In public foundations, however, the adaptations of the curriculum to the needs of future tradesmen or artisans went no further than that of Archbishop Rotherham's provision, in the college he founded in 1483 in his native town, for one of the teachers to be 'learned and skilled in the art of writing and reckoning', or Bishop Stillington's ordinance, for the school he established at Acaster between 1466 and 1483, that one of the masters should 'teche to Write and all such things as belonged to Scrivener Craft'. Before technical or scientific education could evolve, scientific attitudes and the experimental method must emerge; and these were born of the union between the advances of the middle ages in thought and practice, in subtlety of logical analysis and skill in craftsmen's techniques. The feebleness of the appropriate intellectual stimulus in an age of theological preoccupations and the weakness of the practical incentive in an era of closely regulated economic activity had so far prevented such a union in England, and, indeed, Western Europe; but it was just beginning in contemporary Italy.

It would be generations before the results of this seriously affected English schools; but by the end of the century Italy was already transmitting to English education another revolutionary influence, that of humanism, with its enthusiasm for the study of the classical literatures of Greece and Rome instead of the dialectic and scholastic theology of late medieval education. Reform in the teaching of Latin grammar began with the *Accidence* of John Stanbridge, master of the newly-founded Magdalen College School from 1488 to 1494; but the first important impact of the Renaissance on English secondary education came with the refounding of St Paul's School, London, by the humanist Dean, John Colet, in 1510. The first headmaster, William Lily, a humanist recently returned from Italy, wrote for this school his famous grammar, from which all subsequent Latin grammars for English boys were derived; and Erasmus devoted much time to finding teachers and writing text-books for the school. The statutes laid down that classical Latin and Greek were to be taught, and that the best classical authors were to take the place of the old medieval disciplines; and these principles spread slowly to other English schools.

The Italian Renaissance had, however, much wider aims than a change in the character of book-learning, important though that was. In contrast to medieval Christian ideals, it aimed at self-reliance, self-expression, and the development of personality; and the emphasis was transferred from the education of bookish clerks to the production of scholar-gentlemen, cultured laymen trained to be men of affairs. By 1531 these ideals found expression in England in *The Boke named the Governour* by Sir Thomas Elyot, a book on the training, not of clerics for the service of the Church, but of the governing classes for the service of the State. He emphasized the importance of physical training, in both strenuous and courtly exercises, he advocated the use of the mother tongue in learning Latin and Greek, and he appealed often to concrete experiences.

Such ideas as these, together with the ferment in the schools, would in any event soon have transformed the medieval order in education; but the end came with revolutionary suddenness in the thirties and forties, with the dissolution of the monasteries, which involved the disappearance of the numerous elementary schools kept by nuns, of the schools of various grades attached to the almonries of monasteries, and of the training for young gentlemen in the households of the abbots of the larger houses; and moreover, the scattering of valuable monastic libraries. A fresh blow soon followed in 1547 in the dissolution of the chantries which, though not so intended, involved the disappearance of many primary schools. Some of the damage was repaired by Henry VIII and Edward VI, and the middle classes devoted much wealth to the endowment of education in the reigns of Elizabeth and the early Stuarts; but such new or refounded schools bore very clearly the marks of the break with the past.

Signs of change came earlier in the universities than in the schools. Humanism began to develop in Oxford from the days of Thomas Chaundler's Wardenship of New College (1454–75), but at first without arousing hostility. This was partly because in England it was then conceived not as a new outlook on life but as a means of improving some aspects of scholasticism, and partly because many of these earlier

English humanists, like Gunthorpe or Shirwood, valued the New Learning mainly for its usefulness in improving their Latin style and helping their careers as diplomats. By the end of the century, however, a rift appeared between the old learning and the new. Conservatives disliked the introduction of public lectures on Greek at Oxford in the nineties by Grocyn and Linacre, and Erasmus found it hard to sow the seeds of Greek learning at Cambridge during his stay there from 1511 to 1514, in spite of the protection of the Chancellor, John Fisher. Not only were new methods introduced, as when Colet lectured on the Epistles of St Paul from a historical standpoint, instead of in the scholastic tradition in which each text was isolated and treated literally, allegorically, morally, and anagogically, but the younger generation of humanists insisted that the New Learning must influence conduct. Conservatives suspected that such novel ideas must lead either to heresy or to the substitution of this world for the next as the object of life. They felt their fears justified when Erasmus made a new Latin translation of the Bible, differing from the Vulgate, or Linacre obtained in 1518 the foundation of the Royal College of Physicians, for a profession whose education and organization had been hitherto entirely under ecclesiastical control.

This natural but obscurantist hostility tended to drive the next generation of humanists into alliance with the advocates of religious change. The Act of Supremacy of 1534 was therefore followed by Royal Injunctions in 1535 which made important educational changes in the Universities. The study of canon law was suppressed, but classical Greek and Latin, Hebrew, mathematics, and medicine were to be encouraged. The standard medieval compendium of Christian doctrine, the *Sentences* of Peter Lombard, was abolished in favour of direct reading of the Bible, whose exposition should be in harmony with the new exegesis. Aristotle and logic were to be studied with the help of humanist writers, putting aside 'the frivolous questions and obscure glosses' of the schoolmen. Visitors appointed by Thomas Cromwell were sent to the universities to enforce these Injunctions with vigour. Duns Scotus, for example, had been one of the revered authorities of late medieval learning; yet Dr Layton, one of the visitors, wrote to Cromwell '. . . the seconde tyme wee came to New Coleege affter we hade declarede your injunctions we founde all the gret quadrant court full of the leiffes of Dunce, the wynde blowying them into evere corner.' Those fluttering leaves symbolized the end of the medieval order in the English universities. Henceforth medieval scholarship was to be despised, and a new order in University studies began to unfold, more critical and more empirical than the old, less authoritarian and less united.

## CHAPTER V

# The Arts

A REVOLUTIONARY influence in religion and education was the art of printing, which made it possible to multiply books with a speed, an accuracy, and a cheapness hitherto inconceivable. Yet this revolutionary technique, discovered in Germany about 1450, was introduced into England by a man of thoroughly conventional outlook. William Caxton (?1422–1491) was no humanist, and not even a professional scrivener. When he set up his printing press in 1476 in the precincts of Westminster Abbey he was a successful mercer with literary tastes, who had picked up the idea of printing while living in Flanders. Caxton's patrons were important persons – Edward IV, Earl Rivers, the Earl of Arundel; but neither they nor the growing literate public, avid for more reading-matter than manuscript methods of production could supply, were Renaissance scholars. The few Englishmen who wanted the Latin or Greek classics could get them from French or Italian presses. Hence Caxton devoted himself almost entirely to translating and publishing in English a wide range of books likely to appeal to his conservative public. Most of his books were therefore didactic or religious, the biggest and most popular of them being the *Golden Legend*, a compendium of Saints' lives which had been a favourite for nearly three centuries; but he also published works of Chaucer, Lydgate, and Gower, and some of the great medieval romances. His successor, Wynkyn de Worde, continued his policy, and the great circulation thus given to old favourites may have helped to prolong medieval tastes in literature. Certainly Caxton's publication of Malory's *Morte d'Arthur* helped to ensure its survival as a living classic until the present day.

The great medieval tales of Troy, Alexander, and the Romans were soon to be killed by the revival of classical studies; and the Charlemagne cycle, which celebrated the triumph of Christendom over the infidel, seemed out of date to the nationalist England of Spenser and Shakespeare. King Arthur and his knights were, however, like the ballads, acclaimed as one of the glories of English tradition; and the Tudors deliberately encouraged popular love of the Arthurian stories to enhance the antiquity and renown of their house. Neither national pride nor royal policy would, however, probably have sufficed to keep alive the Arthurian romances had not Malory retold them in a work of genius. In his work, completed in 1469, Malory claims merely to be translating a French book, though in fact he used various Arthurian romances, English as well as French. But his work is far from being simply a compilation; he adapted his sources to the needs of his time. The decay of the old chivalric social order and the horrors of civil war made men look back nostalgically to the idealized chivalry of a remote and fabulous past; but they wanted its fantasies to be presented in a coherent, credible, and sympathetic form. Malory condensed and simplified his material, and eliminated the supernatural and mysterious whenever possible. Usually matter-of-fact, he was indifferent to the theological significance of the Quest for the Holy Grail, though not to its mystical appeal; he was interested in adventures for their own sake and in the conflict of loyalties which led finally to tragedy. He enhanced the importance of Arthur, and made him not only a chivalrous but a national hero. And just as in the structure of his stories Malory stands as a link between two ages, so he does in his inimitable style. In the difficult task of retelling an old tale he achieves a wonderful blend of archaism and straightforwardness, pathos and simplicity, majesty and ease, cadence and clarity. A new text of his work, discovered by Mr W. F. Oakeshott in 1934 and published by Professor Vinaver in 1947, enables us to see more vividly how Malory's style has wrought a subtle beauty out of his materials. His book is England's first work in poetic prose; and some measure of his achievement is the contrast between France, where the Arthurian cycle, so popular with ten generations of

Frenchmen, withered away in the Renaissance, and England, where the Arthurian legends never died.

Malory's stories shine the more brightly against the general mediocrity of English literature in the late fifteenth century. The only creations which displayed vitality were those apparently intended for a popular audience – ballads like *The Nut-Brown Maid* or morality plays like *Everyman*. The former, with its elaborate rhymes and rhythms, may be the work of a courtly poet, but its style is simple and sincere, and the dramatic liveliness of the poem outweighs the moralizing of its opening and closing stanzas. The play *Everyman* is the most impressive of all the morality plays, and a masterpiece of its kind. The metre may be imperfect and the language lacking in brilliance, but this allegory of Christian death is so powerfully sincere and poignantly constructed that it has the strength and drama of Greek tragedy.

The courtly tradition derived from Chaucer had been declining throughout the century, until with Stephen Hawes (?1474–?1523) it was buried under a heap of erudition and morality. The allegories and the chivalric elements in which he delighted were as outworn as the scholasticism and the feudal order which had given them birth. The platitudinous and unrhythmical verses of Hawes are of interest chiefly as a link between the *Roman de la Rose* and Spenser.

The last two poets in the medieval tradition, Alexander Barclay (1474–1552) and John Skelton (?1460–1529), showed more originality. Barclay's translation and expansion in 1509 of Brant's *Ship of Fools*, which pilloried savagely the follies of mankind, had a great success. His verses are usually crude and unrhythmical, but his style had the merit of sincerity and realism. These qualities are also marked in the far more vigorous verses of John Skelton. A learned Oxford graduate and tutor to the future Henry VIII, he was famous for his Latin verses and well known as a grammarian. Faithful to the outworn tradition in which he was reared, he was nevertheless too original to be content with it; so that his energy produced a torrent of short, irregular lines, whose rhymes he himself acknowledged to be 'ragged, tattered, and jagged'. In his use of allegory and alliteration he adhered to the old forms; but, unlike Hawes, he succeeded in revivifying those traditions by his brutal satire, his sophisticated tenderness, his immense vigour. No Protestant attacked proud prelates more savagely than Skelton, and he had to spend several years in sanctuary at Westminster because of his daring attacks on Wolsey.

The next two court poets, Sir Thomas Wyatt (1503–42) and the Earl of Surrey, were thoroughly imbued with Renaissance learning, which they showed not only in the matter of their poetry, but in their conscious, humanist attention to form, which their medieval predecessors had either achieved, like Chaucer, by instinct and experience, or not at all. In other spheres of literature besides poetry great changes were taking place in this generation. The morality plays with their allegorical types waned with the old scholastic metaphysics; and the anti-papal John Bale in his *Kynge John* (*c.* 1536) adapted the morality to create our first history play. By about 1540 Nicholas Udall, headmaster of Eton, could write *Ralph Roister Doister*, the first English comedy inspired by the classical tradition.

The new spirit had appeared earlier in the prose of Sir Thomas More (1478–1535). His greatest literary work, *Utopia* (1516), was in Latin; but his humanism manifested itself in the English tongue in his incomplete *History of Richard III*. This is the first history in the English language which is not merely an artless collection of facts, but a deliberately designed and carefully executed composition. Sir Thomas More's own life inspired a biography (*c.* 1535) by his son-in-law William Roper, which marks an advance in clarity and construction on More's own writings. In the same decade Sir Thomas Elyot showed in his *Governour* (1531) that English could be moulded into a classical restraint and lucidity.

But the most important developments in English literature were due to the religious changes which began in this decade. On the one hand, the new generations of writers and readers lost touch with the oldest and most copious stream of English prose, that of medieval devotional works, now shunned as papistical and superstitious. On the other, the breach with Rome led to the creation of Cranmer's beautiful liturgy and the dissemination of the great translation of the Bible, begun by Tyndale (1525) and completed by Coverdale (1535), the basis of the Authorized Version of 1611. Both Bible and Prayer Book were translated by great scholars familiar with medieval religious works, but the incomparable influence of the English Bible and Prayer Book increasingly separated English prose henceforth from its medieval predecessor.

It was not only in literature that medieval traditions were dying in our period. The early printers could help to create a standard English vocabulary and orthography, but they could find no great book-making craft to guide them. Their type and lay-out were mediocre and their wood-cuts crude. Yet English wood-carvers had been second to none, and English illumination and calligraphy had formerly been unsurpassed. But English illumination was now producing only shop-work, and since the middle of the century had had to draw copiously on Flemish art for its ideas. While English lords had been fighting one another, or devastating France, the Duchy of Burgundy had been an oasis of peace and prosperity in Europe, and the munificent patronage of the Burgundian dukes or the Flemish towns had enabled a great succession of Flemish painters to become the leaders of Northern Europe. When, for example, Edward IV in his exile of 1470–1 spent some months as the guest of the great patron and connoisseur, Louis, Lord of Gruthuyse, he was enchanted by that noble's collection of manuscripts, and after his restoration bought as many Flemish manuscripts as he could.* The striking advances in technique inaugurated by Jan Van Eyck enabled his Flemish successors to paint with a realism which captivated not only the Yorkist kings

---

*The beautiful Hastings Book of Hours, bequeathed to the British Museum in 1968 by Mrs C. W. Dyson Perrins, shows that when Lord Hastings wanted to make a fine gift to Edward V, he commissioned artists in Ghent to write and illuminate the manuscript for him.

and Henry VII but other English patrons too. Flemish artists like Hugo van der Goes and Hans Memling painted for Englishmen; and if English illuminators were to attract any lucrative business they had to adopt Flemish fashions. One of the best late-fifteenth-century manuscripts, for example, the *Pageant of Richard Beauchamp, Earl of Warwick*, made about 1493, takes the landscapes for its pleasing pen-and-ink drawings from Burgundian manuscripts, and its figures are drawn with the heavy realism and thick draperies of the Flemish style. Against the competition of Flemish illumination and easel painting, and of the new art of printing, English manuscript production, enfeebled by the civil war, could not recover. By the early sixteenth century, expect for uninspired shop-work, it was nearly dead; though something of the great traditions of English illumination may have descended to the later miniaturists, such as Nicholas Hilliard.

English wall- and panel-painting of this period also shows Flemish influence, but not to the same weakening extent. There are undeniably strong Flemish traits in the finest English wall-paintings of the late fifteenth century, those depicting the Miracles of the Virgin in Eton College Chapel, executed between 1479 and 1483 by William Baker; yet the types depicted are strongly English in character. The grisaille colouring and the realistic detail are borrowed from Flanders; but the simple grace and dignity are in the best English tradition. In portrait painting, too, the English tradition could still produce fine work. The English feeling for line-composition, going back to the tenth century, is well displayed in the fine portrait of Margaret Beaufort (1488), now in the National Portrait Gallery. The growing individualism of the period produced an increasing demand for portraits; and the taste for exact realism has given us what are probably fair likenesses of the Yorkist kings and Henry VII and some of their subjects, even if their artistic merit is usually not very great. The lack of good native painters caused the early Tudors to welcome foreign painters to their court; Henry VII invited the

Fleming Mabuse and Henry VIII Holbein the Younger.

Flemish influence in this period was as dominant in stained glass as in other branches of painting. Amongst the Flemish glaziers imported by Henry VII was Bernard Flower. He was in charge of the glazing of Henry VII's Chapel in Westminster Abbey (c. 1510–15), which must have been as magnificent as Flower's later work in King's College Chapel, Cambridge, still is. He also had a hand in making the splendid windows (c. 1500) of Fairford Church, paid for by the Cotswold woolman, John Tame. Gorgeous as these Flemish productions were, they nevertheless contained the seeds of a decadence which quickly showed itself. The glaziers tried to produce in glass the perspective and naturalistic effects of the painters in oils in the Netherlands, and the sense that the design should fit into the stone-work was fading. Subjects began to spread over several lights, enamelling replaced leading and pot metals, and glaziers began to overstep the limits of their medium. Even where more remote places retained the native tradition, as at Malvern Priory or St Neots, Cornwall, glazing became heavy and crude in colour and execution. After the fifteen-thirties there was an end to nearly all glass-painting for churches, and the art was henceforth restricted mainly to heraldic work for private houses. The growing substitution of glass for horn or wooden shutters in the windows of private houses provided increasing business for glaziers; but after the fifteen-thirties the art of stained glass quickly withered, and great quantities of medieval stained glass were destroyed.

Henceforth the crafts which could cater for more secular needs, such as furniture, metal-work, embroidery, and tombs, throve best; and this meant that one form of sculpture at least survived better than the art of stained glass. Even before the thirties the growing individualism meant that much of the best work went into tombs and chantries; but fine wall statues were still possible. Two wonderful early-sixteenth-century stone heads are preserved in the libraries of Winchester Cathedral and Westminster Abbey; and the hundred or more statues (c. 1502–12) in Henry VII's Chapel are full of character and variety, as well as very skilfully executed. The symbolism of the thirteenth century has been replaced by an anecdotal realism – some of the figures wear spectacles. Nevertheless, patrons often felt that technically competent but uninspired shop-work was good enough for wall statues, whereas they wanted effigies of themselves as well done as they could afford. There was, for example, a marked degeneration in this period in the alabaster retables which in the early fifteenth century had been so good; whereas alabaster tombs of quite high quality were produced in large quantities until the Reformation and after it. A few tombs began to have kneeling effigies of the deceased knight or merchant, his wife, and his usually numerous children, in the style so beloved in Elizabethan and Jacobean days; but the usual type was still the stone or alabaster chest surrounded by canopied weepers and surmounted by recumbent effigies carved in a very realistic style which recorded minutely the changes in fashion. Before the break with Rome Renaissance influence on figure sculpture in England was still small and limited mainly to Italian work, such as Torrigiano's tombs of Margaret Beaufort and Henry VII, or Majano's fine terracotta medallion busts at Hampton Court. Occasionally Renaissance motifs began to be carved on Gothic structures, as in the case of some of the chantry chapels at Christ Church, Hampshire; but no important change occurred before the thirties. A great deal of medieval sculpture perished when the monasteries were dissolved; and more still was soon to be destroyed when images in all churches were removed. With the religious changes Italian and French sculptors began to be replaced by Germans and Flemings. Gothic feeling lingered for many years to come, but the thirties form the most distinctive ending to medieval sculpture.

The last phase of medieval England saw a higher level of excelence maintained in wood-carving than in sculpture. Not only were fine roofs, screens, and reredoses produced, but also particularly charming misericords. Here the fancy of the carvers, less confined than elsewhere by their clerical patrons' wishes, took advantage of the contemporary love of anecdotal realism. Scenes from everyday life were often treated in a satirical and humorous vein, and even the most sacred subjects were handled with levity; for example, animals are depicted conducting one or other of the services of the Church. The technical level of these misericords was usually high; but skill in wood-carving and carpentry was not limited to church furniture. The old aristocracy had sought magnificence, the display of gorgeous fabrics concealing very simple walls and furniture; but the rising middle classes were more interested in solid comfort, and did not have the problem of frequent removals. They not only wanted more furniture, but they wanted it better made, and this prompted the discovery that framed and panelled construction allows for shrinking much better than simple planked furniture. Hence the simple planked chests and walls began to be replaced by the panelled chests and walls which we associate with the Tudors. The varying width of the panels, thicker in the middle than at the inset-edges, stimulate the woodcarvers to evolve the linen-fold and parchemin forms of decoration now so much admired. Renaissance details, such as a carved head surrounded by a classical circular wreath (Romayne panelling), started to creep in from the beginning of Henry VII's reign; but the first full-blooded Renaissance wood-carving now extant in England is the wonderful Italian-wrought organ-screen (c. 1531–35) in King's College Chapel, Cambridge. This fine screen may fitly signal the end of medieval English wood-carving, for not only did the style change hereafter until the Gothic had disappeared, but much of the achievement of medieval wood-carving was destroyed; and the art was henceforth for a while needed much less in churches than it had been in late medieval England.

In architecture, too, the fifteen-thirties mark the transition from medieval to modern times, although, as in other spheres, signs of fundamental change had appeared and old forms lingered long after this decade. The gradual suppression of disorder by the Yorkists and Tudors (except on the Scottish border) reduced the need for massive walls, whose value was in any case declining with the improvement of cannon. By Henry VIII's day such features as battlemented turrets and fortified gateways were erected, if at all, for ornament rather than defence, as at Compton Wynyates or Layer Marney. Now that the countryside was more peaceful, the wealthy could pay more attention to comfort – bigger windows filled with glass, gardens of formal design, better and more abundant furniture; and, with the invention of printing, wall-papers appeared. Sanitation was not yet improved, and cleanliness may even have been diminishing; but in upper-class houses the number of rooms increased. These more private rooms grew in importance at the expense of the hall, as the military retainer system was restricted, the old aristocracy impoverished and its hospitality reduced, and the new aristocracy preferred comfort rather than display in the old style. Halls were still impressive in the houses of this period, with their panelled walls, their great bay windows adorned with heraldic glass, their carved fire-places, and their hammer-beam roofs; but they were used in the old way only on great occasions, such as Christmas, when the family and its guests came to join the rest of the household in feasting and fun. Otherwise the master and his family and guests ate in a private dining-room and slept in private bedrooms, which grew in number so that at Hengrave Hall, Suffolk (1538) there were no fewer than forty. This withdrawal of the master of the house from the old communal life of the great hall meant his increasing separation from the life and interests of his servants. Lower down the social scale there was still close contact between the classes; the apprentice still ate at his master's table, and farm-hands still slept in the yeoman's hall by the open hearth, near their master's bedstead. But higher standards of comfort were sought in the numerous manor-houses which reflected commercial prosperity or royal favour. The many houses dating from this period, ranging from charming black and white timbered halls, built by country gentry, such as Bramall Hall, Cheshire, or Speke Hall, near Liverpool, to that magnificent palace of mellow red brick, Hampton Court, are a vivid reminder of the increasing attention paid to domestic comfort and beauty.

Domestic architecture, though of growing importance, had not yet eclipsed church-building. It is true that little was done to cathedrals, except to finish a tower, to construct a vault, or to add chantry chapels, as was done at Durham, Oxford, and Winchester. It was also true that Bath Abbey Church (c. 1500–39) is the only large monastic church begun in this period, though additions were made to existing buildings, such as Abbot Hoby's graceful tower (1510–25) at Fountains or the beautiful fan-vault (c. 1475–90) of the nave of Sherborne Abbey. But this was because the main streams of pious generosity were now directed to parish churches, schools and colleges, chantries, and royal chapels. The prosperity of the cloth industry produced splendid parish churches, such as those at Lavenham (1486–1523) and Long Melford (1470–96); and many additions were made to parish churches, such as those in Stratford-on-Avon's richly windowed chancel (1465–91) or Louth's stately tower (c. 1460–75). The educational zeal of the age gave to Oxford and Cambridge many of their most beautiful buildings, of which perhaps the finest are Christ Church Hall, Oxford, and King's College Chapel, Cambridge. College towers such as that of Magdelan College (c. 1490–1509) or Lupton Tower (1516–20) at Eton vied in excellence with those of churches. This was a period when kings built magnificent royal chapels; Edward IV began the rebuilding of St George's Chapel, Windsor (1473–1537) and Henry VII founded at Westminster Abbey the superb chapel (1503–19) which bears his name.

These two royal chapels, together with King's College Chapel, are three of the finest examples of Perpendicular Gothic ever built. Both in their purpose and in their style they give scarcely any indication that medieval England was about to disappear. Indeed, of all the many religious buildings of this period only a few chantry chapels, such as that at Boxgrove Priory, Sussex, show signs of Renaissance influence. Yet for church architecture the middle ages were nearly at an end. In the fifteen-thirties church building came to a sudden stop, and in the next few years the suppression of the monasteries, friaries, and chantries meant the sudden destruction or gradual ruin of a considerable part of the church architecture of medieval England. For the rest of the sixteenth century there was virtually no church building; and though the early seventeenth century saw the slight Laudian revival, and the erection of several Gothic chapels in Oxford Colleges, where Gothic lingered until the Civil War, Gothic was now a mere survival, whose spirit and forms were ebbing away. By the time Wren re-erected one or two London churches in Gothic style, medieval church architecture was dead; for him Gothic was no longer a living tradition but a conscious, antiquarian exercise, 'in the Gothick mode'.

The religious changes bore more hardly on the visual arts than on music, which had been flourishing after its setback in the Wars of the Roses. Edward IV established a fine choir in connexion with his rebuilt St George's Chapel, Windsor; and Richard III, Henry VII, and Henry VIII all maintained and fostered the choir of the Chapel Royal. This was of greater importance than may at first appear, for it offered the best prospects to composers, and hence was the centre of the musical revival of this period, as it had been of the efflorescence of Henry IV's day. Most of the art-music of the time, from masses and motets to carols and songs, emanated from members of the Chapel Royal, such as that insufficiently appreciated master, Robert Fayrfax. Such composers were sometimes directors of the king's music; sometimes they sang or accompanied it. Edward IV organized in his household a band of minstrels which flourished under his successors. The court minstrels of this age bore no resemblance, except in name, to the unspecialized wandering entertainers of the twelfth century. They were skilled instrumentalists, often with university degrees in music; and some of them, like John Redford (1486–1540), organist of the Chapel Royal, composed music which is still played or sung. Companies of such minstrels were maintained, not only by the king, but by noblemen and towns. Companies of noblemen's minstrels began to tour the country, and writers like Hugh Aston (1485–1522?) began to develop instrumental music, as distinct from a mere transference to instruments of the already well-developed contrapuntal choral style. The improvement of virginals, lutes, and viols encouraged music-making in the home, where more privacy was now possible, at any rate among the upper and middle classes. By the end of our period there was developing the Renaissance ideal of the cultured gentleman, who ought to be able either to sing or to play; and there was much encouragement of music at the court of Henry VIII, who was both a performer and a composer.

Secular music was thus thriving, and the seeds were being sown of the remarkable musical flowering of the Elizabethan age. But church music continued to flourish as well, even after the fifteen-thirties, for the Church of England had less objection to even elaborate church music (provided the words were intelligible) than either the Puritans or the Council of Trent. Distinguished musicians such as Tallis and Merbecke not only wrote masses for the old order but composed fine settings for the reformed services. Nevertheless, when the services of the Church were revised, simplified, and translated into English, a new style was required, and the Church music of the middle ages was neither usable nor desired. Moreover, the Reformers' insistence on syllabic setting of the words strengthened the Renaissance emphasis on fitting of the music to speech rhythms. This change hastened the development of new secular forms, such as the madrigal and the air, in Elizabeth's day. In music, too, the fifteen-thirties may therefore be made the most appropriate ending to the story of medieval England.

# BOOK LIST

THE following list is in general confined to secondary works; but even a casual reader should explore some of the writings of the period as soon as possible. A great number of extracts (730), some of them lengthy, from original sources, are given in translation in my *English Historical Documents, 1327–1485* (1969, Vol. IV of the Eyre and Spottiswoode series, general editor D. C. Douglas). This volume also provides annotated bibliographies of original sources as well as detailed lists of secondary books and articles. Volumes VII and VIII of the *Cambridge Medieval History* include long and valuable classified bibliographies; though much has been written on this period since they were published in the 1930s. More up-to-date bibliographies, classified and annotated, will be found in *A Bibliography of English History to 1485*, edited by E. B. Graves (Oxford, 1975) and *Bibliographical Handbooks: Late Medieval England, 1377–1485*, compiled by D. J. Guth (Cambridge, 1976). Apart from my *English Historical Documents*, titles of recent works on this period, whether original sources, secondary books, or the more important articles, will be found in the *Annual Bulletin of Historical Literature*, published by the Historical Association. Just as it is a mistake to think that original sources are only for the researcher, so it is an error to suppose that articles in periodicals are only for the pedant. Both kinds of reading can often be fascinating for the general reader.

## GENERAL

BAGLEY, J. J., *Historical Interpretation: The Sources of English History 1066–1540* (Harmondsworth, 1965).

CHRIMES, S. B., *Lancastrians, Yorkists and Henry VII* (London, 1964).

COULTON, G. G., *Medieval Panorama* (London, 1940).

GREEN, V. H. H., *The Later Plantagenets* (London, 1955).

HOLMES, G. A., *The Later Middle Ages, 1272–1485* (Edinburgh, 1962).

HUIZINGA, J., *The Waning of the Middle Ages* (London, 1924).

KEEN, M. H., *England in the Later Middle Ages* (London, 1973).

KINGSFORD, C. L., *Prejudice and Promise in Fifteenth Century England* (Oxford, 1925).

LANDER, J. R., *Conflict and Stability in Fifteenth-Century England* (London, 1969).

*London University Source Books*, Nos. I, II, III, and VI, compiled by D. HUGHES (1918), J. H. FLEMMING (1921), I. D. THORNLEY (1921) and C. H. WILLIAMS (1925) respectively.

PERROY, E., *Le Guerre de Cent Ans* (Paris, 1945).

ed. POOLE, A. L., *Medieval England*: a new edition of Barnard's Companion to English History (2 vols., Clarendon Press, 1958).

ed. POOLE, R. L., *Historical Atlas of Modern Europe* (Oxford, 1900).

ENGLAND IN THE LATE MIDDLE AGES

POWICKE, F. M., *Medieval England* (London, 1931).
SALZMAN, L. F., *English Life in the Middle Ages* (Oxford, 1926).
SALZMAN, L. F., *England in Tudor Times* (Cambridge, 1926).
WILKINSON, B., *The Later Middle Ages in England* (London, 1969).

## THE POLITICAL FRAMEWORK

Useful surveys, incorporating the results of recent research in many
fields and giving full bibliographies, will be found in the relevant volumes
of the Oxford History of England; M. McKisack, *The Fourteenth
Century* (1959), E. F. Jacob, *The Fifteenth Century* (1961), and J. D. Mackie,
*The Earlier Tudors* (1952). Especially stimulating for the early Tudor
period is G. E. Elton's *England under the Tudors* (1955), with its annotated
bibliography. Still of value are Sir J. H. Ramsay's *The Genesis of Lancaster*
(2 vols., Oxford, 1913), his *Lancaster and York* (2 vols., Oxford, 1892), and
the political narratives of this period given by Bishop W. Stubbs in his
*The Constitutional History of England* (3 vols., Oxford, 1873–8, frequently
reprinted). For the European background, see C. W. Previté-Orton,
*History of Europe 1198–1378* (3rd edn., 1951), W. T. Waugh, *History of
Europe 1378–1494* (3rd edn., 1949), and A. J. Grant, *History of Europe,
1494–1610* (2nd edn., 1938) in the Methuen series; the *Cambridge Medieval History*, Vols. 7 and 8 (1932, 1936), and the *New Cambridge Modern
History*, Vol. I (1957), (though the usefulness of the latter is impaired by
the lack of any bibliographies); and the *Histoire du Moyen Age*, ed. G.
Glotz, Vols. 6 to 8 (Paris, 1941). Biographies and studies of single reigns
are often attractive and stimulating, such as T. F. Tout, *The Place of the
Reign of Edward II in English History* (2nd edition, revised by H. John-
stone, Manchester, 1936); J. R. Maddicott, *Thomas of Lancaster* (Oxford,
1970); K. Fowler, *The King's Lieutenant: Henry of Grosmont* (London,
1969); J. A. Tuck, *Richard II and the English Nobility* (London, 1973);
R. H. Jones, *The Royal Policy of Richard II* (London, 1968); S. Armitage
Smith, *John of Gaunt* (London, 1904, reprinted 1964); J. L. Kirby,
*Henry IV of England* (London, 1970); Sir J. E. Lloyd, *Owen Glendower*
(London, 1931); E. F. Jacob, *Henry V and the Invasion of France* (London,
1947); E. Carleton Williams, *My Lord of Bedford, 1389–1435* (London,
1963); K. Vickers, *Humphrey, Duke of Gloucester* (London, 1907); C. D.
Ross, *Edward IV* (London, 1974); P. M. Kendall, *Richard the Third*
(London, 1955); R. L. Storey, *The Reign of Henry VII* (London, 1968);
S. B. Chrimes, *Henry VII* (London, 1972); A. F. Pollard, *Wolsey* (London,
1929); R. W. Chambers, *Sir Thomas More* (London, 1935, Penguin
Books, 1963); J. J. Scarisbrick, *Henry VIII* (London, 1968, Penguin Books
1971).

## THE GOVERNMENT OF THE REALM

ed. BAYNE, C. J. and DUNHAM, W. H., *Select Cases in the Council of Henry
VII* (Selden Society, 1958).

BELLAMY, J. G., *The Law of Treason in England in the Later Middle Ages* (Cambridge, 1970).

BIRD, R., *The Turbulent London of Richard II* (London, 1949).

CHRIMES, S. B., *English Constitutional Ideas in the Fifteenth Century* (Cambridge, 1936).

CHRIMES, S. B. and BROWN, A. L., *English Constitutional Documents, 1307–1485* (London, 1961).

ELTON, G. R., *The Tudor Constitution* (Cambridge, 1960).

GREEN, A. S., *Town Life in the Fifteenth Century* (London, 1894).

LYON, B., *A Constitutional and Legal History of Medieval England* (New York, 1960).

MCKISACK, M., *The Parliamentary Representation of English Boroughs during the Middle Ages* (Oxford, 1932).

ed. MORRIS, W. A., WILLARD, J. F., DUNHAM, W. H., *The English Government at Work 1327–1336* (3 vols., 1940–50, Cambridge, Mass.).

MYERS, A. R., *The Household of Edward IV* (Manchester, 1959).

OTWAY-RUTHVEN, J., *The King's Secretary and the Signet Office in the XVth Century* (Cambridge, 1939).

PICKTHORN, K., *Early Tudor Government: Henry VII* (Cambridge, 1934).

PLUCKNETT, T. F. T., *A Concise History of the Common Law* (London, 5th edition, 1955).

PUTNAM, B. H., *Proceedings before the Justices of the Peace in the 14th and 15th centuries* (London, 1938).

ROSKELL, J. S., *The Commons in the Parliament of 1422* (Manchester, 1954).

SCHRAMM, P. E., *A History of the English Coronation* (Oxford, 1937).

STEEL, A., *The Receipt of the Exchequer* (Cambridge, 1954).

TASWELL-LANGMEAD, T. P., *English Constitutional History* (10th edition, revised and enlarged by T. F. T. Plucknett, London, 1946).

THOMPSON, A. H., *The English Clergy and their Organization in the Later Middle Ages* (Oxford, 1947).

THOMPSON, F., *A Short History of Parliament, 1294–1642* (Minneapolis, 1953). In conjunction with this one may consult a useful survey of recent work on the early history of Parliament, G. Templeman's article 'The History of Parliament in the Light of Modern Research', in the *University of Birmingham Historical Journal*, Vol. I (1948) pp. 202–31.

TOUT, T. F. T., *Chapters in the Administrative History of Medieval England* (6 vols., Manchester, 1920–33).

WILKINSON, B., *Constitutional History of Medieval England*, Vols. II and III (London, 1952 and 1958).

WILKINSON, B., *The Constitutional History of England in the Fifteenth Century* (London, 1964).

WOLFFE, B. P., *The Crown Lands, 1461–1536* (London, 1970).

WOODCOCK, B. L., *Medieval Ecclesiastical Courts of the Diocese of Canterbury* (Oxford, 1952).

# ENGLAND IN THE LATE MIDDLE AGES

## ECONOMIC AND SOCIAL DEVELOPMENTS

ABRAM, A., *English Life and Manners in the Later Middle Ages* (London, 1913).

BEAN, J. W. M., *The Decline of English Feudalism, 1215–1540* (Manchester, 1968).

BENNETT, H. S., *Life on the English Manor* (Cambridge, 1937).

BENNETT,, H. S., *The Pastons and their England* (Cambridge, 1922).

BERESFORD, M., *The Lost Villages of England* (London, 1954).

BRIDBURY, A. R., *Economic Growth, England in the Later Middle Ages* (London, 1962).

CARUS-WILSON, E. M., *Medieval Merchant Venturers* (London, 1954).

ed. CHRIMES, S. B., ROSS, C. D., and GRIFFITHS, R. A., *Fifteenth Century England, 1399–1509* (Manchester, 1972).

ed. CLAPHAM, J. H., POWER, E., POSTAN, M. M., RICH, E. E. and MILLER, E., *The Cambridge Economic History of Europe* (3 vols., 1942–63). Good bibliographies.

COULTON, G. G., *Chaucer and his England* (London, 1908, 1937).

ed. DARBY, H. C., *An Historical Geography of England* (Cambridge, 1936).

DOBSON, R. B., *The Peasants' Revolt of 1381* (London, 1970).

DU BOULAY, F. R. H., *An Age of Ambition: English society in the late Middle Ages* (London, 1970).

DUNHAM, W. H., *Lord Hastings' Indentured Retinues, 1461–83* (New Haven, 1955).

FERGUSON, A. B., *The Indian Summer of English Chivalry* (Durham, N. C., 1960).

FOWLER, K., *The Age of Plantagenet and Valois* (London, 1967). Concerned especially with war and society and well illustrated.

HEWITT, H. J., *The Organization of War under Edward III* (Manchester, 1966).

HILL, J. W. F., *Medieval Lincoln* (Cambridge, 1948).

HOLMES, G. A., *The Estates of the Higher Nobility in Fourteenth Century England* (Cambridge, 1957).

JUSSERAND, J. J., *English Wayfaring Life in the Middle Ages* (new edition, London, 1920).

KEEN, M. H., *The Laws of War in the Late Middle Ages* (London, 1965).

LANDER, J. R., *Conflict and Stability in Fifteenth-Century England* (London, 1969).

LIPSON, E., *Introduction to the Economic History of England*, Vol I (11th edition, London, 1956).

LLOYD, T. H., *The English Wool Trade in the Middle Ages* (Cambridge, 1977).

McFARLANE, K. B., *The Nobility of Later Medieval England* (Oxford, 1973).

POWER, E., *The Wool Trade in Medieval English History* (Oxford, 1941).

# BOOK LIST

ed. POWER, E. E., and POSTAN, M. M., *Studies in English Trade in the Fifteenth Century* (London, 1933).

RAFTIS, J. A., *The Estates of Ramsey Abbey* (Toronto, 1957).

REES, W., *South Wales and the March, 1284-1415* (London, 1924).

ROSENTHAL, J. T., *Nobles and the Noble Life 1295-1500* (London, 1976).

SALUSBURY, G. T., *Street Life in Medieval England* (2nd edition, Oxford, 1948).

STOREY, R. L., *The End of the House of Lancaster* (London, 1966).

STRUTT, J., *Sports and Pastimes of the People of England* (ed. Cox, J. C., London, 1903).

TAWNEY, R. H., *The Agrarian Problem in the Sixteenth Century* (London, 1912).

THOMPSON, G. Scott, *Two Centuries of Family History* (London, 1930). On the rise of the Russell family.

THRUPP, S. L., *The Merchant Class of Medieval London* (London, 1948).

ZIEGLER, P., *The Black Death* (London, 1969). Those who want more detail on this subject should consult J. F. D. Shrewsbury's monumental work, *A History of Bubonic Plague in the British Isles* (Cambridge, 1970).

## RELIGIOUS AND EDUCATIONAL MOVEMENTS

ASTON, M. E., *Thomas Arundel* (Oxford, 1967).

BOWKER, M., *The Secular Clergy in the Diocese of Lincoln, 1495-1520* (Cambridge, 1968).

ed. BUTLER-BOWDEN, W., *The Book of Margery Kempe* (Oxford, 1954).

CHARLTON, K., *Education in Renaissance England* (London, 1965).

CUTTS, E. L., *Parish Priests and their People in the Middle Ages* (London, 1898).

DEANESLY, M., *The Lollard Bible* (Cambridge, 1920).

DICKENS, A. G., *The English Reformation* (London, 1964).

EDWARDS, K., *The English Secular Cathedrals in the Middle Ages* (2nd edition, Manchester, 1967).

GREEN, V. H. H., *Bishop Reginald Pecock* (Cambridge, 1945).

HEATH, P., *The English Parish Clergy on the Eve of the Reformation* (London, 1969).

JACOB, E. F., *Essays in the Conciliar Epoch* (2nd edition, 1953).

KNOWLES, M. D., *The English Mystical Tradition* (London, 1961).

KNOWLES, M. D., *The Religious Orders in England* (3 vols., Cambridge, 1948, 1955 and 1959).

ed. LAWRENCE, C. H., *The English Church and the Papacy in the Middle Ages* (London, 1965). Good essays by W. A. Pantin and F. R. H. Du Boulay on the 14th and 15th centuries.

MANNING, B. L., *The People's Faith in the Time of Wyclif* (Cambridge, 1919).

ed. NELSON, W., *A Fifteenth Century School Book* (Oxford, 1956).

ORME, N., *English Schools in the Middle Ages* (London, 1973).

OWST, G. R., *Preaching in Medieval England* (Cambridge, 1926).

PANTIN, W. A., *The English Church in the Fourteenth Century* (Cambridge, 1955).

PARRY, A. W., *Education in England in the Middle Ages* (London, 1920).

POWER, E. E., *Medieval English Nunneries* (Cambridge, 1922).

RASHDALL, H., *The Universities of Europe in the Middle Ages* (revised edition by Powicke, F. M., and Emden, A. B., Oxford, 1936, Vol. 3).

ROBSON, J. A., *Wyclif and the Oxford Schools* (Oxford, 1961).

SMITH, H. Maynard, *Pre-Reformation England* (London, 1938).

STOREY, R. L., *Thomas Langley and the Bishopric of Durham* (London, 1961).

THOMSON, J. A. F., *The Later Lollards* (Oxford, 1965).

THORNDIKE, Lynn, *A History of Magic and Experimental Science*, Vols. 3 and 4 (New York, 1929).

WEISS, R., *Humanism in England during the Fifteenth Century* (Oxford, 1951).

WOOD-LEGH, K. L., *Perpetual Chantries in Britain* (Cambridge, 1965).

WORKMAN, H. B., *John Wyclif* (2 vols., Oxford, 1926).

YOUINGS, J., *The Dissolution of the Monasteries* (London, 1971).

## LITERATURE AND THE ARTS

BENNETT, H. S., *Chaucer and the Fifteenth Century* (Oxford, 1947).

BENNETT, H. S., *English Books and Readers, 1475–1557* (London, 1952).

BLAKE, N. F., *Caxton and his World* (London, 1969).

BROWN, R. A., *English Medieval Castles* (London, 1954).

CHAMBERS, E. K., *English Literature at the Close of the Middle Ages* (Oxford, 1945).

COGHILL, N., *The Poet Chaucer* (Oxford, 1949).

COOK, G. H., *The English Medieval Parish Church* (London, 1956).

COTTLE, B., *The Triumph of English, 1350–1400* (London, 1969).

DAVIES, R. T., *Medieval English Lyrics* (London, 1963).

EVANS, J., *English Art, 1307–1461* (Oxford, 1949).

GARDNER, A., *English Medieval Sculpture* (new edition, Cambridge, 1953).

HARRISON, F. LL., *Music in Medieval Britain* (London, 1958).

HARVEY, J., *Gothic England* (London, 1947).

HASSALL, W. O., *The Holkham Bible Picture Book* (London, 1954).

HOWARD, F. E., and CROSSLEY, F. H., *English Church Woodwork, 1250–1550* (London, 1918).

KELLY, F. M., and SCHWABE, R., *A Short History of Costume and Armour*, Vol. I (London, 1931).

LLOYD, N., *History of the English House* (London, 1931).

MATTHEW, G., *The Court of Richard the Second* (London, 1968).

MILLAR, E. G., *English Illuminated Manuscripts of the 14th and 15th Centuries* (Paris and Brussels, 1928).

RENWICK, W. L., and ORTON, H., *The Beginnings of English Literature to Skelton, 1509* (London, 1939).

RICKERT, M., *Painting in Britain: The Middle Ages* (Penguin Books, 1954).

SALTER, E., *Piers Plowman, an introduction* (Oxford, 1962).

SALZMAN, L. F., *Building in England down to 1540* (Oxford, 1952).

SCATTERGOOD, V. J., *Politics and Poetry in the Fifteenth Century* (London, 1971).

TAYLOR, J., *The Universal Chronicle of Ranulf Higden* (Oxford, 1966).

WICKHAM, G. W. G., *Early English Stages*, Vol. I, 1300–1576 (London, 1959).

WOOD, M., *The English Medieval House* (London, 1965).

WOODFORDE, C., *English Stained and Painted Glass* (Oxford, 1954).

## ENGLAND IN THE LATE MIDDLE AGES

*A map to illustrate the places mentioned in the text*

Legend:

- ✕ Battles
- ◇ Castles
- ‡ Bishoprics
- ✝ Monasteries

*Dover* Cinque Ports
----- Some of the main roads of later
medieval England derived from
the fourteenth-century Gough map

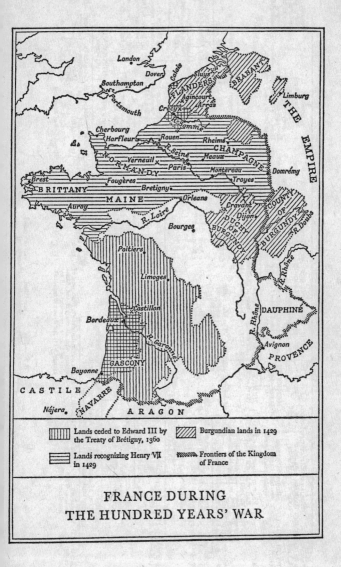

London
Dover
Southampton
Portsmouth
Calais
Sluys
FLANDERS
Agincourt
Crécy
Arras
Somme
BRABANT
Limburg
THE EMPIRE
Cherbourg
Harfleur
Rouen
Rheims
CHAMPAGNE
R. Seine
Meaux
Domrémy
NORMANDY
Verneuil
Paris
Montereau
Brest
Fougères
Troyes
BRITTANY
Bretigny
Orleans
Cravant
COUNTY OF BURGUNDY
MAINE
Auray
R. Loire
Dijon
DUCHY OF BURGUNDY
R. Doubs
Bourges
Poitiers
R. Rhône
Limoges
Castillon
DAUPHINÉ
Bordeaux
R. Garonne
R. Rhône
Avignon
PROVENCE
Bayonne
GASCONY
CASTILE
NAVARRE
ARAGON
Nájera

| Lands ceded to Edward III by the Treaty of Brétigny, 1360 | Burgundian lands in 1429 |
| Lands recognizing Henry VII in 1429 | Frontiers of the Kingdom of France |

# FRANCE DURING
# THE HUNDRED YEARS' WAR

# EDWARD III (1327–77)

EDWARD, The Black Prince d. 1376

WILLIAM OF HATFIELD o.s.p.

ELIZABETH DE BURGH = LIONEL, Duke of Clarence d. 1368

BLANCHE (1) = JOHN OF GAUNT Duke of LANCASTER d. 1399 = (3)CATHARINE SWYNFORD d. 1403

EDMUND, Duke of York d. 1402

THOMAS, Duke of Gloucester murdered 1397, ancestor of the Dukes of Buckingham

---

RICHARD II (1377–99)

ROGER MORTIMER executed 1330 Great-grandfather of

HENRY IV (1399–1413)

(3) THOMAS BEAUFORT Duke of Exeter d. 1427

HENRY BEAUFORT Cardinal, Bishop of Winchester, d. 1447

(1) JOHN BEAUFORT Marquis of Somerset, d. 1410

EDWARD Duke of York k. in battle, 1415

RICHARD Earl of Cambridge, ex. 1415

The Yorkist Line — See to left

EDMUND BEAUFORT Duke of Somerset killed in battle 1455

OWEN TUDOR = KATHARINE OF FRANCE executed 1461 | Widow of Henry V

EDMUND MORTIMER Earl of March d. 1381 = PHILIPPA d. 1382

HENRY V (1413–22) = KATHARINE OF FRANCE d. 1437

THOMAS Duke of Clarence k. in battle, 1421

JOHN Duke of Bedford d. 1435

HUMPHREY Duke of Gloucester d. 1447

JOHN BEAUFORT Duke of Somerset d. 1444 = JANE BEAUFORT = JAMES I King of Scots (1406–37) Royal line of Scotland

EDMUND TUDOR Earl of Richmond d. 1456

MARGARET BEAUFORT d. 1509

(1) HENRY, Duke of Somerset, executed 1464

(2) EDMUND, Duke of Somerset, executed 1471

(3) JOHN BEAUFORT, killed in battle, 1471

ROGER Earl of March k. in battle, 1398 = Daughter of Owen Glendower

EDMUND MORTIMER d. 1409

HENRY VI (1422–61) murdered 1471 = MARGARET OF ANJOU d. 1482

MARGARET = CHARLES Duke of Burgundy killed in battle 1477 d. 1503

ELIZABETH = JOHN Duke of Suffolk d. 1491

HENRY VIII (1509–47) = MARGARET = CHARLES BRANDON Duke of Suffolk d. 1545

(1) LOUIS XII of France (1498–1515)

RICHARD Duke of York killed in battle 1460 = CECILY NEVILLE

ROGER Earl of March d. before 1415

ANNE MORTIMER = RICHARD Earl of Cambridge executed 1415

EDMUND Earl of March o.s.p. 1424

EDWARD Prince of Wales killed in battle 1471 = ANNE NEVILLE

JOHN Earl of Lincoln killed in battle 1487

EDMUND Earl of Suffolk de la Pole executed 1513 o.s.p. 1525

RICHARD Duke of Suffolk de la Pole killed in battle 1525 o.s.p.

ELIZABETH OF YORK d. 1503 = HENRY VII (1485–1509)

ARTHUR Prince of Wales d. 1502

JAMES IV of Scotland (1488–1513) = MARGARET d. 1541

CHARLES BRANDON Duke of Suffolk d. 1545 = (2) MARY = (1) LOUIS XII of France d. 1533

Royal line of Scotland

---

EDWARD IV (1461–83) = ELIZABETH WYDVILLE d. 1492

EDMUND Earl of Rutland killed in battle, 1460

GEORGE Duke of Clarence executed 1478 = ISABELLA NEVILLE d. 1476

RICHARD III (1483–5) = ANNE NEVILLE d. 1485

EDWARD Earl of Warwick executed 1499

MARGARET Countess of Salisbury executed 1541 = SIR RICHARD POLE d. 1505

EDWARD Prince of Wales d. 1484

HENRY Lord Montague executed 1538

REGINALD POLE Cardinal, Archbishop of Canterbury, d. 1558

SIR GEOFFREY POLE d. 1558

EDWARD V (1483) Murdered

RICHARD Duke of York Murdered 1483

Six other daughters, from one of whom was descended the Marquis of Exeter (executed 1538 by Henry VIII for dynastic reasons).

---

KEY
- d. = died
- o.s.p. = obiit sine prole (died without issue)
- k. = killed
- ex. = executed
- --- = illegitimate (John of Gaunt's three Beaufort sons were born before he married Catharine Swynford)

# INDEX

Poggio Bracciolini (1380–1459), 180
Poitiers, battle of, 24, 26, 120
Poland, 157
Pole, Reginald (1500–58), Cardinal, 1555, Archbishop of Canterbury, 1556, 241
Police, 51, 219
Pontefract Castle, 35, 116
Ponthieu, 25
Popes, see Papacy
  Boniface IX, 1389–1404, 32
  Calixtus III, 1455–8, 169
  Gregory XI, 1370–78, 83
  Innocent VIII, 1484–92, 236
  Martin V, 1417–31, 169, 170, 171
  Pius II, 1460–66, 169
Portsmouth, 126
Portugal, 159, 161
Praemunire, 83, 84, 170
Printing, 242, 250, 254
Privateering and piracy, 159, 160
Provisions, papal, 50, 83, 84, 170, 181
Pulteney, Sir John (d. 1349), 66, 106

Ramsey, 57, 62
Ranworth, 196
Ravenspur, 34, 130
Redford, John (1486–1540), 261
Renaissance, Italian, see Humanism
Renaissance, twelfth century, 86–7
Rheims, 124
Richard II (1367–1400), King of England, 1377–99, 18, 21, 29–36, 38, 41, 42, 45, 47, 48, 49, 50, 66, 69, 86, 100, 105, 109, 110, 115, 116, 132, 136, 156, 165, 189, 191, 195, 214
Richard III (1452–85), Duke of Gloucester, 1461, King of England, 1483, 84, 200, 201, 203, 205, 211, 261

Richmond, 173, 238
Rievaulx, 56, 75
Ripon, 191
Rivers, Earl: Anthony Wydeville (1442?–83), Earl, 1469, 250
Roads, 57, 58
Robert I, King of Scots, see Bruce
Robert II (1316–90), King of Scots, 1371, 25
Rolle, Richard (d. 1349), 85, 97
Romney Marsh, 55
Roos, Lord (d. 1414), 142
Roper, William (1496–1578), 253
Roses, Wars of the, 127–31, 136, 187, 199, 203, 204, 223, 227, 261
Rotherham, Thomas (1423–1500), Archbishop of York, 1480, 245
Rouen, 120, 187
Russells, 163, 231, 235
Russia, 157, 232
Rye, 29

St Albans, 99, 128, 208, 238
St Cloud, 118
St Ives (Huntingdonshire), 57
St Neots (Cornwall), 256
Salisbury, 180, 195, 238
Santiago of Compostella, 159
Scandinavia, 157
Scheere, Herman (fl. 1400–20), 195
Schools, 91, 92, 93, 94, 180–81, 245–6
Scotland, 14, 15, 17, 19, 20, 21, 23, 25, 32, 60, 103, 116, 128, 204, 230, 244
Scrope, Richard (1350?–1405), Archbishop of York, 1398, 117
Sculpture, 111–12, 192, 194, 256–7
Seal, Exchequer, 39
  Great, 39
  Privy, 39, 40, 41, 139, 183
  Signet, 40, 41, 139, 214
Secretary, 41, 139, 214
Serfdom, 55, 58–62, 149, 150, 232

# THE PELICAN HISTORY OF ENGLAND

While each volume is complete in itself, the whole series has been planned to provide an intelligent and consecutive guide to the development of English society in all its aspects.

'As a portent in the broadening of popular culture the influence of this wonderful series has yet to receive full recognition and precise assessment. No venture could be more enterprising or show more confidence in the public's willingness to purchase thoughtful books ...' – *Listener*